Thinking as Computation

A First Course

Thinking as Computation

A First Course

Hector J. Levesque

The MIT Press
Cambridge, Massachusetts
London, England

© 2012 Massachusetts Institute of Technology

MIT Press books may be purchased at special quantity discounts for business or sales promotional use. For information, please email special_sales@mitpress.mit.edu or write to Special Sales Department, The MIT Press, 55 Hayward Street, Cambridge, MA 02142.

This book was set in Palatino by the author using the LATEX document preparation system. Printed and bound in the United States of America.

Library of Congress Cataloging-in-Publication Data

Levesque, Hector J., 1951–
Thinking as computation : a first course / Hector J. Levesque.
    p.   cm.
Includes bibliographical references and index.
ISBN 978-0-262-01699-5 (hardcover : alk. paper) 1. Computational intelligence. I. Title.
Q342.L48   2012
006.3—dc23

2011026394

10 9 8 7 6 5 4 3 2 1

For the late Ray Reiter,
who got me to thinking

Contents

Preface

This book derives from a course that I teach at the University of Toronto entitled Computers and Thought. The syllabus states the following:

> The goal [of the course] is to study one idea in detail, the idea that ordinary thinking as performed by people might be understood as a form of computation. We explore the connection between thinking and computing by examining what it takes to program a computer to perform certain tasks that seem to require thought. A secondary goal is to learn a certain type of computer programming in a language called Prolog.

The course is intended for first-year undergraduate students who are interested in this idea but who have no technical specialization or background other than high school mathematics. This book is intended to serve as the text for such a course.

Background

The faculty of Arts and Science at the University of Toronto decided a few years ago that it would be a good idea to offer seminar-style courses to first-year undergraduates. This would have a number of desirable effects. First, students would be exposed to research ideas very early in their academic careers and perhaps see how a research-intensive university is different from one that concentrates mainly on teaching. It would also allow first-year students to come into contact with senior faculty engaged in research, whom they might not otherwise encounter until they took upper-level (or even graduate-level) courses.

The faculty decided that each department had to offer at least one such seminar per year, guaranteeing that new students would have a wide assortment to choose from. Instructors were free to decide on the specific topic they would cover; they were asked only to provide a short abstract. Incoming students were sent these abstracts and were given the option of indicating which of the seminars they were interested in. At the time of admission, the faculty streamed students into classes according to their top three choices, limiting the enrollment of each seminar to twenty-five students. For many students, this would be the only class they would attend in their first year at the

University of Toronto with fewer than one hundred students. (Some first-year classes go into the thousands.) So another benefit of these classes is that first-year students would come into contact with a faculty member in a very small group. Instructors would get to know their students by name. In a university with over fifty thousand students, this by itself was already quite remarkable.

The first-year seminars typically cover a wide range of topics. The courses last an entire year, and while they do give students breadth and experience, they are not intended to be used as prerequisites for more advanced courses. So the curriculum can be very flexible, and students can take courses on topics that are only distantly related to what they hope to specialize in.

A typical first-year seminar in a science department (such as computer science) looks at ongoing research issues or controversies from a nontechnical point of view. Sometimes high school science or mathematics courses are required by the instructor, but with students coming from all over the world, it is difficult to depend on any specific background preparation. With a nontechnical approach, students can still be engaged in scholarly activity, tracking down references, discussing the ideas that emerge, making presentations, writing essays, and so on.

Computers and Thought

The first time I taught this course, I planned to look at my subarea of artificial intelligence (AI) research in just this way. I thought it would be worthwhile to have students understand what people in this area cared about and how they did their research. I also wanted students to read from the commentators who had written about AI (Turing, Fodor, Dennett, and Pylyshyn among them) and especially from the critics of the field (like Searle and Dreyfus) who felt that the work in AI could never illuminate what was going on in *people*.

The course did not work well. I came to feel that the students were not getting a clear enough picture of AI research to appreciate how there could be conflicting interpretations of it.

I started thinking that it might be better to give them some direct hands-on experience. Instead of having philosophers tell them why AI would never be able to do this or that, I wanted them to see for themselves what computers could do and to get a feel for some of the limitations. In a nutshell, I wanted them to try to program computers to perform activities that required thought.

This would be challenging for the students. The first-year students who take this course are not in a technical stream. I've had students majoring in sociology, criminology, commerce, history, biology, European studies, economics, political science, curatorial studies, cinema, English, and religion. I clearly would have a hard time teaching them to write interesting AI programs in Python or Scheme in a single year.

However, I found that it was possible to teach nontechnical students to program in Prolog provided one did not insist on teaching them algorithms. It is possible, in other words, to get students to express what they need as a Prolog program and let Prolog search for answers. Small examples can be made to work well. The students get a real taste for the strength as well as the limitations of search, and especially the crushing power of combinatorics. *This is where the class had to go!*

At first I did a hybrid course, with a bit of technical work and a bit of philosophical discussion. But in the end, the philosophical part served mainly to give the students a break and keep them engaged. (When a topic is less technical, it is easier for students to feel that they can present their opinions and join in.) I came to believe that with a bit of effort on my part, there could be good class involvement and participation even in the technical part of the course. So Searle and his Chinese Room eventually fell by the wayside.

Cognitive science or artificial intelligence?

Although this book is not intended primarily for students majoring in a technical discipline like computer science or engineering, it is still a book about AI, not its sister discipline of cognitive science.

What is the difference between cognitive science and AI? While there are strong connections and overlap between the two, the main difference is that cognitive science is the interdisciplinary study of *people* as cognitive beings, whereas AI is the study of *intelligent behavior* achieved through computational means. The analogy I like (and take up in chapter 1) is the difference between studying flying animals and studying flight. Before the advent of aircraft, the only large-scale flying objects were animals like birds and bats. Cognitive science is like an interdisciplinary study of these flying animals, whereas AI is more like the study of what is sufficient for flight. Obviously, if one wants to understand flying animals, it helps to know something about flight in general; similarly, if one wants to understand the principles of flight, it helps to know something about the animals that fly. But the two areas have quite different objectives and methods.

Just to be clear, then, this is a book about thinking seen as a computational process and not about the thinkers themselves. As a technically restrained introduction to parts of AI, I believe it has a role to play in a cognitive science program. But it cannot replace the core material on the thinkers: psychology, neuroscience, biology, evolution, the social sciences, and so on.

Having said this, let me add that I do find it somewhat scandalous how far apart cognitive science and AI have drifted in the last twenty years or so. There are students studying AI who are led to believe that cognitive science is too soft and full of polemics to be of use. On the other side, there are students of cognitive science who are told that AI is mostly concerned with engineering applications, and just as well, since philosophers have demonstrated that AI cannot possibly have anything to say about the mind and what goes on in people. This is a very unfortunate state of affairs, and I can only hope that a new generation of students will put aside the prejudices of the past and see what there is to learn from both sides.

Overview of the book

The book follows the sequence of topics that I teach in the first-year course. However, it also includes some additional optional material (indicated by an asterisk before the section or chapter title) that in some cases is more advanced. The twelve chapters of the book are structured as follows:

- Chapter 1 is an introduction to the basic concepts. It talks about thinking and computing, and how they might be related. These topics are taken up again briefly in the philosophical conclusion of chapter 12.

- The next three chapters are related to Prolog. Chapter 2 introduces back-chaining informally; chapter 3 presents Prolog programs and queries; chapter 4 explains how to write the sorts of Prolog programs that will be used in the rest of the book. Additional features of Prolog are introduced as needed, including all of chapter 7 on lists in Prolog.

- The remaining chapters are case studies of various sorts of tasks where thinking appears to be required, and how they can be realized as Prolog programs. The tasks included are these: satisfying constraints (chapter 5), interpreting visual scenes (chapter 6), understanding natural language (chapter 8), planning courses of action (chapter 9), playing strategic games (chapter 10), and extending beyond Prolog to learning, explaining, and propositional reasoning (chapter 11).

Most of the chapters conclude with short bibliographic notes and exercises.

Is the book an introduction to artificial intelligence?

This book is about thinking as a computational process and, as such, falls squarely within the subject matter of AI. I hesitate to call the book an introduction to AI, however, since so much of AI is not even mentioned. Some of the missing topics might have been included in a longer book (for a longer course). Examples are knowledge discovery, Bayesian inference, and cognitive robotics.

But a lot of AI is not concerned with thinking at all (as it is understood here) and would be quite out of place in this book. Examples are sensory learning (like reinforcement conditioning), motor control (like legged locomotion), and early vision (like detecting shape from shading). There is a lot to be said about those topics, and about the interface between them and thinking (between early vision and the sort of visual interpretation seen in chapter 6, for instance). But they are so different from the thinking parts that it might be a mistake to try to combine them in a single introductory course.

Guide for the course instructor

At the University of Toronto, seminar courses like this one are full-year courses, which means two twelve-week terms, with 2 hours of lectures and 1 hour of tutorial each week. So I present the material from the book in 48 hours of lectures. (Tutorials are used for other purposes, such as going over the topics in the appendices, for example.) The breakdown of lectures is roughly as follows:

- 2 weeks to introduce thinking as computation (chapters 1, 2)

- 3–4 weeks for basic Prolog (chapters 3, 4)

- 3–4 weeks for satisfying constraints (chapter 5)

- 2 weeks for lists in Prolog (chapter 7)

- 3–4 weeks for natural language (chapter 8)

- 3–4 weeks for planning (chapter 9)

- 3 weeks for game playing (chapter 10)

- 1 week to conclude with some philosophy (chapter 12)

Because this course is not intended to be part of the students' specializations, I cover the material very slowly and make sure there is plenty of time for discussion, questions, and review in class. I skip over or breeze through many of the optional topics in the book.

I tell the students at the outset that nobody will have to drop out of the course because they find the material too difficult. We discuss how much time I expect them to spend on the course and I tell them that they can get a grade of B (or better) if they *attempt* everything that is asked of them, and get *correct answers* for the very easiest parts. Of course, to get a grade better than a B, they would need to go beyond this.

Here is how I arrange evaluation in the course. Over the entire year, there are five big assignments (requiring the students to write and submit Prolog programs), class participation in each term, and seven small homework tasks. These homework tasks require them to do various things, sometimes using pencil and paper, and sometimes using the computer, but do not require them to hand in anything. Instead, at the next tutorial, the teaching assistant goes over how to do the task, and asks them about what they have done to determine whether they have given the homework their attention. This, I believe, is a terrific way to get students (in a small class) to start thinking about what is needed for an assignment, and to clear up any confusion early in the process. Note that all the exercises in this book have been tested in the classroom.

Alternative courses using this book

The book could also work well for courses with different formats. For a half-year course (one twelve-week term, or 24 hours of lectures), I recommend something like the following:

- 2 weeks to introduce thinking as computation (chapters 1, 2)

- 3–4 weeks for basic Prolog (chapters 3, 4)

- 3–4 weeks for satisfying constraints (chapter 5)

- 2 weeks for visual interpretation (chapter 6)

- 1 week to conclude with some philosophy (chapter 12)

While this does present a somewhat impoverished view of thinking (tied to just constraint satisfaction), it nonetheless spans a range of examples, from recreational (like logic puzzles) to practical (like scheduling), and from artificial (like Sudoku) to natural (like vision).

What about a course for students with somewhat more technical facility, for example, second-year computer science students? For a half-year course with 24 contact hours, I recommend a more ambitious program:

- 1–2 weeks to introduce thinking as computation (chapters 1, 2)

- 2–3 weeks for basic Prolog (chapters 3, 4)

- 2–3 weeks for satisfying constraints (chapter 5)

- 2 weeks for lists in Prolog (chapter 7)

- 2–3 weeks for either natural language (chapter 8) or planning (chapter 9)

- 1 week to conclude with some philosophy (chapter 12)

With 36 contact hours or more, it should be possible to get through the full course, and even some of the more advanced topics like those in chapter 11.

Finally, what about a course for students with still more expertise, like students who already know Prolog? One possibility is to supplement the material in the book with algorithmic content: better algorithms for constraint satisfaction (such as arc consistency), for parsing (such as bottom-up methods), for planning (such as heuristic planning), for game playing (such as alpha-beta search). These are only hinted at in the text. Another possibility is to take the topics of chapter 11 on explanation, learning, and propositional reasoning as a springboard for a whole new section on numerical uncertainty, which has come to dominate so much of current AI research. But maybe the best option here is simply to use a more advanced text: I recommend the comprehensive textbook by Russell and Norvig [11].

Guide for the student

Let me start with a word of reassurance. *This book is not just for techies!* You will definitely need upper-level high school mathematics, and you will also need to know how to operate a computer: create text files, edit them, print them, and save them (see appendix A). You do not need to know how to program a computer, and there is actually not much mathematics in the book, mostly simple arithmetic.

So why is familiarity with mathematics necessary?

- You will need to be able to deal with variables and mathematical notation. Suppose the text refers to "seven words of English, x_1, x_2, ..., x_7." If this looks mysterious to you, you are probably not familiar with mathematical notation.

- You will need to be able to look at large symbolic expressions (or formulas), make sure they are put together correctly, and work on them precisely according to instructions. You need to be able to deal with a lot of tiny details without getting lost or bored. You might have picked up this skill in a variety of ways (like knitting from a complex pattern or building a model ship inside a bottle), but courses in mathematics are terrific practice.

Assuming you are interested in the subject matter of the book, do you have the necessary background to get through it all? There is no easy answer. I suggest you work through the first few chapters until you get to the exercises in chapter 4. If you have no idea of how to do the first few exercises there, then you should certainly consider stopping.

Going through this book as a self-study course is much harder than having an instructor who can answer questions as they come up. But if you are going through it alone, here are some things you definitely need to know:

- Any chapter or section with an asterisk (∗) marking the title is an optional topic that may be more advanced. (A marked section within a marked chapter is even more advanced.) Skip these on first reading, or at least don't be disappointed if they are not clear to you at first.

- The exercises at the end of each chapter range from very simple to much more difficult. You should always be able to answer the first few questions, but don't be discouraged if you can't get through all of them.

Acknowledgments

This book has its genesis in a course that the late Ray Reiter and I first taught together in 1994. It was Ray who had the idea of teaching logic programming, including the concept of recursion, to first-year undergraduates. I owe Ray an enormous debt for his inspiration and intellectual leadership on this, and I can only hope that he would have found this book to his liking.

Over the years, the course evolved and began to be less about programming and more about artificial intelligence. I thank all the students who went through various iterations of the course without a textbook, as well as the teaching assistants: David Mitchell, Mikhail Soutchanski, Ron Petrick, Stavros Vassos, and Tim Capes. I also thank the University of Toronto for giving me the opportunity to teach an experimental and ever-changing course to first-year students.

I was fortunate that a number of people were willing to read drafts of parts of the book and provide me with comments: Ron Brachman, Ernie Davis, Sven Dickinson, Gerhard Lakemeyer, Gerald Penn, Bart Selman, Mikhail Soutchanski, my brothers John and Paul, my daughter Michelle, and three anonymous reviewers. Their comments were invaluable! I thank them all. All the remaining errors and oversights in the book are of course my fault, not theirs.

I also wish to thank the good folks at MIT Press. Ada Brunstein and Marc Lowenthal believed in the project from the very beginning and helped to get me started. Mel Goldsipe saw me through the many final edits and helped to get me stopped. A special thanks to Alice Cheyer for her thorough copyediting.

This book was completed while I was on sabbatical from the University of Toronto. I thank my hosts Gerhard Lakemeyer at the Technical University of Aachen, Maurice Pagnucco at the University of New South Wales, and Jim Delgrande at Simon Fraser University for providing such wonderful environments for writing. I also thank the Natural Science and Engineering Research Council of Canada who generously funded me throughout the writing of the book, and in fact, throughout my academic career.

Finally, I would like to thank my family and friends who supported me most enthusiastically throughout the project, and especially Pat, my dearest wife and proofreader *extraordinaire*, who might have heard "Working on the book!" a bit too often as the answer to the question "What are you doing today?" Well guys, it's all done!

Toronto, August 2011

1 · Thinking and Computation

Consider the following scenario:

> A professor enters a classroom where a group of undergraduates is sitting, and announces "There is free pizza in the hall!" Suddenly, the students stand up and stampede toward the classroom door.

The events described here seem so ordinary that it is easy to miss how truly remarkable they are. But step back from them for a moment and imagine that you are studying these students as a curious scientist from another world. You observe that a certain sound emanates from the professor and that this causes a flurry of activity in the students. Now, as a scientist, ask yourself this: What sort of *physics* would explain how acoustic energy can be transformed into kinetic energy in this way? In particular, note that a very small change in the acoustic energy (like the professor's saying "There is free pizza in Nepal.") can result in *no* kinetic energy being produced at all, except maybe for some puzzled head shaking.

This is the wonder of *intelligent behavior*, perhaps the single most complex natural phenomenon that we are aware of. As a sheer mystery, it easily overshadows topics like dark matter, the source of gravity, and the mechanics of cancer.

One striking aspect of intelligent behavior of this sort is that it is clearly conditioned by *knowledge*: for a very wide range of activities, people make decisions about what to do based on what they know (or believe) about the world, effortlessly and often unconsciously. It's certainly not the *sounds* themselves that cause the students to stand up like animals that have been trained to respond to a bell. This is easy enough to confirm. The professor could have brought in a *sign* with a pizza message on it written in big letters, and the effect would have been just the same. In fact, one can imagine a situation where the following is written on the whiteboard at the front of the classroom:

> As part of a psychology experiment, the professor will soon enter and tell you that free food is available. This is just a test. Please remain seated.

In this case, neither the sounds nor the sign would have any effect at all. One can try other small variations, and it will become clear that what makes the difference is whether the students come to *believe* there is free pizza to be had nearby.

Using what we believe or know in this way is so commonplace that we only really pay attention to it when it is not there. When we say that someone behaved *unintelligently*, for instance, when someone uses a lit match to see if there is any gas in a car's gas tank, what we usually mean is not that there is something the person did not know but rather that the person has failed to use what he or she *did* know. We might say: "You weren't thinking!" Indeed, it is *thinking* that is supposed to deliver what we know to the decisions we need to make. The students head toward the door because they *think* that is the way to free pizza. It is thinking, in the end, that makes human behavior intelligent.

But what is thinking, and how does it work? What exactly goes on in people's heads when they think about where to go for free pizza, or about who will win the Academy Award for Best Actor, or about whether a free market needs to be regulated?

The purpose of this book is to suggest where to look for an answer. It proposes that thinking is a form of computation. In the same way that digital computers perform calculations on representations of numbers, human brains perform calculations on representations of what is known.

This chapter is an introduction to this idea. The first section reviews very briefly the notion of thinking. The process of computation is somewhat less familiar, so more time is spent on it, in the second section. The third section introduces the (somewhat controversial) idea of thinking as a form of computation.

1.1   Thinking

Are brains like computers? In a word, *no*. It is true historically that in trying to understand the brain, people have proposed models that seem to mirror the most advanced technology of the time. Over the years, the brain has been described as clockwork, a steam engine, a telephone switchboard, and (these days) a computer. But in time, these descriptions are found to be much too simplistic to say anything useful about what is inside our heads. There is no reason to believe that the computer analogy will be any different in this regard.

In fact, this book has very little to say about the brain itself. Rather it focuses on thinking. But thinking is what the brain does. How can one study the relation between computers and thinking without studying the brain?

Here is a useful analogy. Consider the study of flight (in the days before airplanes). One might want to understand how certain animals like birds and bats are able to fly.

One might also want to try to build machines that are capable of flight. There are two ways to proceed:

- study flying animals like birds, looking very carefully at their wings, their feathers, their muscles, and then construct machines that emulate birds;

- study aerodynamics—how air flows above and below an airfoil, and how this provides lift—by using wind tunnels and varying the shapes of airfoils.

Both kinds of studies lead to insights, but of a different sort. The second strategy is the more general one: it seeks to discover the principles of flight that apply to anything, including birds.

It is this second strategy that is used here to study thinking. While there is a lot to be learned by studying the brain, this book focuses on the *thinking process* itself to determine general principles that will apply to brains and to anything else that needs to think.

1.1.1   What is thinking?

What exactly is thinking? For humans, it is clearly some sort of process that occurs in our heads over time. The easiest way to understand it is to observe it in action.

Read the following sentence:

> *The trophy would not fit into the brown suitcase because it was too small.*

Pause for a moment to make sure you understand it. Now answer this question: What was too small? What does *it* refer to? Clearly, *it* refers to the suitcase, not the trophy.

Now, how did you get the right answer?

Observe that there is nothing in the sentence itself that gives away the answer. This is easy to demonstrate. Simply replace the word *small* by *big*:

> *The trophy would not fit into the brown suitcase because it was too big.*

What was too big? Now the answer goes the other way: *it* now refers to the trophy, not the suitcase.

What this shows is that in making sense of the sentence, in particular, in determining what *it* refers to, you had to use what you already knew about the sizes of things, things fitting inside other things, and so on, even if you were unaware of doing so.

This is thinking.

Thinking is bringing what you know to bear on what you are doing. This is what you had to do to understand the sentence. The process happens in the brain, sometimes very quickly, and you may or may not be aware that it is taking place. (You may not have felt the change that happened in your thinking when the word was changed from *small* to *big*.)

Thinking is clearly a biological process, since we are biological creatures. Does this mean that thinking is like digestion? Or like mitosis in cells? Or is it different still?

The central conjecture of this book is this:

> *Thinking can be usefully understood as a computational process.*

Thinking has perhaps more in common with multiplication or sorting a list of numbers than with digestion or mitosis.

This conjecture is *controversial*. Not all philosophers, psychologists, evolutionary biologists, and neuroscientists are lined up to support it. Some do, some don't, and some struggle with the concept of thinking in the first place.

Nonetheless this is the conjecture that this book pursues.

1.2   Computation

Computer science as a field of study has two branches: hardware and software. Hardware is the concern of engineers who study and build the physical machines (computers) themselves. Software is the written instructions—programs—specifying what those machines should do. And what the machines do is *computation*, a certain manipulation of symbols. Birds "produce" flight, musicians "produce" music, and computers "produce" computation according to a program.

This book focuses on computation itself as the primary subject of computer science. What (or who) is performing the symbol manipulation is a secondary concern. Modern electronic computers happen to provide a fast, cheap, and reliable way to do this computation, but other devices can do it as well. (The Dutch computer scientist Edsger Dijkstra once said that computer science is no more about the computers than astronomy is about telescopes.)

1.2.1   Symbols and symbolic structures

In their simplest form, *symbols* are just characters from some alphabet, like the following:

- digits: *3, 7, V* (the last one is a Roman numeral)
- letters: *x, R, β* (the last one is a Greek letter)
- operators: $+$, $\leq$, $\cap$

They can be strung together into more complex forms:

- numerals: *5874, –3.75*

- words: *John, don't*

They can be grouped in certain ways:

- mathematical expressions: *247 + 4(x – 1)³*

- English phrases: *the woman John loved*

Finally, some of these groupings can be thought of as being true or false:

- mathematical inequalities: $247 + 4(x - 1)^3 \leq \dfrac{n!}{4}$

- English sentences: *The woman John loved had brown hair.*

It is _symbolic structures_, arrangements of symbols like those just illustrated, that are the medium of computation.

1.2.2   What is computation?

For present purposes, _computation_ is the process of taking symbolic structures, breaking them apart, comparing them, and reassembling them according to a precise recipe called a _procedure_. The symbols at the start of the procedure are called the _inputs_. The symbols at the end of the procedure are called the _outputs_. The procedure is _called_ on the inputs and _returns_ the outputs. It is important to keep track of where you are and to follow the instructions in the procedure _exactly_. (You may not be able to figure out _why_ you are doing the steps involved. No matter.)

1.2.3   Some arithmetic procedures

Imagine explaining to someone (a young child) how to do subtraction:

$$\begin{array}{r} 53 \\ -\ 17 \\ \hline \end{array}$$

One might say something like this:

> First subtract the 7 from 3. But since since 7 is bigger than 3, borrow 10 from the 5 on the left. That changes the 3 to a 13 and changes the 5 to a 4. So subtract 7 not from 3 but from 13, which gives 6. Write the 6 as the first digit of the answer on the right, under the 7. Then subtract 1 not from 5 but from 4, which gives 3. Write the 3 as the second digit of the answer, under the 1. So the answer is 36.

Figure 1.1. Adding two single-digit numbers

Procedure PROC0:

You are given two digits as input and will return two digits as output. To do so, use this table.

	0	1	2	3	4	5	6	7	8	9
0	00	01	02	03	04	05	06	07	08	09
1	01	02	03	04	05	06	07	08	09	10
2	02	03	04	05	06	07	08	09	10	11
3	03	04	05	06	07	08	09	10	11	12
4	04	05	06	07	08	09	10	11	12	13
5	05	06	07	08	09	10	11	12	13	14
6	06	07	08	09	10	11	12	13	14	15
7	07	08	09	10	11	12	13	14	15	16
8	08	09	10	11	12	13	14	15	16	17
9	09	10	11	12	13	14	15	16	17	18

To add the two digits, find the *row* for the first digit in the table, and find the *column* for the second digit, and return as output the two digits that appear at their intersection in the table.

These are the kinds of detailed instructions one wants in a procedure.

PROC0

Maybe the simplest job in arithmetic, the one learned before any others, is the addition of two single-digit numbers. Figure 1.1 shows a procedure called PROC0 that gives explicit instructions for adding two digits.

Notice that it makes use of an *addition table*. (Typically, young children are not taught addition in this way, but most of us were taught multiplication using a table like this, which we had to memorize.) One can see that if PROC0 is called on 7 and 6, it will return *13*, and if it is called on *3* and *5*, it will return *08*. (It will be handy for the answer returned here to be the two digits *08* and not simply *8*.)

Figure 1.2. Adding three single-digit numbers

Procedure PROC1:

>   You are given three digits as input, a, t, and b.
>   You will return two digits as output, c and s.

1. Call PROC0 on t and b, and let u and v be the answers returned.
    (The u is the left digit returned by PROC0, and the v is the right one.)

2. Call PROC0 on a and v, and let u' and v' be the answers returned.
    (The u' is the left digit returned, and the v' is the right one.)

3. If $u = u' = 0$, then return with $c = 0$ and $s = v'$.
    If $u = u' = 1$, then return with $c = 2$ and $s = v'$.
    Otherwise, return with $c = 1$ and $s = v'$.

PROC1

Now, building on this procedure, consider adding three digits. Intuitively, one should add the first two digits and then take the sum and add the last digit to it. However one needs to worry about the carry digits to get the answer right. The procedure PROC1 in figure 1.2 does this. It calls PROC0 twice and then decides whether the final carry digit to return should be *0, 1,* or *2*.

Trace the behavior of this procedure in detail to make sure you understand how it works. Suppose PROC1 is called with inputs *7, 4,* and *5.*

>   At the start, $a = 7$, $t = 4$, and $b = 5$. Determine the values of c and s to return.
>
>   1. Call PROC0 on *4* and *5*, which returns *09*. So $u = 0$ and $v = 9$.
>
>   2. Call PROC0 on *7* and *9*, which returns *16*. So $u' = 1$ and $v' = 6$.
>
>   3. Then $u \neq u'$, so return with $c = 1$ and $s = 6$.

The output returned by PROC1 in this case is *16*, as desired.

Here are some other examples to make sure you understand how this works:

-   If PROC1 is called on *3, 4,* and *1*, it will return *08*: u and v will be *0* and *5*, and u' and v' will be *0* and *8*, so c will be *0* and s will be *8*.

-   If PROC1 is called on *8, 9,* and *2*, it will return *19*: u and v will be *1* and *1*, and u' and v' will be *0* and *9*, so c will be *1* and s will be *9*.

Figure 1.3.   Adding two multidigit numbers

Procedure PROC2:

You are given two multidigit numbers as input, each with the same number of digits:

$$x_1 \ x_2 \ \ldots \ x_k$$
$$y_1 \ y_2 \ \ldots \ y_k$$

You will return a number with one additional digit as output:

$$z_0 \ z_1 \ z_2 \ \ldots \ z_k$$

1. Start at the right-hand side of the inputs (looking at x_k and y_k).
    Call PROC1 with a as 0, t as x_k, and b as y_k.
    Let z_k be the s returned. (Keep the c returned for the next step.)

2. Move over one step to the left (looking at x_{k-1} and y_{k-1}).
    Call PROC1 with a as the c from the previous step, t as x_{k-1}, and b as y_{k-1}.
    Let z_{k-1} be the s returned. (Keep the c returned for the next step.)

3. Continue in this way through all the digits, from right to left, filling out in turn,
    $z_{k-2}, z_{k-3}, \ldots, z_3, z_2, z_1$.

4. Let z_0 be the final c returned by PROC1 (with x_1 and y_1).

- If PROC1 is called on *8, 9,* and *6,* it will return *23*: u and v will be *1* and *5,* and u' and v' will be *1* and *3,* so c will be *2* and s will be *3.*

Note that it is not the business of the procedure to explain *why* the operations are done. It needs to make a decision about a final carry digit c. But as far as the procedure is concerned, the only thing that matters is what the final answer should be.

PROC2

Now, building on the procedure PROC1, consider instructions for adding two multidigit numbers. In this case, you know that you have to go from right to left, keeping track of the carry digits along the way. A procedure PROC2 for doing this is shown in figure 1.3. Trace the behavior of this procedure when the inputs are *747* and *281* (so that $k = 3$):

1. Starting at the right side, call PROC1 with $a = 0$, $t = 7$, and $b = 1$.
    It will return $c = 0$ and $s = 8$. So z_3 will be *8.*

Figure 1.4. Adding any list of numbers

Procedure PROC3:

You are given a list of numbers $n_1, n_2, \ldots$.
You will return a single number *sum* as output.

1. Let *sum* start off being the single digit *0*.

2. Start with the first number n_1 and *sum*. Make sure they both have the same number of digits by inserting *0* symbols on the left as needed. Then call PROC2 on these two numbers, and let the new value of *sum* be the number it returns.

3. Do the same thing with n_2 and the current value of *sum*, to produce the next value for *sum*.

4. Continue in this way with the rest of the numbers, $n_3, n_4, \ldots$.

5. Return as output the final value of *sum*.

---

2. Call PROC1 with $a = 0$ (the c from the previous step), $t = 4$, and $b = 8$. It will return $c = 1$ and $s = 2$. So z_2 will be *2*.

3. Call PROC1 with $a = 1$ (the c from the previous step), $t = 7$, and $b = 2$. It will return $c = 1$ and $s = 0$. So z_1 will be *0*.

4. Finally, z_0 will be *1* (the last c returned).

So the answer returned by PROC2 on *747* and *281* will be the four digits *1028*. And sure enough, 1028 is the sum of 747 and 281. Again observe that the procedure does not explain itself. Nowhere does it say that each digit stands for a power of ten (units, tens, hundreds, thousands, and so on) with the unit digits on the right. However, even if you do not know what the symbols are supposed to mean or why you are doing the operations, if you follow the directions in PROC2 exactly, keeping track of where you are at each step, you will add the two numbers correctly.

PROC3

Now consider a general addition procedure that will add any list of numbers, each with any number of digits. The procedure for this is in figure 1.4. It is easy to see that it does the right thing, repeatedly adding two numbers using PROC2 and keeping a running total. (PROC3 is not explicit about how to pad the shorter numbers with *0* symbols on the left. Imagine there is a PROC4 that does that.)

Going from here

Given a procedure that can do addition, it is not too hard to imagine doing subtraction the same way. Given those two, one can define procedures that do multiplication and division. Building on these, one can have a procedure to tell whether a number is prime. One can use pairs of numbers to represent fractions (rational numbers) and do arithmetic on them. One can arrange rational numbers into matrices and have procedures that operate on them to solve systems of equations. One can use systems of equations to model complex physical systems and have procedures that perform numerical simulations of these systems.

And on it goes.

So starting with simple symbolic operations (such as table lookup, putting together and taking apart sequences of symbols, comparing them, and so on), one can assemble the operations into ever larger procedures and develop an extremely wide range of behaviors as computational processes. This is what computer science is about.

1.2.4   The lesson

The key observation on these arithmetic procedures is this:

> *To produce meaningful answers, you do not have to understand what the symbols stand for or why the manipulations are correct.*

Although one can certainly understand the procedures as doing arithmetic, one does not need this understanding to actually carry out the procedures.

Here is a simple thought experiment to support this claim. Imagine replacing the symbols *0* through *9* everywhere by new symbols that do not look at all like digits, for example, a heart shape for *0*, a star for *1*, an anchor shape for *2*, and so on. Now give the procedures PROC0–PROC3, including the table for PROC0 with the new symbols, to a friend without saying what these new symbols mean or what the procedures are supposed to be doing. By following PROC2, the friend should still be able to do addition: take as input two sequences of new symbols representing numbers, and return as output the sequence of new symbols that represents their sum.

So symbols can be processed purely mechanically and still end up producing the right results. This might be called the trick of computation:

> *Computers can perform a wide variety of impressive activities precisely because those activities can be described as a type of symbol processing that can be carried out purely mechanically.*

This "trick" has turned out to be one of the major inventions of the twentieth century, allowing devices that perform computation to permeate almost all areas of our modern lives. And note: It has nothing to do with electronics or physics.

1.3 Thinking as computation

One might still ask, though, just what does computation have to do with ordinary thinking? Recall the central conjecture of this book:

Thinking can be usefully understood as a computational process.

What does this conjecture amount to?

- *Not* that the brain is something like an electronic computer (which it is in some ways perhaps, but in most ways is not).

- The process of thinking can be usefully understood as a form of *symbol processing* that can be carried out purely mechanically without having to know what the symbols stand for.

Why is this so controversial? Perhaps the idea that *some* types of thinking are computational is not so surprising. Consider activities like doing a homework problem in algebra, or filling out an income tax form, or estimating a grocery bill as you are shopping. These all involve thinking and are clearly computational.

The problem is that so much of our thinking seems to have very little to do with calculations or anything even remotely numerical. You can think about anything you want, not just numbers. Consider this example:

I know my keys are in my coat pocket or on the fridge.
That's where I always leave them.
I felt in my coat pocket, and there's nothing there.
So my keys must be on the fridge, and that's where I should look.

This is an example of thinking that appears to have nothing to do with numbers. But it is about something: keys, coat pocket, refrigerator. In fact, thinking always seems to be about *something*. Computation, on the other hand, seems to be about *nothing*: it is the process of manipulating symbols in a mechanical way without taking into account what the symbols stand for. So there is certainly a conceptual gap between the two that needs to be bridged. Fortunately, the bulk of the groundwork was already done by Leibniz.

1.3.1 Leibniz and his idea

The idea that thinking can be seen as a kind of computation is one of the rare ideas in Western culture that does not go back to the ancient Greeks. The first person to take this idea seriously was the German philosopher Gottfried Leibniz (1646–1716).

Leibniz was an amazing thinker. Among many other ideas and discoveries, he invented the calculus at the same time as Isaac Newton did. While Newton was interested in problems in physics and chemistry, Leibniz was more interested in symbols and symbol manipulation. He only started doing mathematics seriously later in life. But intrigued by how symbols standing for variables and constants could be shuffled around to solve equations in algebra, he wondered whether there were symbolic solutions to problems involving tangents and areas. And the infinitesimal calculus (derivatives and integrals) came out of this.

When it came to arithmetic, Leibniz observed that it was sufficient to manipulate symbols on a piece of paper according to certain rules to be able to draw conclusions about otherwise abstract numbers. A number (like fourteen, say) might be a completely abstract notion, but the symbols used to represent it (like the symbols *14* or *XIV* or *1110*) are much more tangible: we can write them down, look at them, move them around. We can determine if a certain relation holds among these numbers (for example, determining whether a number is the sum of two others) just by manipulating the symbols. (The symbols *1110* represent the number fourteen in the binary number system invented by Leibniz that is used by digital computers.)

His idea then was this: *Ideas*, that is, the objects of ordinary thought, are like numbers. It will be sufficient to manipulate symbols standing for them according to certain rules. The ideas may be abstract, but the symbols are concrete. One will be able to go from one idea to the next just by doing symbolic manipulation.

In other words, he drew the following analogy:

- The rules of arithmetic allow us to deal with abstract numbers in terms of concrete symbols. The manipulation of those symbols mirrors the relations among the numbers being represented.

- The rules of *logic* allow us to deal with abstract ideas in terms of concrete symbols. The manipulation of those symbols mirrors the relations among the ideas being represented.

What a truly remarkable idea! It says that although the objects of human thought are formless and abstract, we can still deal with them concretely as a kind of arithmetic, by representing them symbolically and operating on the symbols.

In the case of arithmetic, we already know what numbers are and what symbols we should use to represent them. We have all been trained to do this symbolic processing starting at a very early age, without a second thought.

But what about ideas? What symbols should stand for them?

1.3.2   Propositions vs. sentences

A *proposition*, as the word is used in the philosophical literature, is an idea that can be expressed by a declarative sentence of English (or other language). So one can think of the sentence as a symbolic representation of the proposition. Consider these examples:

- *My keys are in my coat pocket.*

- *Dinosaurs were warm-blooded.*

- *The stock market composite index will rise to twice its current value within the next three years.*

- *Hate literature should not be tolerated, even if that impinges on free speech.*

These are all English sentences. The first one uses seven words of English, for example. But apart from being English sentences, they each express an *idea*, an idea that can be expressed in other languages with other sentences. So we have the *sentence*, on the one hand (like the first one with seven words), and the *proposition* it expresses, on the other (like the idea that my keys are located somewhere).

What can be said about the propositions themselves? They are abstract entities, like numbers, but they have some special properties:

- Propositions are considered to *hold* or to *not hold*. A sentence is *true* if the proposition it expresses holds, and *false* if that proposition does not hold.

  This does not mean that there will be no controversy about whether the proposition holds. It just means that it makes sense to ask *if* it holds (or if the corresponding sentence is true). A number is a very different sort of abstract object; we do not ask if a number holds in this sense.

- Propositions are considered to be related to people in certain ways: people may or may not believe them, fear them, regret them, wish for them, worry about them, and so on. These various relationships between people and propositions are what philosophers call *propositional attitudes*.

- Propositions are related to each other in certain ways: a proposition might imply, or provide evidence for, or contradict another proposition.

Uninterpreted sentences

A first clue that one might be able to understand thinking as computation is to look at a sentence of English as a purely symbolic structure made up of a sequence of words. Consider this, for example:

The snark was a boojum.

This is a line from the poem *The Hunting of the Snark,* by Lewis Carroll, that was intended to be nonsense. (What is this snark? What is a boojum?) Observe that if one assumes that the sentence is *true,* even without knowing what the words *snark* and *boojum* mean, one can answer certain questions:

- What kind of thing was the snark?
  (It was a boojum.)

- Is it true that the snark was either a beejum or a boojum?
  (Yes, because it was a boojum.)

- If no boojum is ever a beejum, was the snark a beejum?
  (No, it could not have been.)

- What is an example of something that was a boojum?
  (The snark, of course.)

The point is that one can provide appropriate answers to these questions *without having to know what the two symbols mean.* This is the first step toward linking thinking and computation. Some simple rules of logic make it possible to extract answers directly from the sentence itself (viewed as a symbolic structure) without having to determine first what the symbols *snark* and *boojum* stand for.

Now consider the following three examples:

1. *My keys are in my coat pocket or on the fridge.*
   Nothing is in my coat pocket.
   So: My keys are on the fridge.

2. *Henry is in the basement or in the garden.*
   Nobody is in the basement.
   So: Henry is in the garden.

3. *Jill is married to George or Jack.*
   Nobody is married to George.
   So: Jill is married to Jack.

Observe that in all these cases the thinking is the same. The pieces are put together in exactly the same way, even though the sentences are about quite different things. There could just as easily be a fourth example:

4. *The frumble is frimble or framble.*
   Nothing is frimble.
   So: The frumble is framble.

Again, one does not need to know what *frimble* means to get the correct conclusion. It does not really matter whether the subject is keys, Henry, Jill, or the frumble. What does matter is the *form* of the sentences in terms of the other connecting words, and the conclusion based on that form. For example, it would be wrong in the last case to conclude that the frumble was frimble.

Logical entailment

Telling us what to conclude in such examples is the job of logic. A collection of sentences $S_1, S_2, \ldots, S_n$ <u>logically entails</u> another sentence S if the truth of S is implicit in the truth of the S_i sentences. In other words, no matter what certain terms (like *boojum, garden, framble*) in the S_i sentences really mean, if they are all true, then the S sentence is also true. So, in determining if a collection of sentences logically entails another, it is not necessary to know what the terms in those sentences mean. (Certain keywords in sentences, such as *and*, do have specific functions.)

So, for example, the sentence

   The snark was a boojum.

logically entails

   Something was a boojum.

Similarly, the sentences

   My keys are in my coat pocket or on the fridge.
   Nothing is in my coat pocket.

logically entail

   My keys are on the fridge.

The fact that these symbols can be used in an uninterpreted way is what allows the connection with computation.

Is thinking logic?

So in the end, is thinking just logic? For anyone who has studied logic, this is not a very plausible notion.

Suppose somebody at a party says,

> *George is a bachelor.*

Here are some of the sentences that this logically entails:

> *Somebody is a bachelor.*
> *George is either a bachelor or a pig farmer.*
> *Not everyone is not a bachelor.*
> *It is not the case that both George and Henry are not bachelors.*

Sure enough, these sentences will all be true if the given sentence is; that is what logical entailment does. But they are so very, very boring!

If you found out at a party that George was a bachelor, it is almost guaranteed that we would not spend time going through logical entailments like these. You might think about *George* (whom you might already know) or about what it means to be a *bachelor*. Thinking seems to be so much richer than just dry logical entailments because thinking seems to depend on what the words in a sentence *mean*.

In fact, the view that thinking is logic may seem so far off the mark that instead of asking what is *wrong* with it, one might be tempted to ask what is *right* with it.

1.3.3   Using what is known: The web of belief

To get a glimmer of what could be right with it, one has to go back to the idea of thinking: bringing knowledge to bear on an activity. In reaching the conclusions about George the bachelor, no other knowledge was used. The search for logical entailments is not from that one sentence alone but rather from that sentence together with everything else that is already known.

Figure 1.5 shows some of the relevant facts that may be known about George the bachelor. In this collection of sentences, the terms *George, bachelor, man,* and so on, appear in many places, linking the sentences together in the same way that the term *frimble* did in the sentences of the earlier example.

It is sometimes helpful to visualize the sentences as forming a kind of *network*, with nodes for each of the terms and links between them according to the sentences in which they appear. The network might look something like the one in figure 1.6. We may not know who George is, for example, but we can see that the node for *George* is connected to the node for *Mary* by way of the node for *son*. We may not know what

Figure 1.5. Some beliefs about George the bachelor

George was born in Boston, collects stamps.

George is the only son of Mary and Fred.

A son of someone is a child who is male.

A man is an adult male person.

A bachelor is a man who has never been married.

A (traditional) marriage is a contract between a man and a woman that is enacted by a wedding and dissolved by a divorce. While the contract is in effect, the man (called the husband) and the woman (called the wife) are said to be married.

A wedding is a ceremony where . . . bride . . . groom . . . bouquet . . .

      and so on.

---

son is supposed to mean, but its node is connected to the nodes for *child* and *male*. Similarly, the *male* node is connected in a different way to the node for *man*. The node for *bachelor* is connected in a complex way to the node for *marriage* and from there, presumably, to *wedding* and *bride*. Although we may not know what any of these terms mean in isolation, the various sorts of links given by the sentences in the network provide a rich set of interdependencies among them.

A network like this is sometimes called a *web of belief* to emphasize that the sentences do not stand alone but link to many others by virtue of the terms they use. The job of logical entailment is to crawl over this web looking for connections among the nodes, sensitive to the different types of links along the way. In figure 1.6 there is a certain path from *George* to *male*, for example, that can lead to the conclusion that George is male. If the fact that George is a bachelor is added to the web, a new set of pathways opens, including some connections from *George* to *marriage* that were not there before.

The logical entailments for the new sentence together with everything previously known gives some additional answers:

> *George has never been the groom at a wedding.*
> *Mary has an unmarried son born in Boston.*
> *No woman is the wife of any of Fred's children.*

These are much more like the ordinary thoughts that people would think when learning that George was a bachelor. They are not exactly poignant, of course, but if some

Figure 1.6.   Some beliefs as a network

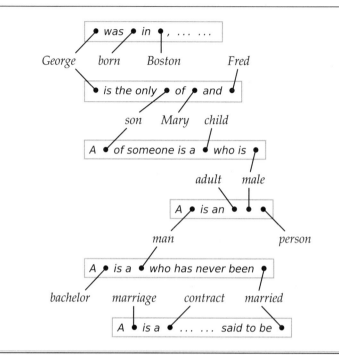

additional facts were added about how parents hope their children end up happily married, one could go in that direction. (Or one might want to include facts about what a bachelor lifestyle is like and get additional entailments about George that would fit into a party setting.)

Observe that to get this richer set of conclusions, one does not need to know in advance what the symbols *George* and *bachelor* mean. What is needed, however, is a much richer collection of sentences over which to apply the rules of logic.

Knowledge bases

At this point, we have to be prepared to make a gigantic leap of the imagination:

> Imagine that we can draw conclusions from *millions* of such facts.

In other words, to make a plausible connection between thinking and computing, we have to imagine that we are considering the logical entailments of a potentially enormous collection of sentences, an entire web of belief. Such a collection is called a *knowledge base* (KB). The collection shown in figure 1.5 is just a very small sample.

So yes, there is a connection between thinking and logic, but it is misleading to think of it as Logic, the subject studied in philosophy. The way Logic is normally taught, one starts with a small set of premises and concentrates on ensuring that the conclusions from them are always correct:

> Socrates is a man.
> All men are mortal.
>
> Therefore, Socrates is mortal.

Thinking is very different. It starts with an enormous collection of premises (maybe millions of them) about a very wide array of subjects. There will be facts in the knowledge base about George and marriage, but also about barber shops, ferris wheels, Academy Awards, hate literature, and so on. The question then is, what are the logical entailments of *all* those sentences?

This leads to two hypotheses:

- Much of the subjective feeling of richness experienced in thinking might be explained as simple mechanical and logical operations, but applied to a very rich collection of sentences.

- To build computer systems with a number of desirable properties (versatile, flexible, extendible, easily maintained, and so on), one must

  - represent much of what the system needs to know as symbolic sentences of some sort, called its knowledge base;

  - perform processing over the knowledge base using the rules of logic to obtain new conclusions;

  - have the system act based on the conclusions it can derive.

Systems built this way are called *knowledge-based systems*.

The big picture

In summary, thinking means bringing what one knows to bear on what one is doing. But how does this work? How do concrete, physical entities like people engage with something formless and abstract like knowledge? What is proposed in this chapter (via Leibniz) is that people engage with *symbolic representations* of that knowledge. In other words, knowledge is represented symbolically as a collection of sentences in a knowledge base, and then entailments of those sentences are computed as needed.

(Actually, there are good reasons to deviate somewhat from strict logical entailment for this. See chapter 3.)

So *computation over a knowledge base* is the direction pursued in this book, although it deals with only tiny knowledge bases. The next chapter studies a procedure that performs this computation for knowledge bases of a certain restricted form.

Want to read more?

This chapter introduced the connection between thinking and computation, an idea that is the subject matter of the rest of this book.

The starting point for this connection is the work of the philosopher Gottfried Leibniz. A good introduction to his thinking can be found in [59]. (His own work is scattered in the thousands of letters he wrote.) There is not much in terms of details, however, as Leibniz did not have the benefit of the modern notions of symbolic logic or computation. These came along in the 1930s, and it took until the 1950s, when John McCarthy, one of the founders of the field of artificial intelligence (AI) [11], became the first person to propose the approach followed in this book, representing what is known as a collection of sentences and computing their logical entailments [47].

An excellent place to begin to explore what psychologists have to say about human thinking is a book by Pinker [9] that is aimed at a broad audience. However, the whole topic of human thinking remains highly controversial, and even Pinker has his detractors [3]. Many find the notion of symbolic computation too limiting because it downplays the effect of the rest of the body on the thinking process [2]. Among the computationalists, many prefer symbolic structures other than sentences that can represent knowledge in a more concrete way [5]. There are also researchers who feel that a lot of thinking needs to be more pictorial or diagrammatic in nature [6].

The general notion of computation used here arose directly out of work on logic in the 1930s. This account of computation is due to Alan Turing, widely considered to be the father of computer science (John von Neumann is often called the father of electronic computers). In 1936, Turing proposed a formal definition of what is here called a procedure in terms of a very simple imaginary device: a *Turing machine* [12]. With this definition, one could now ask questions like whether it was even possible to compute a certain result. Turing was the first to prove that there was a *universal* Turing machine that could compute what any other one could, and remarkably enough, that some results could not be computed by *any* Turing machine.

Turing's carefully worked definition has withstood the test of time. Although different models of computation have been proposed (including a strikingly different one by Alonzo Church), they have all been shown to be equivalent to Turing's. Every computer built so far has been a special case of a Turing machine and subject to the restrictions proved by Turing. The claim that this will be true of *any* physical computer to be built is called the *Church-Turing thesis* [8].

Regarding thinking as computation, there is a superb though somewhat advanced philosophical book on this subject by Pylyshyn [10]. Much of the argument presented here about how actions are conditioned by what is known derives from this insightful book. (In the terminology he uses, those actions are said to be cognitively penetrable.)

Outside of philosophy, there is a subarea of AI called *knowledge representation and reasoning* that starts with the work of McCarthy and is concerned with the issue of representing knowledge in symbolic form and devising computational procedures to reason with it effectively. A graduate-level textbook on this area of research is by Brachman and Levesque [1]. The state of the art in this research area is reviewed in a (quite advanced) technical handbook [4].

Finally, although this book concentrates on small knowledge bases, the CYC project [7] is an example of a project whose goal is to build a large knowledge base along the lines discussed here.

Exercise

Consider the procedure PROCX in figure 1.7. It assumes there are other procedures elsewhere that will do some arithmetic (subtraction, multiplication, and less-than comparisons). It also assumes that one can *concatenate* strings of digits: $x\char`^y$ means the string consisting of the digits in x followed by those in y. It works by repeatedly setting new values to u, v, *bot*, *top*, and *side* as the digits of the input are worked through in pairs from left to right.

Figure out what the procedure PROCX is doing. *Hint:* Trace its behavior when the input is *137641*.

Figure 1.7.   A mystery procedure

Procedure PROCX:

You are given a sequence of digits x as input.
You will return a sequence of digits as output.

1. Group the digits in x into pairs starting from the right. (If x has an odd number of digits, the leftmost group will only have a single digit in it.)

2. Start with u, v, bot, top, and $side$ all having an initial value of 0.

3. Then, working your way from left to right on the groups in x, repeat the following:

   a. Set bot to $(bot - u)$ ^(the next group from x).

   b. Set $side$ to $2 \times top$.

   c. Set v to the largest single digit such that $v \times (side\,\hat{}\,v) \leq bot$.

   d. Set u to $v \times (side\,\hat{}\,v)$.

   e. Set top to $top\,\hat{}\,v$.

4. The answer to return is the final value of top.

---

2   A Procedure for Thinking

Chapter 1 showed that thinking, or at least some simple forms of thinking, could be profitably understood as drawing conclusions from a large collection of sentences called a knowledge base (KB). Leibniz's idea was that the rules of logic would tell how to manipulate these symbolic structures representing propositions the same way that the rules of arithmetic tell how to manipulate symbolic structures representing numbers. This chapter examines this symbolic manipulation as a computational *procedure*, not so different from those for arithmetic.

The procedure studied in this chapter is called *back-chaining*. It works on sentences of English, but sentences that are very restricted in their form. They have none of the niceties found in English or any other natural language. On the other hand, these sentences can be treated as *uninterpreted* symbolic structures: one can operate on them without having to know in advance what they mean. This is in accordance with the view of computation saying that one can produce interesting answers to interesting questions without having to know what the symbols stand for.

This chapter has five sections. The first section looks at the types of sentences included in the knowledge base and introduces a small example. Section 2 examines the notion of logical entailment in a bit more detail. The back-chaining procedure is presented in section 3. Section 4 looks at some complex behavior of back-chaining involving variables. Section 5 summarizes very briefly what is good and less good about this procedure for thinking.

2.1   Atomic and conditional sentences

A special but very useful case of a knowledge base is one consisting of just two sorts of sentences:

- Atomic sentences, that is, simple basic sentences whose exact form is left unspecified for now

- Conditional sentences, that is, sentences of the form *If P_1 and … and P_n then Q,* where the P_i and the Q are atomic sentences

Figure 2.1.   A family example knowledge base

---

john is a child of sue.   *john is a child of sam.*

jane is a child of sue.   *jane is a child of sam.*

  sue is a child of george.   *sue is a child of gina.*

john is male.   *jane is female.*   *june is female.*

sam is male.   *sue is female.*   *george is male.*

If X is a child of Y then Y is a parent of X.

If X is a child of Y and Y is male then Y is a father of X.

If X is male and Y is female then X is of opposite sex from Y.

If X is male and Y is female then Y is of opposite sex from X.

If X is a father of Y and Y is a parent of Z then X is a grandfather of Z.

In both cases, the sentences may contain variables (written here capitalized) and constants (written here uncapitalized). So, for example,

   sue is a child of george.

is an example of an atomic sentence, whereas

   If X is a child of Y and Y is male then Y is a father of X.

is an example of a conditional sentence. In these two sentences, the words *If*, *and*, and *then* are special keywords, *X* and *Y* are variables, and all the other words are considered to be constants.

A complete but small KB in this restricted sublanguage of English is shown in figure 2.1. In this case, the first five lines are atomic sentences (a total of twelve of them), and the remaining five lines are conditional sentences.

At this point, you should not spend too much time trying to make sense of the sentences. They will be treated as a collection of symbols, somewhat like the digits in an arithmetic problem.

2.2   Logical entailment

The computational procedure of interest here is one that computes logical entailments of a knowledge base. More precisely, the procedure will receive an atomic sentence Q (the *query*) as input, and its job will be to determine if the query is logically entailed by the knowledge base.

Before going on to this procedure, it is worthwhile to examine the notion of logical entailment more closely. Recall that a sentence is *logically entailed* if it cannot not help but be true if all the sentences in the knowledge base are true. In determining what is and is not logically entailed, we do not use normal English understanding of the constants that appear in the knowledge base or in the query. In the KB of figure 2.1, there are constants like *sam* and *female*; for purposes of logical entailment, imagine that these names have been changed everywhere to something neutral, like *object13* and *property51*.

Here are some sample logical entailments of this knowledge base:

- *jane is a child of sue.*

  This sentence is in the KB, and therefore if everything in the KB is true, it must be true, too. Note that even if other symbols had been used everywhere in the KB and in the query, like *relation17* instead of *child* and *person53* instead of *jane*, the resulting sentence would still be an entailment.

- *sue is a parent of jane.*

  This sentence is not in the KB, but the following two sentences are there:

  > *jane is a child of sue.*
  > *If X is a child of Y then Y is a parent of X.*

  So if everything in the KB is true, then by virtue of the special keywords *If* and *then*, the query must also be true. Again, this is not because of the relationship between the English words *child* and *parent*; it is because there is a conditional sentence in the KB that makes a connection between the *child* and *parent* symbols.

- *george is a grandfather of jane.*

  This sentence must be true for the same reason as the previous one; the argument is just longer. It requires using these sentences in the KB:

  1. *george is male.*
  2. *jane is a child of sue.*
  3. *sue is a child of george.*
  4. *If X is a child of Y then Y is a parent of X.*
  5. *If X is a child of Y and Y is male then Y is a father of X.*
  6. *If X is a father of Y and Y is a parent of Z then X is a grandfather of Z.*

  If everything in the KB is true, then the following sentences that are not in the KB must also be true:

7. *george is a father of sue.*   (by virtue of sentences 3, 1, and 5)

8. *sue is a parent of jane.*   (by virtue of sentences 2 and 4)

9. *george is a grandfather of jane.*   (by virtue of sentences 7, 8, and 6)

So in all three cases the query is logically entailed by the KB. Now let us consider some examples of sentences that are *not* logically entailed:

- *gina is female.*

  This sentence may indeed be true. After all, Gina is a name that is commonly used by females. However, although the constant *gina* appears in the KB, it could just as well have been *harvey* or *person17d*. No connection to *female* is warranted.

- *john is younger than sam.*

  Someone might say, "If everything in the KB is true, then John is a child of Sam, so he has to be younger than Sam. So the query must be true." This is not quite right, but the reason may not be obvious. It cannot be assumed that the symbol *younger* means the same as it does in English. In deciding what is entailed, the only information that may be used is what actually appears in the KB (see *parent* and *grandfather*). Since the symbol *younger* does not appear in the KB, there is no information to use. The query could be written as *john is in relation239 to sam* which, of course, need not be true. So the query is not logically entailed.

- *sue is a mother of john.*

  This is similar to the previous case. The following two sentences are entailed by the knowledge base:

  > *sue is female.*
  > *sue is a parent of john.*

  But one cannot conclude that the sentence

  > *sue is a mother of john.*

  is true. One might want to make a connection between *mother* and the symbols *female* and *parent*, since that is how it works out in English. But nothing in the KB currently sanctions this. This is quite unlike the *father* case, where sentences in the KB do connect *father*, *male*, and *parent*.

Figure 2.2. The back-chaining procedure

To establish a sentence Q:

1. Try to locate Q itself in the KB. If you can, then return *success*.

2. Otherwise, try to locate a conditional sentence of the form

    If P_1 and ... and P_n then Q

    in the KB. If you cannot, then return *failure*.

3. Otherwise, use back-chaining to try to establish P_1, then P_2, ... , then P_n. If these are all successful, then return *success*.

4. Otherwise, go back to step 2 and look for another conditional.

═══════════════════════════════════════

2.3   Back-chaining

The computational procedure used in this chapter is called *back-chaining*. As mentioned, the procedure is given an atomic sentence Q and attempts to determine if Q is logically entailed by the knowledge base, that is, back-chaining is asked to *establish* the query. So the input will be a query Q (and implicitly, a KB in the background), and the output will be either *success* or *failure*. (Even if a query Q can be successfully established, it is *not* added to the KB. Back-chaining always leaves the KB unchanged. No learning happens here.)

The back-chaining procedure is shown in figure 2.2. It is called back-chaining because it chains backward from a query to the atomic sentences in the KB. Note that the back-chaining procedure for Q depends on using the back-chaining procedure for other sentences (the P_i). This makes it a *recursive* procedure (discussed in chapters 3 and 4). Before looking at back-chaining in action, we need to deal with one complication: *variables*.

2.3.1   Using variables

There are sentences in the knowledge base that include variables, such as the one relating *child* and *parent*. A sentence like

> *If X is a child of Y then Y is a parent of X.*

is intended to work as if the KB included sentences like

If john is a child of sue then sue is a parent of john.
If john is a child of gina then gina is a parent of john.
If gertrude is a child of heathcliff then heathcliff is a parent of gertrude.

and all the (infinitely many) other sentences of this form. So one needs to be able to draw the same conclusions from the one sentence with variables as would be drawn from all the other sentences with constants in them.

From the point of view of back-chaining, here is what this use of variables amounts to. Suppose the query Q is

george is a parent of sue.

Step 2 in figure 2.2 says to check whether the KB has a sentence of the form

If ... then george is a parent of sue.

The KB does not have a conditional sentence for this particular Q, but it does have a sentence

If ... then Y is a parent of X.

This is considered to *match* the Q at step 2, so at step 3, the relevant Y is *george* and the relevant X is *sue*. Here is the result:

- The query Q at step 2 is *george is a parent of sue.*

- The KB contains *If X is a child of Y then Y is a parent of X.*
  This is considered to match for *Y=george* and *X=sue.*

- The query P_1 at step 3 is *sue is a child of george.*

2.3.2 Tracing the back-chaining

The following four examples simulate the execution of the back-chaining procedure on four sample queries. This is called *tracing* the procedure and is very similar to what was done with arithmetic in chapter 1. Note the step numbers as you follow the procedure.

Example 1

Establish the query *jane is a child of sue.*

1. Look for *jane is a child of sue* in the KB. Found.
   Return *success* for *jane is a child of sue.*

Example 2

Establish the query *gina is female*.

1. Look for *gina is female* in the KB. Nothing found.

2. Look for *If . . . then gina is female* in the KB. Nothing found.
   Return *failure* for *gina is female*.

Example 3

Establish the query *george is a father of sue*.

1. Look for *george is a father of sue* in the KB. Nothing found.

2. Look for *If . . . then george is a father of sue* in the KB.
   Found: *If X is a child of Y and Y is male then Y is a father of X.*
   This matches for *Y=george* and *X=sue*.

3. Work on the two if-parts of this matching conditional:
   (Note in figure 2.2 that the two parts are worked on from left to right.)

   - Establish the query *sue is a child of george*.
     (This is the query *X is a child of Y* with *X=sue* and *Y=george*.)

     1. Look for *sue is a child of george* in the KB. Found.
        Return *success* for *sue is a child of george*.

   - Establish the query *george is male*.
     (This is the query *Y is male* with *Y=george*.)

     1. Look for *george is male* in the KB. Found.
        Return *success* for *george is male*.

   Since both parts were successful, return *success* for the original query
   george is a father of sue.

Example 4

Establish the query *jane is of opposite sex from george*.

1. Look for *jane is of opposite sex from george* in the KB. Nothing found.

2. Look for *If . . . then jane is of opposite sex from george* in the KB.
   Found: *If X is male and Y is female then X is of opposite sex from Y.*
   This matches for *X=jane* and *Y=george*.

(This is the first matching conditional found. When looking for a sentence, back-chaining always considers the KB in its entirety from top to bottom.)

3. Work on the two if-parts of the matching conditional:

   ▪ Establish the query *jane is male*.

      1. Look for *jane is male* in the KB. Nothing found.

      2. Look for *If . . . then jane is male* in the KB. Nothing found.
         Return *failure* for *jane is male*.

   Since the first part was not successful, skip the second one.

4. The attempt to establish the two if-parts was not successful.
   So go back to step 2 to see if there is another matching conditional.

2. Look again for *If . . . then jane is of opposite sex from george* in the KB.
   Found: *If X is male and Y is female then Y is of opposite sex from X.*
   This matches for *Y=jane* and *X=george*.
   (This is the second of the two matching conditionals in the KB.)

3. Work on the two if-parts of the matching conditional:

   ▪ Establish the query *george is male*.

      1. Look for *george is male* in the KB. Found.
         Return *success* for *george is male*.

   ▪ Establish the query *jane is female*.

      1. Look for *jane is female* in the KB. Found.
         Return *success* for *jane is female*.

   Since both parts were successful, return *success* for the original query
   jane is of opposite sex from george.

You should reread these four examples carefully and make sure that you follow each of the steps. *They are crucial to understanding how back-chaining works.*

Note in particular how the procedure works backward from the query at step 3 using other queries, and depending on how *they* turn out, either returns *success* or (at step 4) goes back to step 2 to see if there are other conditional sentences that can be used. (Only when there are no more sentences will it return *failure*.)

Although this is a computational procedure, and you do not need to know what the symbols mean, it is absolutely critical to keep track of your place in the procedure. At step 3, you may need to work on another subquery, which itself could get to another step 3, and which could invoke yet another subsubquery. In tracing the procedure, indentation was used to show how *deep* you were in the procedure. When one of the subqueries returns *success* or *failure*, you must be able to decide what to do at one level higher.

This is illustrated in example 3 with the subquery *sue is a child of george*. This subquery returned *success*. But the work was not finished, since at a higher level, it was still necessary to work on the second subquery *george is male*.

In example 4, the first conditional sentence found did not work: the subquery *jane is male* returned *failure*. But again the work was not finished: the procedure was at step 3, and it required going to step 4, which required returning to step 2 to look for another conditional. The second conditional did work, and the entire query returned *success*.

2.4   Variables in queries

In the four examples just considered, the query Q only contained constants. The back-chaining procedure must be generalized so that it also works when Q contains variables. In this case, the interest lies not in whether Q is logically entailed, but *for what values of the variables* the query Q is logically entailed. Note the following:

- If the query is *sue is a child of gina*, it asks if the sentence is logically entailed by the KB. It is a yes/no question, and the *success* or *failure* returned by back-chaining gives the answer.

- If the query is *X is a child of gina*, it asks for what value of *X* is the sentence logically entailed by the KB. It is a *wh* question (who? what? when? where? why? how?). The expected answer is something like *X=sue* (since the sentence *sue is a child of gina* is entailed).

When a query contains a variable, a unique answer is not necessarily expected. If the query is *john is a child of Z*, either of the following answers would work: *Z=sue* or *Z=sam*; each corresponding sentence is logically entailed.

2.4.1   One complication: Renaming variables

One complication raised by the issue of variables within queries is the following: what should be done if a variable in a query has the same name as one in the knowledge base? How can one keep straight which is which?

The answer is simple:

The names of the variables in the sentences of the knowledge base do not really matter; they can be changed at any time.

For example,

If X is a child of Y then Y is a parent of X.

says exactly the same thing as

If U is a child of V then V is a parent of U.

and exactly the same thing as

If Var13 is a child of Var19 then Var19 is a parent of Var13.

All these sentences make precisely the same connection between *child* and *parent*.

So to keep variables in a query distinct from those used in a KB, the variables in the KB can be renamed without changing what the sentences are saying. Thus, during back-chaining, whenever there is a query with variables, the variables in the sentences of the KB will be renamed to ensure that they differ from the ones in the query. (They could be renamed in the query instead, but this is not done here.)

To see this renaming in action, consider the trace shown in figure 2.3 for the query *george is a father of Y*. Let us review the steps:

1. There is nothing in the KB that matches this query.

2. There is a conditional to consider. However, the names of its variables conflict with *Y* in the query, so first change them to *U* and *V*. After this renaming, there is a match as before with *U=Y* and *V=george*.

3. After *U* and *V* are replaced by their matching values, there are two subqueries remaining: *Y is a child of george* and *george is male*. Note that after replacing the variables by their matching values, there is still the variable *Y* to deal with.

    1. Look for *Y is a child of george* in the KB. The KB does not contain this sentence literally. But it does contain a matching sentence, from which *Y* gets the value *sue*. So this query succeeds with *Y=sue*.

    2. The query *george is male* then succeeds straightforwardly.

    Since both of these queries succeed, the query *george is a father of Y* succeeds with *Y=sue*. This means that *george is a father of sue* has been established and is logically entailed by the KB.

Figure 2.3.   A trace of a query with a variable

Establish the query *george is a father of Y.*

1. Look for *george is a father of Y* in the KB. Nothing found.

2. Look for *If ... then george is a father of Y* in the KB.
   Found: *If U is a child of V and V is male then V is a father of U.*
   This matches for *V=george* and *U=Y.*

3. Work on the two if-parts of the matching conditional:

   - Establish the query *Y is a child of george.*

     1. Look for *Y is a child of george* in the KB.
        Found: *sue is a child of george,* which matches for *Y=sue.*
        Return *success* for *Y is a child of george* with *Y=sue.*

   - Establish the query *george is male.*

     1. Look for *george is male* in the KB. Found.
        Return *success* for *george is male.*

   Since both parts were successful, return *success* for the query
   george is a father of Y with *Y=sue.*

2.4.2   Another complication: Backtracking

Another complication can arise with variables in queries because there can be more
than one answer. It is possible that one answer is found, but that later in the back-
chaining procedure, the answer leads to failure. In this case, one must go back to
where the answer was found, and see if there is another answer to use in its place.
This is called *backtracking* and is best illustrated using an example.

   Consider the query *P is a father of john.* The search is for someone whom John
is a child of and who is male, which is to say, Sam. How is the query handled by
back-chaining? A trace for it starts as follows:

1. Look for *P is a father of john* in the KB. Nothing found.

2. Look for *If ... then P is a father of john* in the KB.
   Found: *If X is a child of Y and Y is male then Y is a father of X.*
   This matches for *X=john* and *Y=P.*

3. Work on the two if-parts of the matching conditional:

- Establish the query *john is a child of P*.

  1. Look for *john is a child of P* in the KB.
     Found: *john is a child of sue*, which matches for *P=sue*.
     Return *success* for *john is a child of P* with *P=sue*.

- Establish the query *sue is male*.

Let us stop here and review what has happened so far. The query *john is a child of P* succeeded. But the first answer found, looking from top to bottom in the KB, was *sue*. This answer is going to be a problem later: the subquery *P is male* with *P=sue* will fail. If there were no backtracking, the whole query would fail. So after discovering that the subquery *sue is male* fails, the back-chaining procedure must backtrack to the subquery *john is a child of P* and look for other possibilities. The value *sam* for *P* will then be found, and the rest of the query will eventually succeed.

So just as step 4 of the back-chaining procedure requires going back to step 2 and considering other options if things do not work out for the P_i subqueries, backtracking requires going back and reconsidering the choice of values for variables if things do not work out.

It is possible to redesign the back-chaining procedure in figure 2.2 to make this backtracking explicit, but this is not done here. (The back-chaining procedure shown in figure 3.12 does take this complication into account.) Suffice it to say that the procedure searches the KB for a matching atomic or conditional sentence, from top to bottom and from left to right, and returns the first match found. But it must be able to search for other matches if the first match causes problems later.

2.4.3   A more complex query

Let us now consider a more complex query: *george is a grandfather of john*. The trace is shown in figure 2.4. Although this query does not itself include variables, variables are introduced for subqueries along the way. For example, a matching conditional in step 2 gives us a value for the variables *X* and *Z* but leaves the *Y* unspecified. This is why in the next step there is a subquery with a variable: *george is a father of Y*. So even if a top-level query has no variables, back-chaining would still need to handle subqueries with variables.

Next, in step 3 of figure 2.4, there are two subqueries: *george is a father of Y* and *Y is a parent of john*. The first one was traced in figure 2.3 and succeeds with *Y=sue*. (This is a good value, and no backtracking will be needed.)

Figure 2.4. A trace of a complex query

Establish the query *george is a grandfather of john*.

1. Look for *george is a grandfather of john* in the KB. Nothing found.

2. Look for *If . . . then george is a grandfather of john* in the KB.
   Found: *If X is a father of Y and Y is a parent of Z then X is a grandfather of Z*.
   This matches for *X=george* and *Z=john*.

3. Work on the two if-parts of the matching conditional:

   - Establish the query *george is a father of Y*.

      See the detailed trace in figure 2.3.

      Return *success* for *george is a father of Y* with *Y=sue*.

   - Establish the query *sue is a parent of john*.

      1. Look for *sue is a parent of john* in the KB. Nothing found.

      2. Look for *If . . . then sue is a parent of john* in the KB.
         Found: *If X is a child of Y then Y is a parent of X*.
         This matches for *Y=sue* and *X=john*.

      3. Work on the single if-part of the matching conditional:

         - Establish the query *john is a child of sue*.

            1. Look for *john is a child of sue* in the KB. Found.
               Return *success* for *john is a child of sue*.

      Since this one part was successful, return *success* for the query
      sue is a parent of john.

   Since both parts were successful, return *success* for the top-level query
   george is a grandfather of john.

So for the second subquery in figure 2.4, *Y is a parent of john*, the *Y* already has a value, *sue*. That is why the second subquery to establish is *sue is a parent of john*, with no variables remaining. The rest of the trace is similar to previous ones.

This was a complex enough query that it is worth reviewing the *thinking* that went into it in a less formal way:

> For George to be a grandfather of John, George needs to be a father of somebody who is a parent of John.

George is male and Sue is a child of George, so George is a father of Sue.

Furthermore, John is a child of Sue, so Sue is a parent of John.

Putting these two facts together, George is a father of Sue, who is a parent of John. So George is a grandfather of John.

2.5   Why is back-chaining good?

Why is back-chaining a procedure worth studying? There are really two issues here:

- Why do we want to do logical entailment at all? This is not an unreasonable question. A lot of what is called thinking seems to be quite unlike what is called logic. All one can say about this for now is that at least some simple forms of thinking (like figuring out grandfathers) do appear to involve extracting logical entailments from other things that are known.

- Is back-chaining the only way to compute logical entailments?. The answer is no. There is also *forward-chaining* as well as other procedures that have little to do with chaining. Moreover, back-chaining is only defined for knowledge bases consisting of atomic and conditional sentences. If one wants to deal with negation or disjunction or any other connectives in the knowledge base, one would need to use another procedure (see chapter 11).

What then is so good about back-chaining?

- It is *goal-directed*. One works backward from a goal (the query to be established) toward what is known (the atomic sentences). In forward-chaining, one starts with atomic sentences and then using the conditional sentences to get new atomic sentences, continues looking for new conclusions, hoping to eventually hit the query. So forward-chaining is looser, more like free association. In some cases, this is good, but with a specific target in mind (the query), it can be unfocused and wasteful.

- It is *logically sound*. To say that a procedure is logically sound means that any time it returns *success* to a query, the query is indeed logically entailed by the knowledge base. In other words, it never makes a mistake. Back-chaining has this property (so far).

- It is sometimes *logically complete*. To say that a procedure is logically complete means that any time a query is logically entailed by the knowledge base, the procedure will eventually return *success*. In other words, the procedure does

Figure 2.5. A dog example knowledge base

---

fido is a collie.

If X is a poodle then X is a dog.

If X is a collie then X is a dog.

If X is a poodle then X is a poodle.

===

not miss anything. Back-chaining almost has this property. It does not miss any logical entailments *provided it does not get stuck in a loop* (see the next section).

- It forms the basis of the Prolog programming language. A computer can be programmed to do back-chaining in a very simple and direct way using Prolog (see chapters 3 and 4).

2.5.1 Getting stuck in a loop

Consider the small knowledge base in figure 2.5. It has one atomic sentence and three conditional sentences. The last sentence is a bit strange perhaps, but it is not intuitively false or wrong.

Observe that this knowledge base logically entails *fido is a dog*. (Just ignore the *poodle* sentences.) However, consider establishing this sentence using back-chaining. Here is the first part of the trace:

1. Look for *fido is a dog* in the KB. Nothing found.

2. Look for *If . . . then fido is a dog* in the KB.
   Found: *If X is a poodle then X is a dog.*
   This matches for *X=fido*.

3. Work on the single if-part of the matching conditional:

   - Establish the query *fido is a poodle.*

     1. Look for *fido is a poodle* in the KB. Nothing found.

     2. Look for *If . . . then fido is a poodle* in the KB.
        Found: *If X is a poodle then X is a poodle.*
        This matches for *X=fido*.

     3. Work on the single if-part of the matching conditional:

        - Establish the query *fido is a poodle.*

It is clear that there is a problem here. In trying to establish *fido is a dog*, the first thing the procedure tries is to establish *fido is a poodle*. Not unreasonable. But instead of the subquery's failing (as it should so that *collie* can be tried next), the procedure finds the last sentence in the knowledge base and tries *fido is a poodle* again as a subquery. It is stuck in a loop. It keeps trying to establish *fido is a poodle* over and over. Consequently, the back-chaining continues forever and never returns *success* as it should. Therefore, back-chaining is not logically complete.

What caused the problem here was the odd sentence saying that anything that is a poodle is a poodle. Even though the sentence is true, it does not add anything to the knowledge base. (The technical term is that the sentence is a *tautology*.) So one might say that this odd sentence should never have been included in the KB and that back-chaining is not to blame for the procedure's getting stuck. This is not an unreasonable position. However, back-chaining can also get stuck on sentences that are not quite so odd, so care will be needed to avoid this undesirable behavior.

Want to read more?

This chapter looked at a computational procedure whose inputs were sentences and whose output was *success* or *failure*, according to whether an input sentence, called the query, was logically entailed by a separate collection of sentences, called the knowledge base. It is a simple matter to get a *computer* to perform this logical computation in Prolog (see chapter 3).

Logic itself has a long history that in Western culture goes back to the ancient Greeks. The modern form of symbolic logic is due to Gottlob Frege, with a specific notation due to Giuseppe Peano, in the early 1900s. The motivation for this development was the desire to put all of mathematical reasoning on a sound footing. In the mid 1930s, Kurt Gödel was able to prove in his celebrated Incompleteness Theorem that this project was doomed, and that mathematical truth (in fact, even simple arithmetic) had to go beyond the application of formal logical rules.

Gödel was a genius. But his work, like that of his good friend Albert Einstein, is perhaps outside the reach of beginners. Fortunately, there is a wonderful review of this part of the history of logic in comic book form [13] that anyone can read and enjoy. (Introductory textbooks on modern symbolic logic do exist, including at least two outstanding ones [14, 15], but they necessarily assume some facility with mathematics.)

Although there are many different ways of looking at logic, the focus in this book is on logical entailment, which in turn depends on thinking about sentences as being true or false. Before 1920 or so, it was typical to think of logic only in terms of *axioms* and *rules of inference* for moving in a correct way from premises to conclusions in arguments or proofs. (This would be like studying the properties of back-chaining with no mention of entailment.) Logicians at the time certainly had an intuitive understanding of what it meant for a sentence to be true, and they felt confident that the rules that they were using were correct (logically sound). But it was only in the late 1920s, spurred by the mathematicians David Hilbert and Wilhelm Ackermann, that they began to consider whether the rules they were using were really *sufficient* (logically complete). In fact, before Gödel proved his Incompleteness Theorem, he proved the completeness of a certain set of axioms and rules of inference, as part of his doctoral thesis.

Soon thereafter, the logician Alfred Tarski took on the topic of truth. He was the first to present a mathematically rigorous definition of a sentence's being true according to a precisely laid-out notion of *logical interpretation*. Logical entailment (or logical consequence) could then be given a mathematical account: it held when a conclusion was true in *all* interpretations where the premises were true. Tarski's work revolutionized logic, and these days it is rare to see a textbook on symbolic logic that does not present the two views of the subject: a syntactic side involving axioms and rules of inference (sometimes called a *proof theory*), and a semantic side involving interpretations and truth (sometimes called a *model theory*), with logical soundness and completeness theorems relating the two.

The idea of restricting language to atomic and conditional sentences goes back to the logician Alfred Horn, who, on a suggestion from Tarski, first examined the properties of sentences like these in the early 1950s. They are usually called *Horn clauses* in his honor, and I use them throughout the book until chapter 11, when I enlarge the representation language.

Exercises

Consider the knowledge base in figure 2.6 about the east-west subway stops in a mythical city somewhere. Note that *left of* is used here to mean *directly* to the left of (as it might appear on a subway map).

1. Give an example of an atomic sentence that is not in the knowledge base in figure 2.6 but that is entailed by it.

Figure 2.6.   A subway knowledge base

---

bay is left of yonge.   st-george is left of bay.

spadina is left of st-george.   bathurst is left of spadina.

christie is left of bathurst.

If X is left of Y then X is west of Y.

If X is left of Y and Y is west of Z then X is west of Z.

If X is west of Y then Y is east of X.

---

2. Explain informally why the sentence *spadina is right of bathurst* is *not* entailed by the knowledge base.

3. Trace the back-chaining procedure on the following queries:

    a. *spadina is west of st-george;*

    b. *yonge is east of bay;*

    c. *christie is west of spadina;*

    d. *yonge is west of yonge;*

    e. *st-george is east of bathurst;*

    f. *bay is west of sherbourne.*

4. Suppose the second conditional sentence in the knowledge base is replaced by

    If X is west of Y and Y is left of Z then X is west of Z.

   Would this change what is entailed? What happens now with the back-chaining procedure on the query (3d) *yonge is west of yonge?*

5. Suppose the (incorrect) atomic sentence

    yonge is left of bay.

   were added to the original knowledge base. For what values of *X* would the resulting knowledge base entail *spadina is west of X*? What happens now with the back-chaining procedure on the query (3f) *bay is west of sherbourne?*

3 The Prolog Language

The previous chapter showed how a procedure called back-chaining could draw logical conclusions from atomic and conditional sentences. It was the first demonstration of how a simple form of thinking could be seen as computation. But so far this computation has not involved computers.

This chapter and the next explain how to write computer programs in a language called Prolog. These programs will end up being knowledge bases like those in chapter 2, but formulated in a new way. Queries will direct a computer to perform back-chaining, just as was done "by hand" in the previous chapter. If nothing else, this will confirm that thinking, as presented in this book, really is a procedure that can be carried out purely mechanically.

Prolog, which stands for <u>pro</u>gramming in <u>log</u>ic, is a language for writing programs that was developed by Alain Colmerauer and colleagues. There are several dialects of Prolog with minor notational differences. This book uses a popular one called SWI-Prolog. (See appendix D for details on this and other dialects of Prolog.)

Learning a programming language like Prolog is a bit like learning a foreign language. It is painstaking and often tedious to memorize not just the new vocabulary but all the rules and regulations of the new language.

Consider a French-speaking person learning English. There will be rules of spelling to learn (like "use *'i'* before *'e'* except after *'c'*"), and many more involving grammar. To take just one example, consider talking about the parent of a child. In French, one chooses between the possessive adjectives *son* and *sa* depending on whether the *parent* in question is male or female: *sa mère* (mother), *son père* (father). In English, on the other hand, one learns that the choice of possessive adjective depends on whether the *child* in question is male or female: for a boy, it's his mother, his father; for a girl, it's her mother, her father.

There is good news and bad news about learning Prolog. The good news is that there are only a few rules to be memorized to get all the spelling and grammar of Prolog right. A complete description of the language fits on one page (see figure 3.10).

Figure 3.1.   The family example in Prolog   `family.pl`

```
% This is the Prolog version of the family example
child(john,sue).    child(john,sam).
child(jane,sue).    child(jane,sam).
child(sue,george).    child(sue,gina).

male(john).    male(sam).    male(george).
female(sue).    female(jane).    female(june).

parent(Y,X) :- child(X,Y).
father(Y,X) :- child(X,Y), male(Y).
opp_sex(X,Y) :- male(X), female(Y).
opp_sex(Y,X) :- male(X), female(Y).
grand_father(X,Z) :- father(X,Y), parent(Y,Z).
```

The bad news is that in contrast to natural languages, Prolog usage is extremely strict. The rules of English are quite forgiving. If you write, "I recieved the package," people will still understand what is meant despite the spelling mistake. You can even say, "accident car passenger hospital," and still be understood, more or less.

In Prolog, there is no such flexibility. *Every single character matters!* A missing comma or a misplaced parenthesis can make the difference between a Prolog program that behaves exactly as intended or a program that does nothing even close. So you will need to be very meticulous and precise about all the details of the Prolog notation. If you are ever going to write your own programs, there is really no choice but to get those details just right. If you already know how to program well in Prolog, you can safely skip this chapter and the next. If you don't, you will learn how to write Prolog programs here.

This chapter is divided into three sections. The first section examines the makeup of Prolog programs in detail. The second section does the same for Prolog queries, which are used to run Prolog programs. The third section reexamines the back-chaining procedure that Prolog uses.

3.1   Prolog programs

Prolog programs are simply knowledge bases of atomic and conditional sentences like those of the previous chapter, but with a slightly different notation. The easiest way to get a sense of that notation is to look at figure 3.1, which contains the entire family example from figure 2.1 written as a Prolog program. (Prolog programs are shown in this font.) To write your own Prolog programs, you will need to know what is and is not allowed. So all the pieces are discussed in detail, starting with the smallest ones.

Constants

A Prolog *constant* must start with a lowercase letter and can be followed by any number of letters, underscores, or digits. A constant may also be a *quoted-string*: any string of characters (other than a single quote) enclosed within single quotes. The following are all legal constants:

```
george    grand_father    mamboNumber5    'Who are you?'
```

Variables

A Prolog *variable* must start with an uppercase letter and can be followed by any number of letters, underscores, or digits. The following are all legal variables:

```
X    P12    MyDog    The_biggest_number    Parameter_26b
```

Prolog has other sorts of terms (numbers and lists) and other types of variables (beginning with an underscore), which are discussed later.

Atomic sentences

The Prolog *atomic sentences* have the following form:

$$predicate(argument_1, \ldots, argument_k)$$

where the *predicate* is a Prolog constant and the subsequent *arguments* are either Prolog constants or variables. So, for example,

```
child(john,X)    delivers_package('Fed Ex',Sender,Receiver)
```

are both atomic sentences, whereas

```
Rich(jim)    likes(george,father(bill))
```

are not. (The first one has a variable in the predicate position, and the second one has an argument that is not a constant or a variable.) Atomic sentences are sometimes called *atoms* for short. Note that instead of *john is a child of X*, there is a pared-down version child(john,X), which omits many of the words used in the sentences in chapter 2, puts the predicate at the front, and requires special punctuation:

- Immediately after the predicate, there must be a left parenthesis.

- Between each argument, there must be a comma.

- Immediately after the last argument, there must be a right parenthesis.

When a predicate has no arguments ($k = 0$), the parentheses can be left out.

Conditional sentences

The _conditional sentences_ of Prolog have this form:

$$head \; :- \; body_1, \ldots, body_n$$

where the head and each element of the body is a Prolog atom. In this case, the notation is quite different from the sentences in chapter 2. For one thing, the _head_, which represents the _then_ part, appears first, and the _body_, which represents the _if_ part, appears afterward. So

```
father(Y,X) :- child(X,Y), male(Y)
```

is equivalent to _If X is a child of Y and Y is male then Y is a father of X_. Note that the words _if_, _then_, and _and_ are left out, and special punctuation is required:

- Immediately after the head, there must be a colon and then a hyphen.

- Between each element of the body, there must be a comma.

When the body is empty ($n = 0$), the :- should be omitted. This means that as far as Prolog is concerned, an atomic sentence is really just a special case of a conditional sentence where the body happens to be empty. (The body can also include other things discussed later.)

In sum, a Prolog _program_ is a sequence of clauses, where a _clause_ is an atomic or conditional sentence terminated by a period. To make programs easier to read (without changing what the program does), spaces, newlines, and comments can be inserted at the end of a program or just before a constant or variable. A Prolog _comment_ starts with a % character (the percent sign) and continues to the end of the line. (In this book, comments are shown in gray italics, but they do not have to be. Only the percent sign is required.)

Here is a very short but complete Prolog program:

```
zzz.
```

This is a Prolog program for the following reasons. A program can be a single clause terminated by a period; a clause can be an atomic sentence; an atomic sentence can be a predicate with no arguments or parentheses; a predicate is written as a constant; and finally, zzz is a constant. Here is a somewhat longer program:

```
% The premises for an old tidbit of logical reasoning
man(socrates).                % Socrates is a man.
mortal(X) :- man(X).          % All men are mortal.
```

A still longer one is the family program in figure 3.1. Typically programs like these are stored in computer files with names like `family.pl`, one per file. (All the programs shown in the figures are available online. The name of the file appears at the top right of each such figure. See appendix A for a complete list.)

3.2 Prolog queries

Once a legal Prolog program has been stored in a file, it is ready for use. But a Prolog program by itself does not really do anything; it only acts in response to *queries*. So here is the usual way of running a Prolog program:

1. Prepare a file containing the Prolog program.

2. Start the Prolog system, and ask it to load the program file.

3. Repeatedly do the following:

   a. Pose a query to the system.

   b. Wait for Prolog to return an answer.

   (Often the queries and answers are saved in a separate log file for later.)

4. Exit the Prolog system.

The details of how these steps are actually carried out vary from system to system.

Figure 3.2 shows a typical run of SWI-Prolog under Linux. (Prolog under Windows or Mac OS X is quite similar. See appendix B.) In this chapter, bold like **this** is used to indicate what a user would type to a Prolog system, and gray italics indicate comments. Anything else is what the Prolog system itself produces.

So in this case, the user starts Prolog, loads the `family.pl` file (figure 3.1), and then asks two queries, one that returns *success* and one that returns *failure*. The name of the file to be loaded appears within square brackets but without the final `.pl` part. Here, success of the query is indicated by `Yes` and failure by `No`. (In some versions of Prolog, `true` and `false` appear instead. See appendix D.)

Note that within Prolog, the `?-` is its way of saying, "I am ready. Give me something to do." In this case, the user tells it (using the square brackets) to load a file, respond to two queries about `sam` and `jane`, and then stop (using the special predicate `halt`).

Figure 3.2.   A run of Prolog with the family example

```
[linux]> swipl                         % Start SWI-Prolog.
Welcome to SWI-Prolog (Multi-threaded, Version 5.6.47)
Copyright (c) 1990-2007 University of Amsterdam.
SWI-Prolog comes with ABSOLUTELY NO WARRANTY. This is free software,
and you are welcome to redistribute it under certain conditions.
Please visit http://www.swi-prolog.org for details.

For help, use ?- help(Topic). or ?- apropos(Word).

?- [family].                           % Load the family.pl file.
family compiled 0.00 sec, 2,728 bytes  % The .pl part is not used.
Yes                                    % No errors were detected.

?- father(sam,jane).                   % A first query to Prolog
Yes                                    % returns success.

?- father(jane,sam).                   % A second query to Prolog
No                                     % returns failure.

?- halt.                               % Exit SWI-Prolog.
[linux]>
```

3.2.1   Queries and their outcomes

In its simplest form, a Prolog *query* is just an atom (with or without variables) and terminated with a period. Note that by entering an atom after a ?- the user asks Prolog to *establish* the query, just as was done in chapter 2. This should not be confused with adding the atom to the knowledge base. In other words, father(sam,jane) is not *telling* Prolog that Sam is a father of Jane; it is *asking* if Sam is a father of Jane. (All the telling took place when the family.pl file, containing the knowledge base, was loaded using the square brackets.)

When Prolog is asked to establish a query with no variables, there are only three possible outcomes:

- Prolog answers Yes—this means that the atom can be established by back-chaining as was the case with father(sam,jane).

- Prolog answers No—this means that the atom cannot be established by back-chaining as was the case with father(jane,sam).

- Prolog does not answer—this means that the atom cannot *yet* be established but that Prolog is continuing to try alternatives.

Figure 3.3. Two more queries after loading the family.pl program

```
?- father(sam,X).          % Who is Sam a father of?
X = john
Yes

?- father(U,V).            % Who is a father of whom?
U = sam
V = john        ;          % Any more?

U = sam
V = jane        ;          % Any more?

U = george
V = sue         ;          % Any more?
No
```

For a query with variables, there will also be three possible outcomes:

- Prolog answers No—this means that the atom cannot be established for any values of the variables.

- Prolog does not answer—this means that the atom cannot *yet* be established for any values of the variables but that Prolog is continuing to try alternatives.

- Prolog displays values for the variables for which it *can* establish the query. At this point the user has some choices:

  - If the user types a space or a return, Prolog answers Yes and the query answering is complete.

  - If the user types a semicolon (;), Prolog tries to find new values for the variables, again with the same three possible outcomes.

So if a query with a variable can be established for different values of the variable, these values can be examined one at a time by using the ; command.

To see how this all works, restart Prolog and again load the family.pl program, as in figure 3.2. Then pose some additional queries.

The first query shown in figure 3.3 uses a variable to ask who Sam is a father of. Prolog responds that an answer is John. Then the user typed a space, indicating that he did not want to see if there were any additional possible answers. The user is finished with this query.

The second query asks Prolog who is a father of whom using two variables: U for the father and V for the child. Prolog returns the pair Sam and John (meaning that it can establish that Sam is a father of John). The user then types a ; asking Prolog to see

Figure 3.4.   Conjunctive queries after loading the family.pl program

---

```
?- female(jane), parent(sam,jane).
Yes
?- female(F), parent(sam,F).
F = jane     ;
No
```

---

if there are any additional answers. It returns Sam and Jane as the next answer. (Same father, different child.) The user asks for more with another ; and Prolog answers George and Sue. The users asks for more with another ; and it answers No (meaning it is unable to establish the query for any other values).

3.2.2   Conjunctive queries

So far, queries have been single atoms terminated with a period. Prolog also allows *conjunctive queries*, which are *sequences* of atoms separated by commas and terminated by a period. These queries are understood *conjunctively*, in the sense that Prolog is asked to establish *all* the atoms in a single query (from left to right). So the comma in a conjunctive query plays the role of *and* just as it does in the body of a conditional sentence.

Assuming the family.pl file is loaded as before, consider the two queries in figure 3.4. The first one asks if Jane is female *and* if Sam is a parent of Jane. The answer is Yes. But this is not very useful, since the job could have been done with two separate atomic queries. What makes conjunctive queries useful is when there are variables that appear in more than one atom. So, for example, in the second query in figure 3.4, the variable F appears in both parts. This query asks if there is an F that satisfies two properties: F is female *and* Sam is a parent of F. Another way of saying this: Is there a female that Sam is a parent of? The key point is that the user seeks the *same* person for both atoms. The answer returned by Prolog is Jane, and after the user types the ; command to ask if there are more, Prolog says No (Jane is the only answer).

Chapter 2 did not deal with conjunctive queries like this, but they were there implicitly. The back-chaining procedure (see figure 2.2) contained the following two instructions:

2. Otherwise, try to locate a conditional sentence of the form
   If P_1 and ... and P_n then Q in the KB. If you cannot, return *failure*.

Figure 3.5.   Negative queries after loading the family.pl program

```
?- child(john,george).          % Is John a child of George?
No

?- \+ child(john,george).       % Is John not a child of George?
Yes

?- parent(X,john), female(X).   % Who is a parent of John
X = sue                         % and female?
Yes

?- parent(X,john), \+ female(X).  % Who is a parent of John
X = sam                         % and not female?
Yes
```

3. Otherwise, use back-chaining to try to establish P_1, then P_2, then ... P_n.

   If these are all successful, then return *success*.

This attempt to handle P_1, then P_2, and so on, is treating the body of a conditional sentence like a conjunctive query: they all have to succeed for this use of the conditional sentence to be successful. In fact, if the clause

```
daughter(F,X) :- female(F), parent(X,F).
```

had been included in the Prolog program of figure 3.1, the query daughter(F,sam) could have been used instead of the second conjunctive query in figure 3.4 to find a female that Sam is a parent of.

3.2.3   Negation in queries

Prolog also allows *negated queries*. The special symbol \+ (meaning *not*) can be used in front of an atom in a query to flip from a Yes to a No, and vice versa. Consider figure 3.5. The answer to the second query is the opposite of the answer to the first one. By itself, this is not very useful. It becomes more useful in the context of a conjunctive query like the fourth one in the figure, where the user wants to find a parent of John who is *not* female.

There was nothing like this use of negation in chapter 2. The query male(X) could have been used, but observe that this is not quite the same as \+ female(X). Consider the case of gina, for example. Because the queries male(gina) and female(gina) *both fail* (since the sex of Gina is not specified), the query \+ female(gina) will succeed, whereas male(gina) will fail.

It is worth observing that if one reads the query `\+ female(gina)` as saying that Gina is not female, then the conclusions from Prolog are no longer *logically sound*. Although the query succeeds, it is *not* the case that the family knowledge base logically entails that Gina is not female; the sex of Gina is left unspecified.

3.2.4   Tracing the back-chaining

In considering an extended version of back-chaining to handle negation, it is worthwhile to follow how Prolog answers conjunctive queries with negation like

    parent(X,john), \+ female(X).

to see how Prolog ends up with the answer `X = sam`.

1. Start by replacing variables in the query with new names to make sure that they do not conflict with any variables that appear in the Prolog program:

       parent(_G312,john), \+ female(_G312).

2. Work on the first atom in the query, `parent(_G312,john)`. Find the clause `parent(Y,X) :- child(X,Y)` in the program (figure 3.1) whose head matches the first atom in the query. This leaves the conjunctive query

       child(john,_G312), \+ female(_G312).

   to work on. (The second part of the query is kept unchanged.)

3. Work on the first atom of the new query, `child(john,_G312)`. Find a matching clause `child(john,sue)` with no body in the program (figure 3.1). Tentatively, this part of the query is finished. This leaves the query

       \+ female(sue).

   (Note that the `child(john,sue)` clause in the program was a bad choice. It will be necessary to backtrack, but that is not known yet.)

4. Work on `\+ female(sue)`. Since this is a negated query, remove the `\+` and consider the unnegated version.

   a. Work on the query `female(sue)`, and find a matching atomic sentence in the program. Return *success*.

   Since the unnegated version succeeds, the negated query *fails*. Backtrack to the most recent choice point (step 3) and reconsider.

Figure 3.6. A Prolog trace for a query

```
?- parent(X,john), \+ female(X).
   Call: (8) parent(_G312,john)
   Call: (9) child(john,_G312)
   Exit: (9) child(john,sue)
   Exit: (8) parent(sue,john)
   Call: (8) female(sue)
   Exit: (8) female(sue)
   Redo: (9) child(john,_G312)
   Exit: (9) child(john,sam)
   Exit: (8) parent(sam,john)
   Call: (8) female(sam)
   Fail: (8) female(sam)
X = sam
Yes
```

5. Reconsider the atom child(john,_G312) (from step 3). Find the next matching clause, child(john,sam) with no body in the program. Tentatively, this part of the query is finished. This leaves

   \+ female(sam).

6. Work on \+ female(sam). Since this is a negated query, remove the \+ and consider the unnegated version.

   a. Work on the query female(sam). There is no clause in the program whose head matches this query. Return *failure*.

   Since the unnegated version fails, the negated query *succeeds*.

7. Since there is nothing left in the conjunctive query, return success, noting that the value of X is sam.

One very nice feature of most Prolog systems is that one can ask Prolog itself to do the tracing. This is very helpful when there is a Prolog program that is legal, but where some queries do not yield hoped-for results.

Figure 3.6 shows an example of a Prolog *trace* for the same query. (How to turn on and turn off this tracing behavior varies from system to system. See appendix C.) This trace goes through roughly the same steps as the previous detailed listing. Four types of lines printed:

- A line that begins Call: is printed when Prolog starts to work on an atomic query.

Figure 3.7.   Instantiated variables and negation

```
?- parent(X,john), \+ female(X).
X = sam
Yes

?- \+ female(X), parent(X,john).
No
```

- A line that begins `Fail:` is printed when the atomic query has failed and Prolog needs to look for alternatives.

- A line that begins `Exit:` is printed when the atomic query has tentatively succeeded, pending the remaining conjunctive query.

- A line that begins `Redo:` is printed when Prolog has gone back to a choice point to reconsider an atomic query.

The numbers that appear within parentheses in such traces are worth looking at. They indicate the level at which Prolog is working. In figure 3.6, the lowest level happens to be (8). This is the level at which Prolog finds the `parent` and `\+ female` queries. Once Prolog uses the conditional sentence with `parent` in the head, and starts working on a `child` query from the body, the number is incremented to (9). (If there had been conditional sentences with the `child` predicate in the head, the atoms in the body would have been at level (10), and so on.)

Although the trace generated by Prolog is succinct, with a bit of practice, you can use it to reconstruct a more reader-friendly trace like the detailed one done in this section.

3.2.5   Instantiated and uninstantiated variables

Now that you have seen how Prolog handles negated queries, there is one small quirk to examine in the back-chaining procedure.

Consider the two queries in figure 3.7. The first one is familiar. The second one simply changes the order in the conjunction. It appears to ask for an X such that X is not female and X is a parent of John. But this time the query fails.

Why are the answers different? Here is a rough trace of the second query:

1. The original query is `\+ female(X), parent(X,john)`.

2. Work on `\+ female(X)`. Since this is a negated query, remove the `\+` and consider the unnegated version.

a. Work on the query `female(X)`; this query succeeds. (The value of X will not matter.)

Since the unnegated version succeeds, `\+ female(X)` fails. The back-chaining does not go on to the second atom; it simply returns *failure*.

So the second query fails because its first part, `\+ female(X)`, fails. And that fails because its unnegated version, `female(X)`, succeeds. So the trace never makes it to the step "and X is a parent of John."

The difference between the two queries is this. In the second query, the variable X is *uninstantiated* (does not yet have a tentative value) when the negated portion of the query is handled. In the first query, the variable X is *instantiated* (has a tentative value) before the negation step. Back-chaining with negation handles these two cases differently.

While there may be cases when something like the second query is wanted, they will be very rare. One is much more likely to want to know about the nonfemale parents of John (and to require something like the first query).

When variables appear in a negated query, make sure that they are already instantiated at an earlier stage of the back-chaining.

The most common way to ensure that a variable is instantiated is by using another atom in a query *before* the negated part, as is done in the first query of figure 3.7.

3.2.6 Equality in queries

The final refinement to the language of queries concerns *equality queries*. Prolog allows elements in a query of the form

$$term_1 = term_2$$

where the two terms are either constants or variables. This query succeeds when the two terms can be made equal by instantiating any variables, and fails otherwise. Some examples are presented in figure 3.8.

The first and second queries succeed by instantiating both X and Y to `sam`. The third query fails, since there is no way to instantiate X and Y to satisfy all three requirements. Finally, in the last query, there is a new form of answer to a query with variables: the query succeeds but there is no single constant value for X and Y. Prolog indicates this by putting a *variable* as the value for X and for Y. The fact that the *same* variable is used for both X and Y is Prolog's way of saying that they can be instantiated to anything, but the two values must be the same.

Figure 3.8.   Queries using equality

```
?- X=sam, X=Y.
X = sam
Y = sam
Yes
?- X=Y, sam=X, \+ Y=jack.
X = sam
Y = sam
Yes
?- X=Y, sam=X, \+ Y=sam.
No
?- X=Y.
X = _G180
Y = _G180
Yes
```

As it turns out, *inequality* is more useful than equality in queries. In fact, it is never necessary to use unnegated equality in a query. Instead of writing a query like

```
child(john,X), child(jane,Y), X=Y.
```

one should write

```
child(john,X), child(jane,X).
```

where the same variable is used more than once. However, negated equality does come in handy, as seen in the queries of figure 3.9.

The first query asks if Sam is parent of someone other than John. In the back-chaining required for this query, X will be instantiated by the parent query and the first tentative value happens to be john. The negated equality fails for this value, and so the parent query is reconsidered, and the second tentative value, jane, is found, for which the rest of the query succeeds.

The second query is the first attempt to get the names of three males. Observe that this does not work properly, since all three variables can have the same value. The third query remedies this and insists that the three values must not be equal, using negated equalities. In this case, Prolog reconsiders the male queries and comes up with three *distinct* values, john, sam, and george.

Figure 3.9. Queries using negated equality

```
?- parent(sam,X), \+ X=john.
X = jane
Yes

?- male(X), male(Y), male(Z).
X = john
Y = john
Z = john
Yes

?- male(X), male(Y), male(Z), \+ X=Y, \+ X=Z, \+ Y=Z.
X = john
Y = sam
Z = george
Yes
```

A review of programs and queries

Figure 3.10 reviews progress so far, with a few minor extensions. First, the word *term* is introduced to mean a constant, variable, or number, and the word *literal* to mean a possibly negated atom or equality. More significantly, the notion of a clause is extended so that the body can be *any query*. So equalities and negations can now be part of the body of a clause. These will be handled during back-chaining exactly as they would be if they were part of a conjunctive query. For example, a clause like

```
has_two_children(X) :- child(Y1,X), child(Y2,X), \+ Y1=Y2.
```

can be in a program as a way of defining a new predicate has_two_children that holds when a person X has (at least) two children. (Without the \+ Y1=Y2 literal, the Y1 and Y2 could be the same child.)

3.3 Prolog back-chaining

This section examines in more detail the back-chaining procedure introduced in chapter 2 to characterize exactly how Prolog goes about using a program that has been loaded to establish a query. Figure 3.11 shows a new, simpler example program called likes.pl.

Figure 3.10.   A review of Prolog programs and queries

Here are the pieces that make up Prolog programs and queries:

- A *constant* is either a string of characters enclosed within single quotes or a lowercase letter optionally followed by letters, digits, and underscores.

- A *variable* is an uppercase letter or an underscore optionally followed by letters, digits, and underscores.

- A *number* is a sequence of one or more digits optionally preceded by a minus sign and optionally containing a decimal point.

- A *term* is a constant, variable, or number.

- A *predicate* is written as a constant.

- An *atom* is a predicate optionally followed by terms (called the *arguments* of the predicate) enclosed within parentheses and separated by commas.

- An *equality* is two terms separated by the = symbol.

- A *literal* is an atom or an equality optionally preceded by the \+ symbol.

- A *query* is a sequence of one or more literals separated by commas and terminated with a period.

- A *clause* is an atom (called the *head* of the clause) followed by a period or by the :- symbol and then a query (called the *body* of the clause).

- A *program* is a sequence of one or more clauses.

Figure 3.11.   The likes example   `likes.pl`

```
% This is a program about who likes what kinds of food.
likes(john,pizza).              % John likes pizza.
likes(john,sushi).              % John likes sushi.
likes(mary,sushi).              % Mary likes sushi.
likes(paul,X) :- likes(john,X). % Paul likes what John likes.
likes(X,icecream).              % Everybody likes ice cream.
```

3.3.1   Unification

Clauses in a program are selected during back-chaining through a matching process called <u>*unification*</u>. Two atoms whose variables are distinct are said to *unify* if there is a substitution of values for the variables that makes the atoms identical. Here are some examples:

- A query such as likes(john,Y) unifies with likes(john,pizza) in the first clause of the program, for Y=pizza.

- A query such as likes(paul,pizza) unifies with likes(paul,X) in the fourth clause of the program, for X=pizza.

- A query such as likes(jane,Y) unifies with likes(X,icecream) in the last clause of the program, for X=jane and Y=icecream.

In all three cases, the given queries would eventually succeed.

Note that both the query and the head of a clause from the program may contain variables. In fact, unification is not concerned with where the atoms come from, which one is from the query and which one is from the program.

As further examples, the following pairs of atoms will unify:

- p(b,X,b) and p(Y,a,b) for X=a and Y=b

- p(X,b,X) and p(a,b,Y) for X=a and Y=a

- p(b,X,b) and p(Y,Z,b) for X=_G12, Y=b, and Z=_G12
  (In this case, the substitution that unifies the two atoms is not unique in that, for example, X=c, Y=b, and Z=c also unifies the two atoms.)

- p(X,Z,X,Z) and p(Y,W,a,Y) for X=a, Z=a, Y=a and W=a
  (In this case, the unifying substitution is unique.)

Here are some examples of pairs of atoms that do not unify:

- p(b,X,b) and p(b,Y)
  (The two terms cannot be made identical, since the predicates have different numbers of arguments.)

- p(b,X,b) and p(Y,a,a)
  (The last arguments are constants that clash.)

- p(X,b,X) and p(a,a,b)
  (The two occurrences of X are required to match different constants.)

- p(X,b,X,a) and p(Y,Z,Z,Y)
  (The two occurrences of X force the Y and Z to be equal, but they must also match a and b, respectively.)

3.3.2   Renaming variables

While the unification process is not concerned with where the atoms come from (query or program) during back-chaining, Prolog nonetheless renames the variables in a query before attempting unification to ensure that there are no clashes.

Consider, for example, the `likes.pl` program in figure 3.11 and what happens with a query such as

```
likes(X,pizza), \+ X=john.
```

This works roughly as follows:

1. Work on the atom `likes(X,pizza)`. First find the clause `likes(john,pizza)` in the program (with no body). This eventually fails.

2. After the failure, backtrack and look for other clauses that will unify with `likes(X,pizza)`. Find the clause whose head is `likes(paul,X)`, but this does not (yet) unify with `likes(X,pizza)`, since there is no value for `X` that makes the two atoms identical.

3. Rename the variable `X` in the query (in both literals) to a totally new variable, such as `X1`.

4. The atom `likes(X1,pizza)` now unifies with `likes(paul,X)` in the program, and the query eventually succeeds.

This renaming of variables is evident when Prolog is asked to trace its behavior when establishing a query.

The next section provides a more detailed picture of how back-chaining works in Prolog on conjunctive queries. Most of the time, an informal description of back-chaining is sufficient, but sometimes, it is useful to understand in more detail all the steps involved, to see, for example, how and where backtracking occurs.

* 3.3.3   Back-chaining revisited

To keep things simple, assume that the conjunctive query consists of atoms only; it is not hard to extend it to negations and equalities.

Look at the back-chaining procedure in figure 3.12. The main step where all the action happens in the procedure is step 3d. At that point, a clause of the program has been found whose head H unifies with the first atom of the query, A_1. Potentially, this clause will give what is needed to establish A_1. However, there may be problems. Perhaps the body of that clause, $B_1, \ldots, B_m$, will not succeed for the values of variables

Figure 3.12. The Prolog back-chaining procedure

To establish a query consisting of atoms $A_1, A_2, \ldots, A_n$:

1. If $n = 0$, there's nothing to do, and so exit with success.

2. Otherwise, begin by renaming all the variables in the conjunctive query.

3. Go through each clause of the *program* from top to bottom:

    a. Assume the current clause has head H and body $B_1, \ldots, B_m$, (where for atomic clauses, $m = 0$).

    b. Test to see if the head H *unifies* with A_1, the first atom of the query.

    c. If it does not unify, try the next clause in the program.

    d. If it does unify, try to establish $B_1^*, \ldots, B_m^*, A_2^*, \ldots, A_n^*$, by back-chaining, where the $*$ means the result of replacing the variables by their values after unification.

    e. If the resulting conjunctive query was successful, exit the procedure with success; if it was not successful, then try the next clause in the program (just as if the H had not unified at step 3c).

4. If all of the clauses of the program have been tried without success, then exit with failure.

---

after the unification of H and A_1, or perhaps the rest of the query, $A_2, \ldots, A_n$, will not succeed for the values of variables after that unification, and backtracking is indicated. So even though the H unifies with A_1, this may not be the desired clause, and the procedure will look for alternatives for A_1 in step e.

To deal with such issues, back-chaining is invoked on a new conjunctive query, $B_1^*, \ldots, B_m^*, A_2^*, \ldots, A_n^*$, where two changes have been made to the original:

- A_1 has been replaced in the query by the *body* of the clause whose head matches A_1. Note that if that matching clause had no body (that is, if the clause was atomic), then there are no B_i atoms, the new query starts at A_2, and the first part of the query is finished, at least tentatively.

- After unifying A_1 with H, the procedure considers the values of the resulting variables. Some variables might appear in both the head and the body of the matching clause and the procedure needs to have the right values for those variables. Also, there can be variables in A_1 that appear in the rest of the conjunctive query, and the procedure needs to have the right values for those variables when going on to A_2.

As mentioned in chapter 2, the back-chaining procedure is _recursive_. This means that part of what it takes to execute the procedure (for certain inputs) involves executing that same procedure on some other inputs. In this case, part of what it takes to do back-chaining on a query is to do back-chaining on another query. This is what happens in step 3d.

To establish the query

$$A_1, A_2, \ldots, A_n,$$

the procedure tries to establish the query

$$B_1^*, B_2^*, \ldots, B_m^*, A_2^*, \ldots, A_n^*.$$

How can this possibly work? It might seem that working on this new query, the procedure would get to step 3d again and find another clause whose head matches B_1^* and whose body is $C_1, \ldots, C_k$. Does this not go on forever, producing longer and longer queries?

It might. Back-chaining _can_ get stuck in a loop and never finish.

However, in other cases, the query that arises in step 3d will be easier to solve than the original one. For example, there may be no body at all in the clause that matches A_1, in which case, the procedure goes from a query with n atoms to one with $(n-1)$ atoms (and eventually to $(n-2)$, and so on, until it gets to 0). Or perhaps there is a body, but it may be able to deal with B_1^* directly in one step (when there is a matching clause that has no body).

At any rate, for back-chaining to return _success_, it must first deal with A_1 by dealing with any B_i atoms that it finds, which may result in dealing with C_i atoms (and perhaps D_i atoms, and so on). When these are all done, then (and only then) does back-chaining go on to the A_2 and the procedure continues (possibly leading to new B_i atoms, as before). A_3 is dealt with in the same way. Eventually, one of two things happens: either the procedure cannot establish one of these A_i no matter what it tries, in which case it returns _failure_; or the procedure gets through all the A_i and ends up with the empty conjunctive query, in which case it returns _success_.

Note that in handling A_1, the procedure looks for clauses to use and then tries to establish a new conjunctive query. If this new query fails, it is not yet done. In fact, it may have failed because the clause it chose for A_1 was not a good one. (It may not be a good one even if it has no body; the unification may require bindings for the variables in A_1 that will not work for A_2, say.) So instead of immediately returning _failure_ after the recursive query fails in step 3d, the procedure backtracks and looks for another clause to work with A_1, in step 3e. It is only when it runs out of clauses to use for A_1 that it finally returns *failure*, in step 4.

Want to read more?

This chapter presented Prolog as a language for writing programs and queries, and showed how a Prolog system uses back-chaining to answer queries. Chapter 4 deals with how to write meaningful Prolog programs.

Prolog was developed by Alain Colmerauer at the Université d'Aix-Marseille II and the Université de Montréal in the early 1970s. Philippe Roussel and Robert Kowalski were also early contributors. (See [16] for some of the history.) Many of the ideas in Prolog were proposed independently in a slightly different form by Carl Hewitt at the Massachusetts Institute of Technology in a computer language called Planner [17]. Prolog was originally intended for computer programs that process *natural language inputs* such as English or French, but it is now used for a wide variety of applications, mainly having to do with artificial intelligence or databases.

Prolog is used most commonly in Britain and France but has enthusiastic fans worldwide. It is often studied as a programming language in computer science courses because it presents a unique view of programming compared to the more conventional programming languages like C++, Java, or Python.

Exercises

Make up a simple knowledge base of atomic sentences about movies (not necessarily real ones) using the following predicates:

`acted_in`(*person*, *movie*)	the person acted in the movie
`directed`(*person*, *movie*)	the person directed the movie
`released`(*movie*, *year*)	the movie came out that year

You can use numbers like `2011` as constants. You may also find it convenient to use quoted strings like `'The Big Lebowski'` as constants.

Save your knowledge base as a Prolog program in a file, and load it into Prolog. Then pose the following questions as queries to Prolog, and obtain Prolog's answers:

1. Did Leonardo DiCaprio act in *Babel*?

2. Who directed *District 9*?

3. Did anyone act in both *Click* and *The Aviator*?

4. Was there a movie released in 2010 that did not star Jennifer Anniston?

5. Who directed movies released in 2009?

    Using the ; command, have Prolog list all such movies and their directors.

6. Has anyone directed more than one movie?

7. Does any movie have more than one director?

8. Has anyone acted in more than one movie released in 2008?

9. Has anyone acted in more than two movies in the same year?

10. Who has worked with the same director in different years?

    Using the ; command, have Prolog list all such actors, directors, the movies they worked on together, and the years the movies were released .

Note: There's nothing wrong with getting *failure* answers from Prolog. But to be sure you have formulated the queries correctly, you may want to change some of the names in the queries, or include some additional movies in your knowledge base.

4   Writing Prolog Programs

The previous chapter looked at what it takes for a Prolog program to be grammatically correct and how it is then used to establish queries. But there is more to a language than just getting the grammar right. There is an old saying in computer science, abbreviated as GIGO: garbage in, garbage out. This means that if the program given to Prolog is grammatically correct but garbage, Prolog will use it to answer queries without complaining, but the answers will also be garbage.

This chapter looks at what it takes to write Prolog programs that are not garbage. The first section examines what it means for a program to be fully correct. Section 2 introduces a new program in a blocks world and studies how it was written. This leads to a discussion of recursion in section 3, and to its companion, mathematical induction, in section 4. Section 5 considers the issue of programs that run forever (see section 2.5.1), and how to avoid writing them. Section 6 looks at a more complex predicate as it appears in the blocks-world program. Finally, section 7 introduces the issue of program efficiency.

4.1   The truth in Prolog

How do we know whether a grammatically correct program will do what it is supposed to? In Prolog, the answer is perhaps clearer than in other programming languages. A Prolog program is a knowledge base made up of clauses. Each of those clauses is an encoding of an atomic or conditional sentence. To answer the question, we need to consider the *truth* of these sentences.

4.1.1   The truth, and nothing but

Let us go back to the family example of figure 3.1, which used the predicate child. As far as Prolog is concerned, that name does not mean anything; it could have been boojum. But the writers of the program had a definite idea in mind when they wrote child(john,sue) and that idea is expressed by the English sentence "John is a child of Sue." The programmers put that atom in the program because they believed, or were willing to assume, that the corresponding English sentence was true. If they had thought that John was a child of Gina, they would have put `child(john,gina)` in the program instead.

Similarly, the program had the clause

```
parent(Y,X) :- child(X,Y).
```

because its creators took the English sentence "If x is a child of y, then y is the parent of x" to be true. If, instead, they had used the clause

```
parent(X,Y) :- child(X,Y).
```

Prolog would not have complained; the clause is grammatically correct. The trouble is that the results would say that John is both a child and a parent of Sue. Garbage in, garbage out. So the clause is not correct because the English sentence "If x is a child of y, then x is a parent of y" is not true.

Suppose the following is in the program:

```
my_predicate(X,Y) :- child(X,Y).
```

Is the corresponding sentence true? It depends on what `my_predicate` means. It is always a good idea to include *comments* in the program to help anyone reading it (including yourself) to understand what was meant:

```
% my_predicate(X,Y) holds when X is a child of Y, or vice versa.
my_predicate(X,Y) :- child(X,Y).
```

Now, at least, it is clear that the corresponding sentence is true.

4.1.2   The whole truth

However, it is not enough to make sure that all the clauses are true. If the program includes the clause `child(john,sue)` but does *not* include the clause `child(john,sam)`, it will still not work properly. A query asking if Sam is a parent of John will not get a good answer even if all the clauses are true (that is, if the sentences they represent are true). The problem is that part of the truth is *missing*.

Consider, for example, the two clauses in the family example about `opp_sex`:

```
opp_sex(X,Y) :- male(X), female(Y).
opp_sex(Y,X) :- male(X), female(Y).
```

Suppose the second one had been left out. On the surface, everything looks fine. The program is grammatically correct (Prolog loads it normally), and every clause in the program is true. If one didn't look too carefully, one might read the single clause as, "Two people are of opposite sex if one of them is male and the other is female." But what the single clause actually says is, "*x* is of opposite sex from *y* if *x* is male and *y* is female." It says nothing about the converse, so that information is missing. This is a very easy thing to overlook. It might only come to light when a query like opp_sex(jane,sam) does not produce the expected answer.

Consider the my_predicate clause. How can one tell whether there are enough clauses for it. Again, it depends on what the predicate was intended to mean. From the comment it appears that a second clause is needed:

```
% my_predicate(X,Y) holds when X is a child of Y, or vice versa.
my_predicate(X,Y) :- child(X,Y).
my_predicate(X,Y) :- child(Y,X).
```

With that second clause, the program matches what was intended.

So a Prolog program must include enough clauses to spell out the *whole* truth. There are two additional points to remember:

- A program might not contain all *possible* truths about a matter. The family program did not include the parents of George, for instance. So some truths might be missing, for a variety of good reasons. This must be accepted, and sometimes documented with comments.

- But a program must include all *relevant* truths, explicitly or implicitly. Consider the truth that Sue is a parent of John. Nowhere is the clause parent(sue,john) in the program. The reason is that this clause can be derived from other clauses using back-chaining; its truth is represented *implicitly* by the program. So to capture the whole truth, one needs to allow for the fact that some of it will be calculated by back-chaining over the knowledge base.

In summary, when writing Prolog programs, all the clauses in a Prolog program must be true, and all the necessary clauses must be represented somehow in the program in a way that Prolog can find them using back-chaining.

Writing a Prolog program involves building a knowledge base of clauses that captures
1. *the truth, and nothing but,*
2. *the whole truth,*
3. *in a form suitable for back-chaining.*

Saying that a program is <u>*logically correct*</u> means that it is correct with respect to grammar and to truth: it has exactly the right logical entailments. Saying that a program is

Figure 4.1.   A blocks world

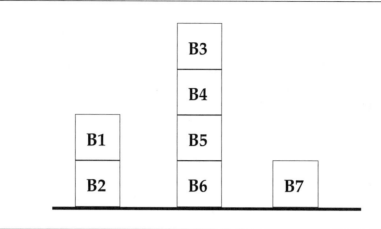

simply *correct* means that it is grammatically correct, logically correct (criteria 1 and 2), and in a form suitable for back-chaining (criterion 3).

4.2   A blocks world

Imagine that we would like to draw appropriate conclusions about a scene like the one depicted in figure 4.1 involving toy blocks on a table. The goal is to describe this scene and get Prolog to determine that

- block B3 is above block B5;
- block B1 is to the left of block B7;
- block B4 is to the right of block B2.

A Prolog program that does this is presented in figure 4.2. (In that figure, the small line numbers on the right are for reference only. They are not part of Prolog.) The program uses five predicates, whose intended meaning is described in the comments. With respect to the scene in figure 4.1, the program handles the on and just_left predicates appropriately, with the six atomic clauses. Similarly, the single clause for the right predicate is correct assuming that the ones for the left predicate are correct. (The program says that right is the inverse of left, just as parent was the inverse of child.)

Figure 4.2. A blocks-world program   `blocks.pl`

```
% on(X,Y) means that block X is directly on top of block Y.          1
on(b1,b2).   on(b3,b4).   on(b4,b5).   on(b5,b6).                    2

% just_left(X,Y) means that blocks X and Y are on the table          4
% and that X is immediately to the left of Y.                        5
just_left(b2,b6).   just_left(b6,b7).                                6

% above(X,Y) means that block X is somewhere above block Y           8
% in the pile where Y occurs.                                        9
above(X,Y) :- on(X,Y).                                              10
above(X,Y) :- on(X,Z), above(Z,Y).                                 11

% left(X,Y) means that block X is somewhere to the left             13
% of block Y but perhaps higher or lower than Y.                    14
left(X,Y) :- just_left(X,Y).                                        15
left(X,Y) :- just_left(X,Z), left(Z,Y).                            16
left(X,Y) :- on(X,Z), left(Z,Y).      % leftmost is on something.   17
left(X,Y) :- on(Y,Z), left(X,Z).      % rightmost is on something.  18

% right(X,Y) is the opposite of left(X,Y).                          20
right(Y,X) :- left(X,Y).                                            21
```

But what about the above predicate? How do we know that the whole truth and nothing but the truth is included for this one? Consider the sentences represented by the clauses in lines 10 and 11:

- If x is directly on y, then x is above y.

- If x is directly on z, and z is above y, then x is above y.

Both these sentences are clearly true. But is this all the necessary information?

Let us first check that the clauses work on some examples by looking at a trace of some queries in figure 4.3. (From now on, user-typed queries are no longer highlighted in bold.)

- For the first query, Prolog determines that block B1 is above block B2 because B1 is directly on B2.

- For the second query, Prolog determines that block B3 is above block B5 because B3 is directly on B4, and B4 is above B5. (It determines that B4 is above B5 because B4 is directly on B5.)

So in trying to establish the query above(b3,b5), Prolog had to first establish above(b4,b5). This means that above is a recursive predicate.

Figure 4.3.   Tracing the above predicate

```
?- above(b1,b2).
  Call: (7) above(b1, b2)    %  The main goal
  Call: (8) on(b1, b2)       %  Try on(b1,b2) using line 10.
  Exit: (8) on(b1, b2)       %  Succeeds because of line 2.
  Exit: (7) above(b1, b2)    %  The main goal succeeds.
Yes

?- above(b3,b5).
  Call: (8) above(b3, b5)    %  The main goal.
  Call: (9) on(b3, b5)       %   - Try on(b3,b5).
  Fail: (9) on(b3, b5)       %     This fails.
  Redo: (8) above(b3, b5)    %  Reconsider.
  Call: (9) on(b3, _L205)    %   - Try on(b3,Z) from line 11.
  Exit: (9) on(b3, b4)       %     This succeeds for Z=b4.
  Call: (9) above(b4, b5)    %   - Now try above(Z,b5) for Z=b4.
  Call: (10) on(b4, b5)      %      - Try on(b4,b5).
  Exit: (10) on(b4, b5)      %        This succeeds.
  Exit: (9) above(b4, b5)    %      This succeeds;
  Exit: (8) above(b3, b5)    %  The main goal succeeds.
Yes
```

4.3   Recursion in Prolog

Most modern programming languages provide recursion, but it is usually considered to be an advanced technique. In fact, it is really quite simple and lies at the heart of Prolog programming.

In the simplest case, a predicate is considered *recursive* when the predicate appears in both the head and the body of a clause, as in line 11. When these are written as English sentences, the predicate is used in both the *if* and the *then* parts of the sentence.

Recursion is needed when there is a predicate that involves using another predicate *some number* of times. In the example with the above predicate, a block x is above a block y when there are *some number* n of intermediate blocks such that x is on b_1, b_1 is on b_2, b_2 is on b_3, ..., b_{n-2} is on b_{n-1}, b_{n-1} is on b_n, and finally b_n is on y. The n here can be any number. When $n = 0$, there are no intermediate blocks: x is directly on y.

Once this pattern of needing to use another predicate some number n of times becomes clear (where the number n is not known in advance), clauses for the predicate are written in a two-step operation:

1. Write a clause to handle the $n = 0$ case. In the example, this means writing a clause for the case where x is above y by virtue of being directly on y:

   ```
   above(X,Y) :- on(X,Y).
   ```

2. Write a clause to handle the $(n + 1)$ case, on the assumption that the n case is already taken care of. In the example, this means writing a clause for **above** when there are $(n + 1)$ blocks between the top and bottom blocks, assuming that **above** already works properly when there are only n blocks between the top and bottom blocks.

   Suppose x is above y with $(n + 1)$ blocks between them. Then there must be a z such that x is directly on z, and z is above y, with n blocks between them. That means that **above**(z, y) will work properly. So the clause

   ```
   above(X,Y) :- on(X,Z), above(Z,Y).
   ```

   will work despite the fact that **above** occurs in both the head and the body.

This explains the two clauses that are used in the program in figure 4.2 . But why does this two-step recipe work? The answer is *mathematical induction*. It is not necessary to understand mathematical induction to write Prolog programs, but it does provide justification for what is done.

---

* 4.4 Mathematical induction

Mathematical induction is a technique for proving that something is true for all natural numbers, $0, 1, 2, \ldots$ The something to be proved is usually expressed as a statement of English that contains a variable, say n, such as, "The sum of the natural numbers up to n is equal to one half of n times $(n + 1)$." Let $S(n)$ denote this statement. So $S(3)$ is the English statement, "The sum of the natural numbers up to 3 is one half of 3 times 4." $S(3)$ is true, since the sum of the natural numbers up to 3 is 6 $(0 + 1 + 2 + 3)$, and one half of 3 times 4 is also 6. Similarly, the statement $S(7)$ is true, since the sum is 28 $(0 + 1 + 2 + 3 + 4 + 5 + 6 + 7)$, and one half of 7 times 8 is also 28. What one would like to do is to *prove* that $S(n)$ is true for every natural number n.

Mathematical induction works in the following way. To prove that for all n, $S(n)$ is true, it is sufficient to do two things:

1. Prove that $S(0)$ is true.

2. Prove that for any natural number n, if $S(n)$ is true, then $S(n + 1)$ is also true.

Step 1 is usually the easy step. Step 2 is typically handled as follows: *assume* that $S(n)$ is true for an arbitrary choice of n, and then use that to *prove* that $S(n+1)$ will also be true.

To see this in action, let us do these proofs. The standard mathematical summation notation (with the Greek letter *sigma*)

$$\sum_{i=0}^{n} i$$

means "the sum of the natural numbers from 0 to n." So the following statement is to be proved by mathematical induction:

$$\text{For all natural numbers } n, \ \sum_{i=0}^{n} i = \frac{n(n+1)}{2}.$$

Here is the proof:

1. Consider the case where $n = 0$. We have

$$\sum_{i=0}^{0} i = 0 = \frac{0 \times 1}{2}.$$

So $S(0)$ is true.

2. Prove that whenever $S(n)$ is true, then $S(n+1)$ is also true.
   Assume that for some arbitrary n, $S(n)$ is true. This means that

$$\sum_{i=0}^{n} i = \frac{n(n+1)}{2}.$$

If this is true, we have

$$\sum_{i=0}^{n+1} i = \left[\sum_{i=0}^{n} i \right] + (n+1) = \frac{n(n+1)}{2} + (n+1).$$

But

$$\frac{n(n+1)}{2} + (n+1) = (n+1) \left[\frac{n}{2} + 1 \right] = (n+1) \frac{(n+2)}{2}.$$

Combining this with the previous equation, we have

$$\sum_{i=0}^{n+1} i = \frac{(n+1)(n+2)}{2}.$$

So this proves that $S(n+1)$ is true.

That completes the proof.

Mathematical induction is not just for arithmetic. Consider a blocks-world setup of colored blocks. Suppose there is a stack of red and green blocks with a red one on the top and a green one on the bottom. Does this mean that there is a red block *directly* on top of a green one? It can be proved that there must be, by mathematical induction:

Let $S(n)$ be the following statement:

> If the top block is red and the bottom one is green and there are n intermediate blocks in between, then there is a red block directly on top of a green one.

Then prove by mathematical induction that $S(n)$ is true for all n.

1. Consider the case where $n = 0$. The top block of the stack is directly on the bottom block, and so a red block is directly on a green block. So $S(0)$ is true.

2. Prove that if $S(n)$ is true, then $S(n+1)$ is also true. Assume that for some arbitrary n, $S(n)$ is true. Suppose there is a stack with $(n+1)$ blocks between the top red and bottom green blocks. Consider the block just below the top one. There are two cases for it:

   a. If that block is green, then there is a red block (namely, the top one) directly on this green one.

   b. If that block is red, then there is a smaller stack, with this red block on the top and the green one on the bottom. There are only n blocks between this red one and the bottom one. Since $S(n)$ is assumed to be true, there must be a red block directly on a green one in this smaller stack.

   Either way, there must be a red block directly on a green one, so $S(n+1)$ is true.

The connection between this style of reasoning and writing Prolog clauses for the above predicate is this. The clauses must work properly no matter how many intermediate blocks there are. Now let $S(n)$ be the following statement:

> The predicate above(x, y) will work correctly when x is above y with n intermediate blocks between them.

If it can be proved that $S(n)$ is true for all n, then the Prolog program for above will work no matter how many blocks there are between the top and bottom ones. To get there, write clauses for the above predicate that duplicate a proof by mathematical induction:

1. Write clauses to ensure that $S(0)$ is true.

2. Assuming there are already clauses making $S(n)$ true, write clauses to ensure that $S(n+1)$ is true.

So proceed in two steps:

1. Write clauses for above(x, y) for those cases where x is above y with no blocks between them. In this case, block x must be directly on y:

```
above(X,Y) :- on(X,Y).
```

2. Assume the above predicate works properly whenever there are n blocks between the top and bottom blocks.

Suppose we have x and y with $n+1$ blocks between them. Then there must be a z such that x is directly on z, and z is above y, with n blocks between them. That means that above(z, y) will work properly. So write the clause

```
above(X,Y) :- on(X,Z), above(Z,Y).
```

Thus, by mathematical induction, the above predicate will do the right thing no matter how many blocks there are.

4.5   Nonterminating programs

Programs where the same predicate appears in the head and the body of a clause open up the possibility that the back-chaining will get stuck in a loop and go on forever. An example is the knowledge base in section 2.5.1 containing the clause

```
poodle(X) :- poodle(X).
```

A clause like this is (trivially) true, so one might think at first that it would not hurt to include it in a Prolog program. But it violates the third programming requirement: a program must be in a form suitable for back-chaining. As shown in chapter 2, this poodle clause can cause back-chaining to run forever (unless it is stopped).

But it is not just clauses like this that are problematic. Consider the following version of opp_sex from the family example:

```
opp_sex(X,Y) :- male(X), female(Y).
opp_sex(X,Y) :- opp_sex(Y,X).
```

At first sight, this looks perfect. Both clauses are true, and together they entail that John is of opposite sex from Jane *and* that Jane is of opposite sex from John. They are logically correct.

But the back-chaining part is a problem. Queries that ought to fail will end up stuck in a loop running forever. The query opp_sex(john,jane) will return *success*, as will the query opp_sex(jane,john) exactly as intended. But consider the query opp_sex(john,george). Here is what happens:

1. The first clause fails because of female(george).

2. The second clause says that the two arguments should be flipped: opp_sex(george,john).

3. The first clause for that query fails because of female(john).

4. The second clause for that query says that the two arguments should be flipped: opp_sex(john,george).

5. Now the program goes right back to step 1, where the first clause fails because of female(george), and so on.

So instead of returning *failure*, the query runs forever. This recursive version of opp_sex is not correct. If the program is to include a clause saying "reverse the arguments if you need to," here is a much better version:

```
male_female(X,Y) :- male(X), female(Y).
opp_sex(X,Y) :- male_female(X,Y).
opp_sex(X,Y) :- male_female(Y,X).
```

This is a nonrecursive program that is correct.

But it is not just queries that are expected to fail that run into trouble with non-terminating programs. To see this, consider again the dog program in figure 2.5. In Prolog, it would look like this:

```
dog(X) :- poodle(X).
dog(X) :- collie(X).
poodle(X) :- poodle(X).
collie(fido).
```

This includes the problematic clause for poodle. Then the query dog(fido) will not succeed as it should because the program never gets past the poodle stage to use the collie clause. So a program that does not fail properly may not get to use the parts of the program where it should find success.

For recursive predicates, like the above predicate, where the same predicate is used in the head and body of a clause, one must be especially vigilant to ensure that the program is in a form suitable for back-chaining.

Consider, for example, this alternative version of line 11 in figure 4.2:

```
above(X,Y) :- above(Z,Y), on(X,Z).
```

This clause says exactly the same thing as the one in the program; it simply changes the order of the conjunction. So from the point of view of truth, it works just as well as the earlier one. It is logically correct. But it does not work well for back-chaining. Consider the query above(b1,b1):

1. The first clause fails because nothing is on block B1.

2. The second clause says to first find a block Z1 such that above(Z1,b1) holds (here renaming the Z variable to Z1).

3. The first clause for above(Z1,b1) fails because nothing is on block B1.

4. The second clause for above(Z1,b1) says to first find a block Z2 such that above(Z2,b1) holds (again renaming the Z variable).

5. The program goes back to step 3, where the first clause fails, and so on.

In terms of conjunctive queries to be established, here is how back-chaining would work with this query:

```
above(b1,b1).
above(Z1,b1), on(b1,Z1).
above(Z2,b1), on(Z1,Z2), on(b1,Z1).
above(Z3,b1), on(Z2,Z3), on(Z1,Z2), on(b1,Z1).
...
```

It is clear that the conjunctive queries will get longer and longer, and so Prolog will eventually produce an error when it runs out of memory.

When writing recursive programs, there is no simple way to *guarantee* that they will terminate. However, a good rule of thumb is that when a clause is recursive, the recursive predicate should appear toward the end of the clause, so that new variables can be instantiated. Instead of

```
above(X,Y) :- above(Z,Y), on(X,Z).
```

write

```
above(X,Y) :- on(X,Z), above(Z,Y).
```

The two sentences mean the same thing. They are both logically correct. But because of the way back-chaining works, the second one will try the recursive predicate only *after* it has found a value for the variable Z using the on predicate.

When the body of a clause contains a recursive predicate, make sure that its new variables are instantiated by earlier atoms in the body.

4.6   A more complex predicate

Having seen how the above predicate works, consider now a more complex predicate: the left predicate in figure 4.2. This is also a recursive predicate, involving four clauses.

- The clauses in lines 15 and 16 in the figure are analogous to those for above except they use the just_left predicate instead of on. One way for $left(x, y)$ to hold is when x and y are on the table, and there are some number of intermediate blocks, each one just left of the next one.

- Line 17 shows the case where $left(x, y)$ holds, but x is not on the table. In that case, there will be an intermediate block z such that x is on z, and z is to the left of y.

- Line 18 shows the case where $left(x, y)$ holds, but y is not on the table. In that case, there will be an intermediate block z such that y is on z, and x is to the left of z.

Understanding why these four clauses are correct takes some work. The best place to start is by looking at a trace of the behavior in figure 4.4. The trace is long, but it is just simple back-chaining, as before:

1. The top-level query in figure 4.4 is left(b1,b7).

2. The program tries the clauses in lines 15 and 16 of figure 4.2, but both fail, since block B1 is not on the table.

3. Next, it tries the clause in line 17. This requires on(b1,Z) for some Z, which succeeds with Z=b2.

4. All that remains is to establish left(b2,b7). Both block B2 and block B7 are on the table, so this is just like the above predicate, but going sideways. The query succeeds by finding an intermediate block, block B6.

To understand how the four clauses for the left predicate do their job, it is useful to reconsider the notion of recursion. This will also help clarify program termination.

∗ 4.6.1   Recursion and termination, reconsidered

The discussion of recursion for the above predicate considered a number n, which was the number of intermediate blocks between a top and a bottom block. The clauses had

Figure 4.4.   Tracing the left predicate

```
?- left(b1,b7).
 Call: (7) left(b1, b7)              % This is the main goal.
 Call: (8) just_left(b1, b7)         %  - Try just_left(b1,b7).
 Fail: (8) just_left(b1, b7)         %     This fails.
 Redo: (7) left(b1, b7)              % Reconsider.
 Call: (8) just_left(b1, _L205)      %  - Try just_left(b1,Z).
 Fail: (8) just_left(b1, _L205)      %     This also fails.
 Redo: (7) left(b1, b7)              % Reconsider.
 Call: (8) on(b1, _L205)             %  - Try on(b1,Z) (line 17).
 Exit: (8) on(b1, b2)                %     This succeeds for Z=b2.
 Call: (8) left(b2, b7)              %  - Try left(Z,b7) for Z=b2.
 Call: (9) just_left(b2, b7)         %      - Try just_left(b2,b7).
 Fail: (9) just_left(b2, b7)         %          This fails.
 Redo: (8) left(b2, b7)              %      Reconsider.
 Call: (9) just_left(b2, _L223)      %      - Try just_left(b2,Z1).
 Exit: (9) just_left(b2, b6)         %        Ok for Z1=b6.
 Call: (9) left(b6, b7)              %      - Try left(b6,b7).
 Call: (10) just_left(b6, b7)        %        - just_left(b6,b7).
 Exit: (10) just_left(b6, b7)        %            This succeeds.
 Exit: (9) left(b6, b7)              %          This succeeds.
 Exit: (8) left(b2, b7)              %      This succeeds.
 Exit: (7) left(b1, b7)              % The main goal succeeds.
Yes
```

to work for any n. The key idea was that there was a measure of some sort of the *size* of the queries; a program had to work for queries of any size. In the case of the above predicate, the size was the number of intermediate blocks between a top block and a bottom block.

Different recursive predicates require different measures of size. Any measure can be considered but it takes practice to find one that works. In the case of the left predicate, the size of a query $left(x, y)$ is the following:

> The number of blocks between x and the table +
>
> the number of blocks between y and the table +
>
> the number of blocks on the table between the base of x and the base of y (where the base means the block on the table below it).

So, for example, the size of left(b6,b7) will be 0, the size of left(b1,b7) will be 3, and the size of left(b1,b4) will be 4.

To capture the whole truth about a recursive predicate, one must make sure that for all n, queries of size n will succeed, just as for the **above** predicate. Again, there is a two-step procedure:

1. Write clauses to handle the $n = 0$ case. For the **left** predicate, this means writing clauses for the case where x is directly to the left of y on the table:

   ```
   left(X,Y) :- just_left(X,Y).
   ```

2. Write clauses to handle the $(n + 1)$ case. For the **left** predicate, assume that queries of size n already work properly. Now suppose there is a query $\text{left}(x, y)$ of size $(n + 1)$. There are only three ways this can happen:

   a. x and y are both on the table, and x is just to the left of a block z. This means that $\text{left}(z, y)$ is of size n, so

      ```
      left(X,Y) :- just_left(X,Z), left(Z,Y).
      ```

   b. x is on a block z, where z is also to the left of y. This means that $\text{left}(z, y)$ is of size n, so

      ```
      left(X,Y) :- on(X,Z), left(Z,Y).
      ```

   c. y is on a block z, where x is also to the left of z. This means that $\text{left}(x, z)$ is of size n, so

      ```
      left(X,Y) :- on(Y,Z), left(X,Z).
      ```

This shows precisely where the four clauses in the program come from. As before, the justification for this two-step procedure is mathematical induction.

One nice thing about using this notion of size is that one can now be more explicit about how to handle the issue of program termination. The idea is simple:

> **Termination.** *A recursive program will terminate if the query that matches the head of a clause is always bigger (according to the size measure being used) than the queries from the body of the clause.*

This is sufficient because as the clause is used over and over, the size keeps going down. Eventually the size will be 0, with no further recursion.

To see this, note that for the recursive clause for the **above** predicate, the program went from a query $\text{above}(x, y)$ of size $(n + 1)$ matching the head, to a query of size n, $\text{above}(z, y)$ in the body. So the size decreases. The **left** predicate is similar.

But consider the nonterminating problematic clause for the **poodle** predicate. In this case, the query from the body is identical to the query matching the head, and so the size (whatever it is) *cannot* be decreasing. Similarly, for the faulty recursive version

Figure 4.5.   The start of a trace of a `left` query

```
?- left(b3,b3).
  Call: (7) left(b3, b3)              % The main goal
  Call: (8) just_left(b3, b3)
  Fail: (8) just_left(b3, b3)
  Redo: (7) left(b3, b3)             % Reconsider.
  Call: (8) just_left(b3, _L205)
  Fail: (8) just_left(b3, _L205)
  Redo: (7) left(b3, b3)             % Reconsider.
  Call: (8) on(b3, _L205)            %    Try on(b3,Z).
  Exit: (8) on(b3, b4)
  Call: (8) left(b4, b3)             %    Then start left(b4,b3).
  Call: (9) just_left(b4, b3)
  Fail: (9) just_left(b4, b3)
  Redo: (8) left(b4, b3)             %    Reconsider. ...
```

of opp_sex, the query from the body is the same as the query matching the head but with the arguments reversed, and so again the size does not decrease.

Finally, consider the incorrect version of the above predicate (where the order of the two conjuncts is changed). It has above(x, y) in the head and above(z, y) in the body, just like the correct version. The difference is that the correct version makes sure that the z is lower than x using the on predicate. This guarantees that above(z, y) will be smaller than above(x, y). There is no such guarantee in the incorrect version, so the program may not terminate.

4.7   Efficiency in Prolog

So far, the blocks-world program is grammatically correct, logically correct, and in the right form for back-chaining. It does exactly what is intended. Yet, while it gives correct results, it does not do so *efficiently*.

Consider, for example, a trace of the query `left(b3,b3)`. The start is shown in figure 4.5. As the trace continues, the query will eventually fail, as it should. But the *eventually* is very far away: a full trace would go on for more than 1500 lines. The reason for this has to do with the way the `left` predicate is defined in the program. A query left(x, y) is handled in three stages:

1. See if x and y are both on the table (using `just_left`).

2. See if x is on another block z, and try `left` with that.

3. See if y is on another block z, and try `left` with that.

The problem is that this scheme forces the program to reconsider the same queries over and over.

Look at the pairs of blocks that will be considered in steps 2 and 3:

- For `left(b3,b3)`, consider `left(b4,b3)` and `left(b3,b4)`.

- For `left(b4,b3)`, consider `left(b5,b3)` and `left(b4,b4)`.

- For `left(b3,b4)`, consider `left(b4,b4)` and `left(b3,b5)`.

So to establish the query `left(b3,b3)`, the query `left(b4,b4)` is considered twice (once for `left(b4,b3)` and once for `left(b3,b4)`). And, by the same argument, the query `left(b4,b4)` requires that `left(b5,b5)` be considered twice, and `left(b5,b5)` requires that `left(b6,b6)` be considered twice. So in trying to answer `left(b3,b3)`, the program will try to establish the query `left(b6,b6)` a total of 8 ($= 2 \times 2 \times 2$) times. If the stack had k blocks in it, the program would try to establish the same bottom query over and over 2^k times.

Why should this matter? There are two reasons:

- Although modern electronic computers can easily deal with stacks of size k, where $k = 20$ and even $k = 30$, no computer can deal with $k = 100$. The number 2^{100} is so incredibly large that the query would not be answered in our lifetimes. Although the program is guaranteed to terminate *eventually*, in practical terms it runs forever.

- Moreover, such prodigious work is unnecessary. All this effort by Prolog is wasted: back-chaining just ends up failing over and over on exactly the same queries.

So in the end, Prolog has not been given very good instructions about *how* to answer these queries, even though it will produce the right answers.

What can be done? Unfortunately, there is no easy way to write Prolog programs and be sure that they will not do more work than necessary. A good part of computer science involves analyzing computational problems and coming up with efficient ways of solving them. By *efficiency* is meant "with as little wasted effort as possible." Among other things, this involves comparing different methods of solving a problem (called *algorithms*) and trying to determine which ones will scale the best as the problem gets bigger.

But each problem needs to be analyzed on its own terms. One needs to think how to structure a Prolog program so that back-chaining can do its job efficiently.

Figure 4.6.   A better procedure for the `left` predicate   left.pl

```
% A new version of the left(X,Y) predicate.
% The rest of the program (for on, just_left, etc.) is elsewhere.
left(X,Y) :- base(X1,X), base(Y1,Y), table_left(X1,Y1).

% base(Z,X) holds if Z is on the table, below or equal to X.
base(X,X) :- \+ on(X,Y).                  % X is not on anything.
base(Z,X) :- on(X,Y), base(Z,Y).          % X is on a block Y.

% table_left(X,Y): X and Y are on the table, X to the left of Y.
table_left(X,Y) :- just_left(X,Y).
table_left(X,Y) :- just_left(X,Z), table_left(Z,Y).
```

This book does not spend much time worrying about the efficiency of different ways of solving a problem. But it is worth remembering that not all procedures that return the same answers to the same queries behave in the same way. The following section suggests a better algorithm for the `left` predicate.

* A better algorithm

One of the reasons the clauses for $left(x, y)$ are not ideal is that the cases handled by the three clauses are not disjoint. When there is a query $left(x, y)$ that should fail when neither block x nor block y is on the table, the program looks at the block below x, generates the `left` query for that, and after failing, looks at the block below y, and generates the `left` query for that. So *both* the third and fourth clauses are used. One should always be concerned about efficiency whenever there is a query of size $(n + 1)$ that can generate *two* recursive queries of size n: there will be two queries of size n, four queries of size $(n - 1)$, eight queries of size $(n - 2)$, and so on. This can lead to an exponential growth in the number of queries.

This exponential behavior can be avoided easily enough. Given a query $left(x, y)$, go directly below x until reaching the table, go directly below y until reaching the table, and then check the `left` relationship for just these two base blocks.

This leads to the clauses redefining `left` in figure 4.6. The predicate $base(z, x)$ holds if z is on the table and is either below x or is x itself. Also, $table\_left(x, y)$ holds if x and y are both on the table, with x to the left of y. (The clauses for on and `just_left` are not included.)

This version returns the same answers as before, but is a *much* better algorithm. There would be no problem dealing with thousands and maybe even millions of blocks. This shows the difference a change in algorithm can make.

Want to read more?

This chapter explained how to write computer programs in Prolog, that is, how to represent knowledge in a form that can be used effectively by back-chaining. This skill is applied throughout the rest of the book.

This chapter is as close as this book gets to traditional computer science. Because Prolog is a somewhat unusual programming language, it is almost never taught as a first language in computer science courses. While there is an excellent introductory programming text that uses Prolog [21], most computer science departments start with languages like Java, Python, or Scheme, for which there are many introductory textbooks. The sort of programming studied here is called *logic programming*, which is often taken up as an advanced topic, using textbooks such as [18, 19, 20, 22].

Computer science goes well beyond programming, however, and one of the topics studied in detail is the notion of *scalability*. How can one manage extremely large computer programs without getting lost in the details? Some of the very large computer programs (such as the program for Microsoft Word, for instance) are among the most complex artifacts ever built by people. How can a team of programmers work on a project of this size without stepping on each other's toes?

In another dimension of scale, it is not just programs that become large; the inputs to the program can also be gigantic. For example, there might be a program that analyzes an enormous geographic database or a genome sequence from biology. A major concern in computer science is *efficiency*. How can one write computer programs that deal with large inputs like these without taking too long or using too much computer memory?

The approach to programming in this chapter was quite informal. Computer scientists learn how to *prove* mathematically that their programs have certain desirable properties, for example, that a certain algorithm will eventually produce an expected result or that it is as good a way as any to calculate a desired result. Mathematical induction often plays a role in this. One of the main topics of theoretical computer science is the analysis of computational tasks themselves, dividing them into *tractable* ones (for which algorithms exist that will scale well as the input grows) and *intractable* ones (for which there are no good algorithms). As noted at the end of chapter 1, there are tasks that are not even *computable*, for which there is no algorithm that is guaranteed to terminate at all.

Exercises

These exercises will give you practice writing and running Prolog programs that reason in a simple way about family relationships, mostly exotic flavors of cousins. Begin your Prolog program by writing a collection of clauses for the `child`, `male`, and `female` predicates for some real or imaginary family. To make things interesting, make sure that more than four generations of people are represented. Note that nobody should have more than two parents (one male and one female), but some individuals will have fewer than two parents recorded. As you work on the following predicates, you should augment your family as necessary so that each of the predicates you define has at least one example in your family.

Figure 3.1 showed clauses for the predicates `parent`, `father`, and `grand_father`. Now write clauses for each of the following predicates (and for any other auxiliary predicates you find useful):

1. `mother`, `grand_parent`, and `great_grand_mother`.

2. `sibling`, `brother`, and `sister`.
   x is a sibling of y if x and y are two different people who share a parent in common. A brother is a sibling who is male; a sister is a sibling who is female.

3. `half_sibling` and `full_sibling`.
   Half siblings are siblings who have exactly one parent in common. Full siblings are siblings who have two parents in common.

4. `first_cousin` and `second_cousin`.
   x is a first cousin of y if some parent of x and some parent of y are siblings. (Note that first cousins will have a grandparent in common.) x and y are second cousins if some parent of x and some parent of y are first cousins. (Second cousins will share a great-grandparent.)

5. `half_first_cousin` and `double_first_cousin`.
   x is a half first cousin of y if some parent of x is a half sibling of a parent of y. x is a double first cousin of y if each parent of x is a sibling of a parent of y. (Note that a first cousin is not the same thing as a double half first cousin. The *double* and *half* do not cancel out.)

6. `first_cousin_twice_removed`.
   Look on the Internet or elsewhere for the definition of a third cousin once

removed or a second cousin twice removed and so on, and fill in the details here.

7. `descendant, ancestor.`
   x is a descendant of y if x is either a child of y or (recursively) of someone who is a descendant of y. x is an ancestor of y if y is a descendant of x.

8. `cousin.`
   x is a cousin of y if some parent of x and some parent of y are either siblings or (recursively) cousins. (The x and y will always end up being nth cousins for some n. For example, fourth cousins will have parents who are third cousins.)

9. `closest_common_ancestor.`
   x is a closest common ancestor of two people y and z if x is an ancestor of both y and z and no child of x is an ancestor of y and z. (A closest common ancestor of two first cousins will be someone who is a grandparent of both.)

10. `write_descendant_chain.`
    Later chapters examine the special predicates `write` and `nl`, which can be used to produce output other than just the values of variables. For example, if there is a clause

    ```
    write_child(X,Y) :-
        write(X), write(' is a child of '), write(Y), nl.
    ```

    then the query `write_child(john_smith,sue_jones)` will always succeed and will also print

    ```
    john_smith is a child of sue_jones
    ```

    on one line. Include this predicate in your program, and write the clauses for a predicate `write_descendant_chain(x,y)` that prints a chain from x to y when x is a descendant of y but prints nothing when x is not a descendant of y. For example, if John Smith is a descendant of William Brown, then `write_descendant_chain(john_smith,william_brown)` should print a sequence of lines something like this:

    ```
    john_smith is a child of sue_jones
    sue_jones is a child of harvey_jones
    harvey_jones is a child of davy_jones
    davy_jones is a child of anna_brown
    anna_brown is a child of william_brown
    ```

Hint: You will not be able to use the `descendant` predicate you defined for this. Use the `child` predicate together with `write_child`. Also, work down from *y* rather than up from *x*.

In case you were wondering, these questions do not exhaust the varieties of cousins people have considered. Anthropologists distinguish between *parallel* and *cross* first cousins, according to whether or not the two parents who are siblings are of the same sex. And once the idea of people being *married* is included, there are new possibilities: step-siblings (children of the spouse of a parent who are not siblings) and siblings-in-law in two varieties (a sibling of a spouse and the spouse of a sibling). This lead to step first cousins and two varieties of first cousins-in-law. And so on.

5   Case Study: Satisfying Constraints

This chapter returns to the central conjecture of the book, namely, that ordinary thinking can be viewed as a form of computation.

One of the difficulties in observing and analyzing our own thinking is that so much of it happens so quickly that it is hard to describe exactly what takes place. An example is resolving the pronoun *it* in the trophy-suitcase sentences in chapter 1. But not all thinking is like this, fortunately. Consider working on a puzzle that appears in a newspaper. There, the reasoning can go on for minutes, even hours. This is the sort of thinking that is the subject matter of this chapter. The thinking needed to solve a wide variety of reasoning puzzles can be formulated in the same way, in terms of *constraint satisfaction problems*. This chapter describes five different constraint satisfaction problems. (Chapter 6 shows that some parts of visual interpretation can also be formulated in this way.)

The approach to constraint satisfaction problems here is not that of an expert but more of a novice, with considerable trial-and-error and guesswork involved. The Prolog programs presented in this chapter work well enough for the easiest forms of the puzzles but will gradually stop working as the puzzles get harder. (What makes a puzzle hard is one of the issues to be discussed.) Some time is spent trying to do better than guessing, but this is not the main focus. Finding ways to cope with challenging puzzles as an expert would is a whole area of research in itself (called constraint programming) that is beyond the scope of this book.

In working through various examples of constraint satisfaction problems, new features of Prolog are introduced as needed, for example, producing output (to display helpful messages), anonymous variables (to avoid having to give names to variables), and numbers (to do arithmetic in Prolog).

The first section of this chapter introduces the idea of constraint satisfaction problems and presents a general way of solving them. Each of the five remaining sections takes on a different constraint satisfaction problem (Sudoku, cryptarithmetic, the eight-queens problem, logic problems, and scheduling) and shows how finding a solution can be cast as a computational task in Prolog.

5.1   Constraint satisfaction problems

It is worthwhile to go back to basic Prolog to recall how certain kinds of queries are handled.

5.1.1   Generate-and-test

Consider again the family example in figure 3.1. To find a male parent of John, the following query can be used:

```
?- male(X), child(john,X).
```

For many purposes, it is quite sufficient to think of this query globally in terms of its overall effect: Prolog will somehow find an X that is both male and has John as a child, or fail trying.

But let's look at how Prolog does this in closer detail. To establish this query, back-chaining will first work on male(X), which will succeed for X=john, and then try to establish child(john,john), which will fail. It will then backtrack and reconsider male(X), find X=sam, consider child(john,sam), which will succeed, giving a final answer. From the point of view of how the variable X is used, there are two stages:

1. Find a candidate value for X, using male.

2. Confirm that value, using child.

Of course, there is nothing special about which predicate is used first. The query could have been

```
?- child(john,X), male(X).
```

In this case, back-chaining uses the child(john,X) query to find a candidate value for X. The first one it finds, X=sue, does not work with male, so it backtracks to get the next value, X=sam, for which male(sam) does work.

This two-stage process is called *generate-and-test*. The idea is that a value is *generated* for a variable and then *tested* to see if the value is the desired one. If it is, the program is done; if it is not, then it backtracks and generates another value, and the process iterates. Of course, generate-and-test also works with more than one variable:

```
?- child(Z,X), male(X).
```

In this case, candidate *pairs* of values are considered. The first pair generated is Z=john and X=sue. But the test male(sue) fails, and so the program backtracks and generates the next pair of values, which is Z=john and X=sam, and which passes the test.

Now consider the following query:

```
?- male(X), child(Z,X), child(jane,Z).
```

Tracing the back-chaining, one can see that generate-and-test is used repeatedly:

1. Using male(X), generate a first value for X, and get X=john.

    a. Generate a Z for this X using child(Z,X), which fails.

2. Backtrack and generate a second value for X, which is X=sam.

    a. Generate a Z for this X using child(Z,X), and get Z=john.
    This fails the test child(jane,Z).

    b. Backtrack and generate the next Z, which is Z=jane.
    This fails the test child(jane,Z).

    c. Backtrack for yet another Z. However, there are no other values for Z, and so the program is unable to generate a Z for this X.

3. Backtrack and generate a third value for X using male(X), which is X=george.

    a. Generate a Z for this X using child(Z,X), and get Z=sue.
    This passes the test child(jane,Z), and so the program is done.

This generate-and-test process, which back-chaining does automatically, is at the root of how constraint satisfaction problems can be solved.

A simple example: Map coloring

Look at the map-coloring problem in figure 5.1. We seek a Prolog program that solves this problem and finds colors for the five countries. A program that does so appears in figure 5.2. This program can be understood by reading the clause for the solution predicate in English:

If a, b, c, d, and e are colors, and if

$$a \neq b, \ a \neq c, \ a \neq d, \ a \neq e, \ b \neq c, \ c \neq d, \text{ and } d \neq e,$$

then these colors are a solution to the given map-coloring problem.

Since the only colors are the three given ones, red, white, and blue, the solution predicate produces correct answers:

Figure 5.1.   A map-coloring problem

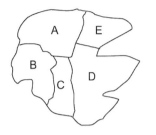

A map is depicted here with countries named A, B, C, D, and E. The goal is to color the countries on the map using just the colors red, white, and blue in such a way that no two countries with a border between them have the same color.

Figure 5.2.   Coloring the map of figure 5.1   map.pl

```
% solution(A,B,C,D,E) holds if A,B,C,D,E are colors
% that solve a map-coloring problem from the text.
solution(A,B,C,D,E) :-
   color(A), color(B), color(C), color(D), color(E),
   \+ A=B, \+ A=C, \+ A=D, \+ A=E, \+ B=C, \+ C=D, \+ D=E.
% The three colors are these.
color(red).
color(white).
color(blue).
```

```
?- solution(A,B,C,D,E).
A = red,  B = white,  C = blue,  D = white,  E = blue
```

(Note: From now on, some figures omit the Yes answer to a query and display the values of variables on a single line.)

This program works by generate-and-test, generating values for the variables A, B, C, D, and E using the color predicate, and then testing whether the values satisfy the required inequalities. If they do, the program is done; otherwise it backtracks and generates new values. (There is more than one correct solution to this problem.)

Note that tracing the behavior of this program would show that Prolog does quite a bit of work before it actually finds a solution. Roughly speaking, this is because all the generating is done before any testing. This issue is discussed in detail in section 5.3.3.

5.1.2 Variables, domains, constraints

Map coloring is a very simple example of a *constraint satisfaction problem*. In general, these are made up of the following three components:

- There are some number of *variables* for which values are to be found. In the case of map coloring, the variables A, B, C, D, E represent the colors of the five countries.

- Each variable gets a value from some finite *domain* of values. In the case of map coloring, each variable has the same domain: the colors red, white, and blue.

- There are *constraints* to be satisfied among subsets of the variables. In the case of map coloring, the constraints are that the colors of countries with borders between them must be different.

A *solution* to a constraint satisfaction problem is an assignment of a value to each variable (taken from the domain of the variable) such that all the constraints are satisfied. In other words, solving a constraint satisfaction problem means finding values for the variables subject to the constraints.

The simplest way to solve a constraint satisfaction problem in Prolog is to use generate-and-test: generate values from the domain for each variable, and then test to see if all the constraints are satisfied, backtracking as necessary.

A Prolog program that solves an arbitrary constraint satisfaction problem using generate-and-test can be constructed using a format somewhat like the following:

```
solution(Variable₁,Variable₂,...,Variableₙ)  :-
    domain₁(Variable₁),
    ...
    domainₙ(Variableₙ),
    constraint₁(Variable,...,Variable),
    ...
    constraintₘ(Variable,...,Variable).
```

This is the form used for the map coloring.

5.1.3 Output in Prolog

When a Prolog query succeeds, it displays values for all the variables. To make the answer easier to read, however, it is often useful to display more. Prolog provides two special predicates that can be used for this in queries or in the bodies of clauses:

- The predicate write(*term*) is considered to always succeed, and it has the effect of printing the value of the *term*.

- The predicate nl (for *newline*) with no arguments is considered to always succeed, and it has the effect of going to a new line of output.

To see how these work, look at how the following queries are answered:

```
?- X=joe, write('variable X is '), write(X), write('!!').
variable X is joe!!
X = joe
Yes
?- write('Paris in the'), nl, write('   spring.').
Paris in the
    spring.
Yes
```

So with these predicates, the solution to the map-coloring problem can be displayed better by adding the following clause to the program of figure 5.2:

```
print_colors :-
    solution(A,B,C,D,E), nl,
    write('Country A is colored '), write(A), nl,
    write('Country B is colored '), write(B), nl,
    write('Country C is colored '), write(C), nl,
    write('Country D is colored '), write(D), nl,
    write('Country E is colored '), write(E), nl.
```

The predicate print_colors first finds a solution to the constraint satisfaction problem using solution, and then prints it in a readable form:

```
?- print_colors.
Country A is colored red
Country B is colored white
Country C is colored blue
Country D is colored white
Country E is colored blue
```

Note that the query in this case no longer has variables. All the variables are within the clause for the print_colors predicate and are displayed explicitly using write and nl. This does not change the *thinking* involved in producing a solution. But it results in a much more convenient program, since anyone running the program does not have to know in advance how to use or interpret the variables.

Figure 5.3. A 4 × 4 Sudoku problem

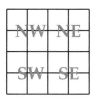

You are given a 4 × 4 grid, where some of the cells are blank and some contain numbers between 1 and 4. Fill in all the blank cells with numbers between 1 and 4 so that

- the numbers in each row (1, 2, 3, 4) are unique,
- the numbers in each column (1, 2, 3, 4) are unique,
- the numbers in each 2 × 2 quadrant (NW, NE, SW, SE) are unique.

5.2 A first example: Sudoku

Figure 5.3 shows a 4 × 4 Sudoku problem. It is a simpler version of Sudoku than the 9 × 9 version that appears in newspapers and puzzle books. (Section 5.2.3 discusses the 9 × 9 version.)

5.2.1 The anonymous variable in Prolog

A certain feature of Prolog, the *anonymous variable*, is useful for solving the Sudoku problem. Prolog allows the underscore character _ to be used as a variable in those cases where the goal is not finding the value of the variable but ensuring that there is one:

```
?- child(X,sue).      % Who is a child of Sue?
X=john
Yes

?- child(_,sue).      % Does Sue have a child?
Yes

?- child(_,john).     % Does John have a child?
No

?- child(_,_).        % Does anyone have a child?
Yes
```

Note that each occurrence of the anonymous variable can be for a different value. So the last query behaves like child(X,Y), rather than like child(X,X).

Figure 5.4.   Using the sudoku predicate

```
?- sudoku(              % Note the anonymous variables in the query.
    1, 4, _, _,
    _, _, 4, _,
    2, _, _, _,
    _, _, _, 3
).
A solution to this puzzle is
    1 4 3 2
    3 2 4 1
    2 3 1 4
    4 1 2 3
```

This anonymous variable can be used to explain what a Sudoku program should do. The user provides a *partial* solution to the problem and asks the program to print a *complete* solution. A query is posed with some of the entries filled in the grid, and the program will print all sixteen entries in a tabular format (see figure 5.4). The top-level predicate is sudoku. Note that the solution shown in the figure satisfies all the constraints: each row, column, and quadrant uses the numbers 1, 2, 3, and 4.

5.2.2   Sudoku as constraint satisfaction

It is easy to see Sudoku as a constraint satisfaction problem:

- There are sixteen variables, one for each entry in the grid.

- The domain for each variable is $\{1, 2, 3, 4\}$.

- The constraints to be satisfied are the following: for each row, column, and quadrant, the four variables must have distinct values.

Assuming there is a solution predicate that takes sixteen arguments and solves the constraint satisfaction problem, it is not hard to define the top-level sudoku predicate that does the printing (see the top half of figure 5.5, above the dashed line). The sudoku predicate uses solution to find a solution, then prints a one-line message, and finally uses the predicate printrow four times to print out each of the rows. As with print_colors, all the thinking happens in the solution predicate.

Let us now turn to this solution predicate. The easiest way to write the predicate is to first define a predicate uniq that takes four arguments and ensures that they are all different from each other:

```
uniq(P,Q,R,S) :- \+ P=Q, \+ P=R, \+ P=S, \+ Q=R, \+ Q=S, \+ R=S.
```

Figure 5.5. A Sudoku solver   sudoku.pl

```
% The main predicate. Solve the puzzle and print the answer.
% The variable Rij stands for the number in row i and column j.
sudoku(R11,R12,R13,R14,R21,R22,R23,R24,R31,R32,R33,R34,
       R41,R42,R43,R44) :-
   solution(R11,R12,R13,R14,R21,R22,R23,R24,R31,R32,R33,R34,
            R41,R42,R43,R44),
   nl, write('A solution to this puzzle is'), nl,
   printrow(R11,R12,R13,R14), printrow(R21,R22,R23,R24),
   printrow(R31,R32,R33,R34), printrow(R41,R42,R43,R44).
```

```
% Print a row of four numbers with spaces between them.
printrow(P,Q,R,S) :- write(' '), write(P), write(' '), write(Q),
   write(' '), write(R), write(' '), write(S), nl.
```

```
%-------------------------------------------------------------------
solution(R11,R12,R13,R14,R21,R22,R23,R24,R31,R32,R33,R34,
         R41,R42,R43,R44) :-
   uniq(R11,R12,R13,R14), uniq(R21,R22,R23,R24),      % rows 1,2
   uniq(R31,R32,R33,R34), uniq(R41,R42,R43,R44),      % rows 3,4
   uniq(R11,R21,R31,R41), uniq(R12,R22,R32,R42),      % cols 1,2
   uniq(R13,R23,R33,R43), uniq(R14,R24,R34,R44),      % cols 3,4
   uniq(R11,R12,R21,R22), uniq(R13,R14,R23,R24),      % NW and NE
   uniq(R31,R32,R41,R42), uniq(R33,R34,R43,R44).      % SW and SE
```

```
% uniq holds if P,Q,R,S are all distinct nums (from 1 to 4).
uniq(P,Q,R,S) :- num(P),  num(Q),  num(R),  num(S),
                 \+ P=Q, \+ P=R, \+ P=S, \+ Q=R, \+ Q=S, \+ R=S.
```

```
% The four numbers to go into each cell
num(1).  num(2).  num(3).  num(4).
```

So uniq(1,3,2,4) succeeds, but uniq(1,3,2,3) fails. (This idea of having a certain number of values that are different from each other shows up in many constraint satisfaction problems.)

As written, however, the uniq predicate can only be used to *test* the four arguments for uniqueness, not to *generate* them. This is because negation needs its arguments to be instantiated (see section 3.2.3). Assuming there is a predicate num that can test or generate the numbers from 1 to 4, the uniq predicate can be rewritten so that it will test or generate a group of four numbers from 1 to 4 that are unique. Then, using this predicate for each row, column, or quadrant, one can test or generate a group of sixteen numbers that solves the Sudoku problem. This is shown in the bottom half of figure 5.5.

How does this `solution` predicate work? It needs to generate sixteen values. It starts by using `uniq(R11,R12,R13,R14)` to generate four distinct values for the variables of row 1. Then it does the same for rows 2, 3, and 4. At this point, all sixteen variables have values. It then tests `uniq(R11,R21,R31,R41)`, which is for the variables of column 1. If these four values are distinct, it continues and tests the distinctness of columns 2, 3, and 4; if they are not distinct, the test fails, and it backtracks to generate new values for the variables in row 4 or 3 or 2 or perhaps all the way back to row 1, as necessary. Once all the column tests succeed, the `solution` predicate tests `uniq(R11,R12,R21,R22)`, which is for the variables of the NW quadrant. If these four values are distinct, it tests the quadrants NE, SW, and SE in turn; if they are not distinct, it again backtracks all the way to the rows and tries to generate new values. If all the column and quadrant tests are successful, a solution has been found, and the program is done.

5.2.3   Search spaces

It is easy to generalize this 4×4 solution to 9×9 Sudoku puzzles. Instead of having twelve constraints (for rows, columns, and quadrants) over sixteen variables, there would be twenty-seven constraints over eighty-one variables.

Will this work? The answer is, in *principle*, definitely yes; in *practice*, definitely no. The problem is that the 9×9 Sudoku puzzle is *much larger* than the 4×4 one. Just how much larger is worth investigating further.

A useful measure of the size of a constraint satisfaction problem is the size of its search space. The _search space_ is the collection of all the different ways the variables of a problem can be assigned values from the domain before taking the constraints into account.

- For a 4×4 Sudoku, each of the sixteen variables can take on four possible values. So there are $4 \times 4 \times \cdots \times 4 = 4^{16}$ possible assignments to the variables, which is about 4×10^9 (four billion). This is considered to be small (for computers).

- For a 9×9 Sudoku puzzle, each of the eighty-one variables can take on nine possible values. So there are $9 \times 9 \times \cdots \times 9 = 9^{81}$ possible assignments to the variables, which is about 2×10^{77}. This is considered to be enormous.

To understand the insurmountable difficulty this second number poses even for the fastest supercomputers, it is useful to do a thought experiment:

1. Imagine that there is a supercomputer capable of exploring a billion variable assignments per second in the search space. (No existing computer is fast enough to do this.)

2. Imagine that by virtue of new technology received from outer space, this super-computer suddenly becomes one billion times faster. This means that jobs that used to take it ten years to do can now be done in under one second.

3. Imagine that there are one billion of these supercomputers and that they can all be made to work together, sharing the job of exploring the search space.

Then,

- How many variable assignments can be explored per second?
  The answer is $10^9 \times 10^9 \times 10^9 = 10^{27}$.

- So how long would it take to go through the 9×9 Sudoku search space?
  The answer is $9^{81} \div 10^{27} = 2 \times 10^{50}$ seconds, or about 6×10^{40} centuries.

Given these sorts of numbers, it should be no surprise that the generate-and-test program to solve the 9×9 Sudoku problem does not work very well.

5.2.4 Guessed values and forced values

This analysis of the search space seems to be suggest that even the fastest computers would not be able to solve a 9×9 Sudoku problem. But this is not quite right. The analysis shows that no computer (or person) would be able to explore the entire Sudoku search space because it is too large. But, in fact, computers and people *are* able to solve Sudoku problems. How they do so is very different from the method used in the 4×4 case.

The problem with the way the Sudoku and map-coloring problems were solved is that there was far too much *guessing*: making a random selection from the search space and then backtracking if it was not right. Sudoku experts do not think this way. They do very little guessing, and only for the most difficult puzzles (the ones sometimes called devilish). Instead, they repeatedly try to see if the constraints of the puzzle *force* the values for certain entries based on the known values of other entries.

For example, figure 5.6 shows a 4×4 Sudoku problem with a 3 located at position $(1, 1)$ (top left) and at position $(4, 4)$ (bottom right). It is not hard to see that there must be a 3 at $(2, 3)$ and another at $(3, 2)$. These two entries are forced.

Programming this type of algorithm for Sudoku would take some work. The basic idea of using forced values to minimize the guesswork is explored in the next constraint satisfaction problem, cryptarithmetic.

Figure 5.6. Forced values in Sudoku

There is only one possible location for a 3 on the second row: it must be located at position $(2,3)$. The other three locations are ruled out by the 3 at position $(1,1)$ and the one at position $(4,4)$.

The 3 on the third row is similar.

5.3 A second example: Cryptarithmetic

Cryptarithmetic problems are of the following form. Given is an equation using letters like this:

$$
\begin{array}{r}
\text{SEND} \\
+ \text{ MORE} \\
\hline
\text{MONEY}
\end{array}
$$

A distinct digit must be found for each letter such that the equation holds. (Also, the leading leftmost digits, S and M, must not be 0.) A solution for this example is

$$S = 9,\ E = 5,\ N = 6,\ D = 7,\ M = 1,\ O = 0,\ R = 8,\ Y = 2$$

since $9567 + 1085 = 10652$. As a preliminary to solving problems like this in Prolog, the next section examines the facilities Prolog provides for arithmetic.

5.3.1 Arithmetic in Prolog

Numbers in Prolog were first mentioned in the review in figure 3.10, which said that a Prolog term is either a constant, variable, or number, and that a *number* is a sequence of one or more digits optionally preceded by a minus sign and optionally containing a decimal point (for rational numbers).

Since numbers are terms, they can appear in programs and queries anywhere a constant or variable can appear. So Prolog program can have clauses like

```
age(donna,23).
age(andy,22).
current_temperature(-5.2).
```

and queries like the following:

```
?- age(donna,N).
N = 23
Yes

?- age(X,N), \+ N=23.
X = andy, N = 22
Yes
```

But what makes numbers especially useful is that Prolog provides arithmetic operations over them. Specifically, going back to figure 3.10, the notion of a literal (the building block of queries and bodies of clauses) can be generalized to include the following *arithmetic relations*, optionally preceded by the negation sign:

- less than: $E_1 < E_2$
- greater than: $E_1 > E_2$
- less than or equal: $E_1 =< E_2$
- greater than or equal: $E_1 >= E_2$
- equal: $E_1 =:= E_2$
- equal: *Variable* is E

The E_i mentioned here are *arithmetic expressions*, that is, formulas built out of numbers and variables using parentheses and the operations + (addition), - (subtraction), * (multiplication), / (division), ** (exponentiation), and others. So here is an arithmetic expression in Prolog:

```
(X-Y)**2 + 3*(X/Y)
```

Note that this is *not* a Prolog term, atom, or literal; the grammar is clearly all wrong. Arithmetic expressions like these can only be used within Prolog programs and queries in very specific contexts. In particular, they can only be used as an E in one of the arithmetic relations just listed.

Here then are some legal Prolog queries that use arithmetic expressions and the answers they produce:

```
?- X=3, (X+4) > 2*X.
X = 3
Yes

?- X=3, (X+2) >= 2*X + 1.
No
```

One restriction on the use of arithmetic expressions is that the variables in them must already have values:

```
?- X=4, X > 2.
X = 4
Yes

?- X > 2, X=4.
ERROR: Arguments are not sufficiently instantiated
```

In requiring variables to be instantiated, arithmetic expressions are like the \+ operation. One exception to this rule is the is operation: the left-hand side must be a variable and it need not have a value; the right-hand side is an arithmetic expression, where all the variables must have values:

```
?- Y=2, X=5, X is Y+4.
No

?- Y=2, X is Y+4.
X = 6,   Y = 2
Yes
```

Using the is relation is the normal way of getting the value of an arithmetic expression to use with another predicate. In other words,

```
q(Y), p(Y+4,Z).
```

is *not* a legal query, since Y+4 is not a term (it is an arithmetic expression). But

```
q(Y), X is Y+4, p(X,Z).
```

is correct (assuming q is being used to generate a numeric value for Y).

Arithmetic programs

With arithmetic expressions, Prolog programs can perform numeric calculations. Suppose, for example, that a program has the following clauses:

```
birth_year(donna,1986).
birth_year(andy,1987).
current_year(2012).
```

Then the following clause *calculates* the age of a person from the current year:

```
% Age of a person P is the current year minus the birth year.
age(P,X) :- birth_year(P,Y1), current_year(Y2), X is Y2-Y1.
```

This gives the following behavior:

Figure 5.7.   A program for n!   factorial.pl

```
% factorial(N,M) holds when M=Nx(N-1)x...x2x1.
factorial(1,1).
factorial(N,M) :- N > 1, N1 is N-1, factorial(N1,K), M is N*K.
```

```
?- age(andy,N).
N = 25
Yes
```

Although they are not the focus of this book, one can also write more traditional numerical programs in Prolog, for example, a program to compute the value of $n!$, defined as $n \times (n-1) \times (n-2) \times \cdots \times 2 \times 1$. What is needed is a predicate factorial(n,m) that holds when $n! = m$. This can be written as a recursive predicate, observing that for $n > 1$, the factorial $n! = n \times (n-1)!$. The entire program for the factorial is shown in figure 5.7.

5.3.2   Cryptarithmetic as constraint satisfaction

Let us now return to the cryptarithmetic problem. The solution to this problem uses arithmetic expressions that deal with integers, in particular, // (integer quotient) and mod (integer remainder). For instance,

```
?- X is 11/3,   Y is 11//3,   Z is 11 mod 3.
X = 3.66667,  Y = 3,   Z = 2
```

Whereas / does full division, the // operation produces the integer part of a division, and mod produces the remainder after an integer division. When these two operations are used with 10, the result is the sum and carry digits of an addition:

```
?- S is (2+5) mod 10,   C is (2+5) // 10,
S = 7,   C = 0
Yes

?- S is (8+5) mod 10,   C is (8+5) // 10,
S = 3,   C = 1
Yes
```

In the first case, the sum digit for $(2+5)$ is 7 with a carry digit of 0 (that is, the sum is 7), and in the second, the sum digit for $(8+5)$ is 3 with a carry digit of 1 (that is, the sum is 13).

Figure 5.8.   SEND+MORE=MONEY v1   sendmore1.pl

```
% solution(...) holds for a solution to SEND+MORE=MONEY.
solution(S,E,N,D,M,O,R,Y) :-
    uniq_digits(S,E,N,D,M,O,R,Y), S > 0, M > 0,
    Y is (D+E) mod 10, C1 is (D+E) // 10,
    E is (N+R+C1) mod 10, C10 is (N+R+C1) // 10,
    N is (E+O+C10) mod 10, C100 is (E+O+C10) // 10,
    O is (S+M+C100) mod 10, M is (S+M+C100) // 10.
```
```
% uniq(...) holds if the arguments are all distinct digits.
uniq_digits(S,E,N,D,M,O,R,Y) :-
    dig(S), dig(E), dig(N), dig(D), dig(M), dig(O), dig(R), dig(Y),
    \+ S=E, \+ S=N, \+ S=D, \+ S=M, \+ S=O, \+ S=R, \+ S=Y,
            \+ E=N, \+ E=D, \+ E=M, \+ E=O, \+ E=R, \+ E=Y,
                    \+ N=D, \+ N=M, \+ N=O, \+ N=R, \+ N=Y,
                            \+ D=M, \+ D=O, \+ D=R, \+ D=Y,
                                    \+ M=O, \+ M=R, \+ M=Y,
                                            \+ O=R, \+ O=Y,
                                                    \+ R=Y.
```
```
% The digits
dig(0). dig(1). dig(2). dig(3). dig(4).
dig(5). dig(6). dig(7). dig(8). dig(9).
```

The $SEND + MORE = MONEY$ equation gives a series of equations involving the sum and carry digits. For example, for the units digits, the sum digit for $(D + E)$ must be Y. If the carry digit for this sum is C_1, then for the tens digit, the sum digit for $(N + R + C_1)$ must be E. The hundreds and thousands digits will be similar.

It is not hard to see this cryptarithmetic problem as a constraint satisfaction one:

- The variables will be the letters that are mentioned in the puzzle, $S, E, N, D, M,$ $O, R, Y,$ as well variables for the carry digits.

- The letter variables will take their values from 0 to 9; the carry-digit variables will be 0 or 1.

- The constraints to be satisfied are that the digits are unique; that $S > 0, M > 0$; and that all the digit equations for the sum and carry digits are satisfied.

A Prolog program that solves this puzzle is shown in figure 5.8. The predicate `uniq_digits` ensures that all its arguments are distinct digits (using the predicate `dig`). The `solution` predicate checks for uniqueness and ensures that the digit equations are satisfied using `//` and `mod`. It uses variables for the carry digits, `C1`, `C10`, `C100`, coming from the units, tens, and hundreds columns, respectively.

One can confirm that this program does the right thing:

```
?- solution(S,E,N,D,M,O,R,Y).
S = 9,  E = 5,  N = 6,  D = 7,  M = 1,  O = 0,  R = 8,  Y = 2
```

There is a problem, however. It takes too long, over ninety seconds even on a fast computer. To do better, guesswork must be minimized.

5.3.3 Minimizing the guesswork: Two rules

There are two rules that help minimize guesswork in this and other constraint satisfaction problems. They allow the solution of much more challenging problems with large search spaces. Here is the first:

> **Rule 1.** *If a value is fully determined by other values, then avoid guessing the value and later testing if it is correct.*

For example, suppose there are two predicates uniq2 and uniq3 that can test or generate two or three distinct values, respectively. Then instead of writing this:

```
uniq3(A,B,C),        % Guess at A,B,C.
B is (A+C) mod 10    % Then test if B is ok.
```

write this:

```
uniq2(A,C),          % Guess at A and C.
B is (A+C) mod 10,   % Calculate B once.
uniq3(A,B,C)         % Test that all values are unique.
```

The first version has a search space of $10 \times 10 \times 10 = 1000$, but the second has a search space of only $10 \times 10 = 100$.

The second rule is this:

> **Rule 2.** *Avoid placing independent guesses between the generation and the testing of other values.*

Then instead of writing this:

```
dig(A), dig(B),      % Guess at A and B.
dig(C), dig(D),      % Guess at C and D.
A > B                % Test for A and B.
```

write this:

```
dig(A), dig(B),      % Guess at A and B.
A > B,               % Test for A and B.
dig(C), dig(D)       % Guess at C and D.
```

Figure 5.9. SEND+MORE=MONEY v2   sendmore2.pl

```
% solution(...) holds for a solution to SEND+MORE=MONEY.
solution(S,E,N,D,M,O,R,Y) :-
    dig(D), dig(E),
    Y is (D+E) mod 10, C1 is (D+E) // 10,
    dig(N), dig(R),
    E is (N+R+C1) mod 10, C10 is (N+R+C1) // 10,
    dig(E), dig(O),
    N is (E+O+C10) mod 10, C100 is (E+O+C10) // 10,
    dig(S), S > 0, dig(M), M > 0,
    O is (S+M+C100) mod 10, M is (S+M+C100) // 10,
    uniq_digits(S,E,N,D,M,O,R,Y).

% The rest of the program is as before.
```

In the first case, the program guesses at values for C and D between the generating and the testing for A and B, whereas in the second case, it finishes the generate-and-test for A and B before going on to C and D.

Why avoid the first version? Suppose the guess for A and B was bad. The next guess is on values for C and D, and this gets to A > B, which will fail. At this point, back-chaining will go through all the combinations of values for C and D to see if any of them allow the query A > B to succeed. Of course, none of them will, and after all this needless work, the program will eventually backtrack to look for the next possible values for A and B. If these new values still fail, back-chaining will again go through all the values for C and D, and so on.

There is a similar problem with the version of map-coloring presented in figure 5.1. The program guesses at the colors of all five countries before it even begins to check that adjacent countries have different colors. So instead of writing this:

```
color(A), color(B), color(C), color(D), color(E),
\+ A=B, \+ A=C, \+ A=D, \+ A=E, \+ B=C, \+ C=D, \+ D=E.
```

it is better to write this:

```
color(A), color(B), \+ A=B, color(C), \+ A=C, \+ B=C,
color(D), \+ A=D, \+ C=D, color(E), \+ A=E, \+ D=E.
```

This is still generate-and-test, but it *interleaves* the generate and the test.

This analysis leads to a second version of the cryptarithmetic puzzle, shown in figure 5.9. This version has exactly the same constraints as the first version in figure 5.8, but they appear in a different order. Note, for example, that there is no guessing at the value of Y, since it can be calculated from D and E. Also, one column is

Figure 5.10. The eight-queens problem

The task is to place eight queens on a 8×8 chessboard such that no queen can capture any other according to the rules of chess. So each queen must be in its own

— row

| column

\ left diagonal

/ right diagonal

handled at a time: generate-and-test is used for D, E and Y, before going on to the next column. The predicate `uniq_digits` is still used to *test* that all the values are distinct but not to *generate* them.

The end result of this shuffling of constraints is that the program will now run in under one-tenth of a second. Can one do even better? Yes, much. But this is not pursued here except to note that the inequality constraints (hidden in `uniq_digits`) could be moved closer to where the variables are being generated.

The next section considers another constraint satisfaction problem, the eight-queens problem. While this does not really introduce any new concepts, it shows how to approach a different sort of problem and what needs to be *known* (in the knowledge base) to solve it.

∗ 5.4   A third example: The eight queens

Consider the eight-queens problem presented in figure 5.10. Assume one queen is placed in each row. So the problem is really to choose a *column* for each queen in such a way that no queen can capture any of the others.

This constraint satisfaction problem has eight variables: C_1, C_2, C_3, C_4, C_5, C_6, C_7, and C_8, where the variable C_i is to be understood as "the column for the queen that is placed in row i." The domain for these variables is also clear: it is a number between 1 and 8 that represents the chosen column for the queen. So, for example, $C_5 = 3$ means that the queen that is in row 5 is located in column 3.

As to the constraints in this problem, what is required is that if the queen in row 1 is in column C_1, and the one in row 2 is in column C_2 and so on, then no queen can

Figure 5.11.   Diagonals in the eight-queens problem

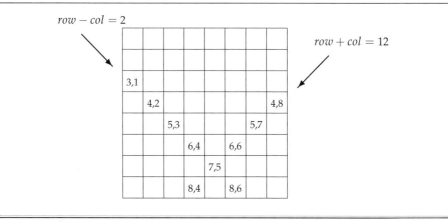

capture any other. All the queens will be in different rows, so that part is automatic. They must be in different columns, too, so that means including $C_1 \neq C_2$, $C_3 \neq C_7$, and so on. (Ensuring that all the columns are unique can be done using the `uniq` predicate, as in previous problems, or some other way.)

But what about diagonals? How can one make sure that each queen has its own left diagonal and its own right diagonal? It takes some advanced detective work to see what happens along the diagonals.

Figure 5.11 shows the row and column numbers for some of the squares on the chessboard. Observe that along a left diagonal (one that rises to the left), the *difference* between the row and column of the square stays constant. The square $(4, 2)$ is in the same left diagonal as the square $(7, 5)$, since $(4 - 2) = (7 - 5)$. The right diagonals are similar, except using the *sum*: the square $(4, 8)$ is in the same right diagonal as square $(7, 5)$, since $(4 + 8) = (7 + 5)$.

Putting these ideas together, one can now state the general principle. A queen that is located on (row_1, col_1) can capture a queen that is located on (row_2, col_2) if and only if one of the following conditions holds:

- They are in the same row: $row_1 = row_2$.

- They are in the same column: $col_1 = col_2$.

- They are in the same left diagonal: $(row_1 - col_1) = (row_2 - col_2)$.

- They are in the same right diagonal: $(row_1 + col_1) = (row_2 + col_2)$.

Figure 5.12. Testing if one queen can capture another   cap.pl

```
% cap(r1,C1,E2,C2) tests if a queen placed on an 8x8 chess board
%    at position (R1,C1) can capture another at position (R2,C2).
cap(R,_,R,_).                              % Note the use of the _ here
cap(_,C,_,C).                              % and here, too.
cap(R1,C1,R2,C2) :- R1-C1 =:= R2-C2.
cap(R1,C1,R2,C2) :- R1+C1 =:= R2+C2.
```

Figure 5.13. A solution to the eight-queens problem   queens.pl

```
% Solve the 8-queens problem.
solution(C1,C2,C3,C4,C5,C6,C7,C8) :-
  col(C1),
  col(C2), \+ cap(2,C2,1,C1),
  col(C3), \+ cap(3,C3,1,C1), \+ cap(3,C3,2,C2),
  col(C4), \+ cap(4,C4,1,C1), \+ cap(4,C4,2,C2), \+ cap(4,C4,3,C3),
  col(C5), \+ cap(5,C5,1,C1), \+ cap(5,C5,2,C2), \+ cap(5,C5,3,C3),
        \+ cap(5,C5,4,C4),
  col(C6), \+ cap(6,C6,1,C1), \+ cap(6,C6,2,C2), \+ cap(6,C6,3,C3),
        \+ cap(6,C6,4,C4), \+ cap(6,C6,5,C5),
  col(C7), \+ cap(7,C7,1,C1), \+ cap(7,C7,2,C2), \+ cap(7,C7,3,C3),
        \+ cap(7,C7,4,C4), \+ cap(7,C7,5,C5), \+ cap(7,C7,6,C6),
  col(C8), \+ cap(8,C8,1,C1), \+ cap(8,C8,2,C2), \+ cap(8,C8,3,C3),
        \+ cap(8,C8,4,C4), \+ cap(8,C8,5,C5), \+ cap(8,C8,6,C6),
           \+ cap(8,C8,7,C7).

% The columns
col(1). col(2). col(3). col(4). col(5). col(6). col(7). col(8).

% cap(R1,C1,R2,C2): a queen on (R1,C1) can capture one on (R2,C2).
cap(R,_,R,_).                              % Note the use of the _ here
cap(_,C,_,C).                              % and here, too.
cap(R1,C1,R2,C2) :- R1-C1 =:= R2-C2.
cap(R1,C1,R2,C2) :- R1+C1 =:= R2+C2.
```

Before writing the solution predicate for this problem, it is a good idea to write
the clauses for a predicate $cap(r_1,c_1,r_2,c_2)$, which holds when a queen placed on
(r_1,c_1) can capture one that is placed on (r_2,c_2). The predicate will need four clauses
that mirror the four conditions. The resulting small program is shown in figure 5.12.
(Always test that an auxiliary predicate like cap is working properly before including
it in a larger program.)

Figure 5.14.   Running the eight-queens program

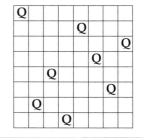

```
?- solution(C1,C2,C3,C4,C5,C6,C7,C8).
C1 = 1,    C2 = 5,    C3 = 8,    C4 = 6
C5 = 3,    C6 = 7,    C7 = 2,    C8 = 4
```

The complete solution predicate for the eight-queens problem is shown in figure 5.13. It says that a solution is generated as follows:

1. Generate a column for the queen in row 1 using col.

2. Generate a column for the queen in row 2 using col, and then test using cap that this queen cannot capture the one in row 1.

3. Generate a column for the queen in row 3 using col, and then test using cap that this queen cannot capture the one in row 1 nor the one in row 2.

4. Generate a column for the queen in row 4 using col, and then test using cap that this queen cannot capture the one in row 1, row 2, or row 3.

5. Continue in this way for row 5, row 6, row 7, and row 8.

Note how the negation of the cap predicate is used at each stage.

There are many arrangements of the queens on a chessboard that will satisfy all the constraints. The first one found by the solution predicate is displayed in figure 5.14. It is worth noting that because of how the col predicate is defined, this program always tries columns in numeric order, 1, 2, 3, and so on. So not surprisingly, the first solution has a queen on (1,1). However, it does not have a queen on (2,3). This means that although a queen on (2,3) is safe from the queen on (1,1), there is no way to place the remaining six queens safely if one starts with (1,1) and (2,3). Similarly, a queen on (2,4) leads to a dead end, and (2,5) is the first choice for the second queen that works with the remaining six queens. Then for the third queen, the (3,2) and (3,7) positions would be safe, but again this would not allow the remaining five queens to be positioned safely, and so (3,8) is the first choice that works with the rest of the queens.

Given the amount of searching and backtracking required to properly place queens on even an 8×8 board, computer scientists have looked for more efficient ways of solving this problem. One method that works well involves placing the queens randomly on a board and then repeatedly moving one of the queens to reduce its conflicts with the others.

5.5 A fourth example: Logic problems

This section considers a very different sort of puzzle, often called a *logic problem*, although it is no more connected to logic than the others. It is a word problem involving several clues about the identities of individuals playing certain roles. A simple example illustrates the form:

In conversation, Sandy, Chris, and Pat discovered that they had distinct occupations and also played distinct musical instruments. Their occupations are doctor, lawyer, and engineer, and the instruments they play are piano, flute, and violin. Also,

1. Chris is married to the doctor.

2. The lawyer plays the piano.

3. Chris is not the engineer.

4. Sandy is a patient of the violinist.

Who plays the flute?

To solve logic puzzles like these as constraint satisfaction problems, one needs to determine what the variables are, what the domains should be, and how the given information leads to constraints on the desired solution.

For this example, to determine who plays the flute, it is necessary to figure out who (among Sandy, Chris, and Pat) plays what instrument and has what job. So the problem can be characterized as follows:

- Variables: `Doctor, Lawyer, Engineer, Piano, Violin, Flute`

- Domain: {`sandy, chris, pat`}

To encode the given information as constraints, these two implicit facts must somehow be included:

- If x is married to y, then $x \neq y$.

- If x is a patient of y, then $x \neq y$ and y is the doctor.

Figure 5.15.   A solution to the first logic problem   `logic1.pl`

```
% A logic puzzle involving jobs and musical instruments,
solution(Flute) :-

    % Distinct occupations and instruments
    uniq_people(Doctor,Lawyer,Engineer),
    uniq_people(Piano,Violin,Flute),

    % The four clues
    \+ chris = Doctor,     % Chris is married to the doctor.
    Lawyer = Piano,        % The lawyer plays the piano.
    \+ Engineer = chris,   % The engineer is not Chris.
    Violin = Doctor,       % Sandy is a patient of
    \+ sandy = Violin.     %    the violinist.

% uniq(...) is used to generate three distinct people.
uniq_people(A,B,C) :- person(A),  person(B),  person(C),
                      \+ A=B, \+ A=C, \+ B=C.

% The three given people
person(chris).    person(sandy).    person(pat).
```

Putting such facts into a knowledge base is tricky, since the conclusions involve equality. For present purposes, it is much easier to embed the information directly in the `solution` predicate, as shown in figure 5.15. The rest of the program is similar to previous examples.

5.5.1   Hidden variables

The main challenge in logic problems like these is typically to determine how to express the constraints. Often the only way to do this is to imagine that there are *hidden variables* that are not mentioned but whose values need to be taken into account. This was the case with the carry digits in the cryptarithmetic problems. They had to be introduced in order to express the constraints among the mentioned digits.

For example, suppose there is exactly the same logic problem as before, except that constraint 3 is

3. Pat is not married to the engineer.

How should this piece of information be handled? At first it seems that it places no constraint on either Pat or the engineer. However, it is useful to think in terms of new variables, for Pat's spouse, Chris's spouse, and Sandy's spouse. Assuming they can only be married to each other, the domain for these variables will be the three people (sandy, chris, pat) or none, to handle the case where the person is not married. The

Figure 5.16. A solution to the second logic problem `logic2.pl`

```
% A second logic puzzle involving jobs and musical instruments
solution(Flute) :-
    uniq_people(Doctor,Lawyer,Engineer),
    uniq_people(Piano,Violin,Flute),

    % Generate values for the three spouse variables.
    spouses(Chris_spouse,Sandy_spouse,Pat_spouse),

    Chris_spouse = Doctor,       % Chris is married to the doctor.
    Lawyer = Piano,              % The lawyer plays the piano.
    \+ Pat_spouse = Engineer,    % Pat is not married to the engineer.
    Violin = Doctor,             % Sandy is a patient of
    \+ sandy = Violin.           %     the violinist.
uniq_people(A,B,C) :-
    person(A),  person(B),  person(C), \+ A=B, \+ A=C, \+ B=C.

person(chris).   person(sandy).   person(pat).

% spouses(X,Y,Z): X,Y,Z can be spouses of Chris,Sandy,Pat.
spouses(none,none,none).      % Nobody is married.
spouses(sandy,chris,none).    % Chris and Sandy are married.
spouses(pat,none,chris).      % Chris and Pat are married.
spouses(none,pat,sandy).      % Sandy and Pat are married.
```

constraints that these spouse variables must satisfy derive from the fact that there are only four marriage possibilities:

- Nobody is married.

- Chris and Sandy are married.

- Chris and Pat are married.

- Sandy and Pat are married.

These four possibilities can be handled with four clauses, as shown in figure 5.16.

* 5.5.2   A more complex logic problem

This section considers an old classic logic problem, called the zebra problem, sometimes attributed to Albert Einstein:

On a street there are five houses of different colors, occupied by five individuals of different nationalities, who own five different pets, drink five different beverages, and smoke five different brands of (American) cigarettes. Also,

1. The occupant of the red house is English.

2. The Spaniard owns a dog.

3. The coffee drinker lives in a green house.

4. The Ukrainian drinks tea.

5. The ivory house is to the left of the green one.

6. The snail owner smokes Winstons.

7. The person in the yellow house smokes Kools.

8. The occupant in the middle house drinks milk.

9. The Norwegian lives in the leftmost house.

10. The Chesterfield smoker lives next to the fox owner.

11. The Kool smoker lives next to the horse owner.

12. The orange juice drinker smokes Lucky Strikes.

13. The Parliament smoker is Japanese.

14. The Norwegian lives next to a blue house.

Who owns the zebra?

Observe that most of these clues will end up being statements of equality among the variables:

4. The Ukrainian drinks tea.
   ```
   Ukrainian = TeaDrinker
   ```

6. The snail owner smokes Winstons.
   ```
   SnailOwner = WinstonSmoker
   ```

The question is what to do about the constraints involving *position*:

5. The ivory house is to the left of the green one.

(Note that *left* here means directly to the left.) This fact needs to relate to other positional constraints like the following:

8. The occupant in the middle house drinks milk.

9. The Norwegian lives in the leftmost house.

10. The Chesterfield smoker lives next to the fox owner.

First determine what *domain* to use for the variables. As long as the appropriate equality and inequality constraints are enforced, the values can be taken from any set. The

Figure 5.17. A solution to the zebra problem   zebra.pl

```
% This is a solution to the classic zebra puzzle.
solution(Zebra,England,Spain,Ukraine,Japan,Norway) :-

    % The fourteen clues
    England=Red, Spain=Dog, Coffee=Green, Ukraine=Tea,
    left(Ivory,Green), Winston=Snail, Kool=Yellow,
    middle_pos(Milk), leftmost_pos(Norway),
    next_to(Chesterfield,Fox), next_to(Kool,Horse),
    LuckyStrike=OJ, Japan=Parliament, next_to(Norway,Blue),

    % The five lists: houses, nations, pets, drinks, cigarettes
    uniq_pos(Green,Red,Yellow,Ivory,Blue),
    uniq_pos(England,Spain,Ukraine,Japan,Norway),
    uniq_pos(Dog,Snail,Zebra,Fox,Horse),
    uniq_pos(Tea,Milk,OJ,Coffee,OtherDrink),
    uniq_pos(Winston,Kool,Parliament,Chesterfield,LuckyStrike).

%-------------- The positional predicates  ------------------
uniq_pos(P1,P2,P3,P4,P5) :-
    pos(P1), pos(P2), pos(P3), pos(P4), pos(P5),
    \+ P1=P2, \+ P1=P3, \+ P1=P4, \+ P1=P5, \+ P2=P3,
    \+ P2=P4, \+ P2=P5, \+ P3=P4, \+ P3=P5, \+ P4=P5.

pos(1). pos(2). pos(3). pos(4). pos(5).

leftmost_pos(1).   middle_pos(3).

left(1,2). left(2,3). left(3,4). left(4,5).

next_to(X,Y) :- left(X,Y).
next_to(X,Y) :- left(Y,X).
```

positional constraints suggest that values be taken from a *positional ordering* of the five houses: 1 (leftmost), 2 (left middle), 3 (middle), 4 (right middle), 5 (rightmost). The knowledge base can include facts about which position is leftmost, which is middle, which position is directly to the left of another, and which position is next to another. These positional facts together with the clause for the solution predicate (from the fourteen puzzle clues and the uniqueness constraints) are shown in figure 5.17.

Since the values of all the variables are just positional numbers, it takes some extra work to get a more descriptive answer. A query with the solution predicate brings the following result:

```
?- solution(Zebra,E,S,U,J,N).
Zebra = 5,  E = 3,  S = 4,  U = 2,  J = 5,  N = 1
Yes
```

Figure 5.18.   A scheduling problem

The task is to schedule a new class to meet five hours each week.

Meeting times are on the hour from 9am to 4pm, on weekdays.

Some of the periods will be taken by previously scheduled activities.

Classes must not meet on successive hours on the same day, or for more than two hours total on any one day.

===

This says that the zebra is in house 5, the rightmost house. But who lives there? To find out, use a `print_solution` predicate defined as follows:

```
print_solution :-
    solution(Zeb,E,S,U,J,N), pmatch(Zeb,E,'English'),
    pmatch(Zeb,S,'Spanish'), pmatch(Zeb,U,'Ukrainian'),
    pmatch(Zeb,J,'Japanese'), pmatch(Zeb,N,'Norwegian').

pmatch(X,X,Name) :-                  % Write when there is a match.
    nl, write('The zebra owner is '), write(Name).
pmatch(X,Y,Name) :- \+ X=Y.          % Write nothing in this case.
```

The `print_solution` predicate uses the positional information to print the nationality that *matches* the zebra house number:

```
?- print_solution.
The zebra owner is Japanese
```

---

* 5.6   A fifth example: Scheduling

The constraint satisfaction problem in this section is not a puzzle at all, but rather a much more practical problem, *scheduling*. Examples of scheduling include assigning people to jobs, or meetings to rooms, or courses to final exam periods. Solving problems like these still requires thinking of course, but now the thinking is not done just for the fun of it, as with puzzles.

A scheduling problem involving the timetable for a course is shown in figure 5.18. The task is to find *periods* (that is, the days and times) for the five classes. This can be formulated as a constraint satisfaction problem as follows:

- Variables: P_1, P_2, P_3, P_4, P_5, where each P_i is a period for the course.

- Domains: Each period is a certain time on a certain day. A period can be encoded as a number: $(100 \times day) + 24\,hr.\,clock$. So, for example, for Monday at 9am, the period would be 109; for Tuesday at 2pm, it would be 214; and for Friday at 4pm, it would be 516.

- Constraints: The five chosen periods must be available (not already taken), non-consecutive, and with no more than two per day. In addition (although it is not stated explicitly), the five periods must all be distinct.

The following generates five available periods:

```
% P1,P2,P3,P4,P5 are five distinct available periods.
uniq_periods(P1,P2,P3,P4,P5) :-
    per(P1), per(P2), per(P3), per(P4), per(P5),
    \+ P1=P2,  \+ P1=P3,  \+ P1=P4,  \+ P1=P5,  \+ P2=P3,
    \+ P2=P4,  \+ P2=P5,  \+ P3=P4,  \+ P3=P5,  \+ P4=P5.

% per(P): P is a period that is not already taken.
per(P) :- day(D), time(T), P is 100*D+T, \+ taken(P).

day(1).  day(2).  day(3).  day(4).  day(5). % The five days

time(9).   time(10).  time(11).  time(12).  % The eight times
time(13).  time(14).  time(15).  time(16).
```

This assumes that the taken predicate is defined separately to tell which periods have been taken by previously scheduled activities.

The solution predicate for this scheduling problem is shown in figure 5.19. The constraints are handled by two predicates: not_2_in_a_row ensures that there is not a pair of periods where one is an hour earlier or later than the other; and not_3_same_day ensures that there are not three periods that are on the same day. (The day of a period is obtained by doing integer division by 100.)

All that remains is to specify which periods are unavailable using the taken predicate. An example specification appears in figure 5.20. Adding those clauses to the scheduling program gives the following:

```
?- solution(P1,P2,P3,P4,P5).
 P1 = 111,  P2= 113,  P3 = 213,  P4 = 409,  P5 = 411
% Mon 11am  Mon 1pm   Tue 1pm    Thu 9am    Thu 11am
```

The scheduling constraints are somewhat loose in this example, so the solution displayed here is not unique.

Figure 5.19. A classroom scheduler   schedule-top.pl

```
% This program solves a classroom scheduling problem.
solution(P1,P2,P3,P4,P5) :-
  uniq_periods(P1,P2,P3,P4,P5),      % All different periods.
  not_2_in_a_row(P1,P2,P3,P4,P5),    % Not two consecutive hrs.
  not_3_same_day(P1,P2,P3,P4,P5).    % Not three on the same day.

not_2_in_a_row(P1,P2,P3,P4,P5) :-
  \+ seq(P1,P2), \+ seq(P1,P3), \+ seq(P1,P4), \+ seq(P1,P5),
  \+ seq(P2,P3), \+ seq(P2,P4), \+ seq(P2,P5), \+ seq(P3,P4),
  \+ seq(P3,P5), \+ seq(P4,P5).

seq(A,B) :- A =:= B-1.
seq(A,B) :- A =:= B+1.

not_3_same_day(P1,P2,P3,P4,P5) :-
  \+ eqday(P1,P2,P3), \+ eqday(P1,P2,P4), \+ eqday(P1,P2,P5),
  \+ eqday(P1,P3,P4), \+ eqday(P1,P3,P5), \+ eqday(P1,P4,P5),
  \+ eqday(P2,P3,P4), \+ eqday(P2,P3,P5), \+ eqday(P2,P4,P5),
  \+ eqday(P3,P4,P5).

eqday(A,B,C) :- Z is A // 100, Z is B // 100, Z is C // 100.

% The definition of uniq_periods is elsewhere.
```

Figure 5.20. Previously scheduled periods   schedule-aux.pl

```
% Monday: only 11am and 1pm are available.
taken(X) :- X // 100 =:= 1, \+ X=111, \+ X=113.
% Tuesday: only 1pm and 2pm are available.
taken(X) :- X // 100 =:= 2, \+ X=213, \+ X=214.
% Wednesday: nothing available.
taken(X) :- X // 100 =:= 3.
% Thursday: all available, except for 10am, 12pm, and 2pm.
taken(410). taken(412). taken(414).
% Friday: nothing available.
taken(X) :- X // 100 =:= 5.
```

Want to read more?

This chapter was about the thinking required to solve constraint satisfaction problems. As noted, the subarea of AI called *constraint programming* studies how to do this efficiently. Work in this area began in the 1970s when Montanari [27] and Mackworth

[26] first formulated constraint satisfaction problems in the form considered here. They also proposed methods of solving them that appear to work much better in practice than generate-and-test. An excellent graduate-level textbook about this area of research is by Dechter [24]. (Note: Scheduling has a history of its own outside of computer science in the area of operations research.)

Constraint satisfaction is connected to many areas of computer science, for example, answering queries in databases [28]. As it turns out, it also raises a very fundamental question about computation itself. To take Sudoku as an example, each Sudoku puzzle is of size $n^2 \times n^2$ for some n (like 9×9 or 121×121), and the search space grows very quickly, in fact, exponentially with n. The question is whether there is a way to solve these puzzles that is *guaranteed* to do better than generate-and-test over this enormous space.

This question can be reformulated in a mathematically precise way using the notion of a Turing machine (mentioned at the end of chapter 1). Is there a Turing machine M and a polynomial P such that M can solve any Sudoku puzzle of size $n^2 \times n^2$ (or report that there is no solution) in no more than $P(n)$ steps? The answer, remarkably enough, is that nobody knows. The question is equivalent to the famous $\mathsf{P} = \mathsf{NP}$ question, first posed by Stephen Cook [23] in the 1970s, and despite the best efforts of thousands of computer scientists and mathematicians since then, it has remained unanswered. Anyone who can answer it will become instantly famous and receive a $1 million reward from the Clay Mathematics Institute. What *is* known about the question is that no matter how the answer turns out, it will affect the view of thousands of other computational tasks, some of which have direct economic significance [25].

Exercises

1. This chapter presented three different ways of handling equality in Prolog: =, =:=, and is. For each of the three, explain briefly what its purpose is, and present an example setting where it should be used but where the other two should not be used.

2. Draw a map of central Europe consisting of the following seven countries: France, Switzerland, Italy, Belgium, Holland, Germany, and Austria. Color the countries on the map using just red, yellow, and orange; no two countries with a border between them can be the same color. Look at an existing map to see where the borders are, and then write a Prolog program that will find a color for each country.

3. Use Prolog to solve the cryptarithmetic puzzle CROSS + ROADS = DANGER.
   Note: If you are not careful with the ordering of constraints in your program, the program could run for hours. With a proper ordering, it should only take a second or so. Explain briefly the order you have chosen.

4. Consider the following problem:

   Donna, Danny, David, and Doreen were seated at a table in a restaurant. The men sat across from each other, as did the women. They each ordered a different main course with a different beverage. In addition,

   - Doreen sat beside the person who ordered steak.
   - The chicken came with a Coke.
   - The person with the lasagna sat across from the person with milk.
   - David never drinks coffee.
   - Donna only drinks water.
   - Danny could not afford to order steak.

   Who ordered the pizza?

   Write a Prolog program that solves this problem by displaying who ordered each of the main courses and each of the beverages. *Hint:* Begin by writing clauses defining predicates $beside(x, y)$, which holds if person x is sitting beside person y, and $across(x, y)$, which holds if person x is sitting across from person y.

5. Many newspapers feature a puzzle called KenKen in the recreational section. The KenKen puzzle is similar to Sudoku except that arithmetic relations are involved. Write a Prolog program that solves a 4×4 KenKen puzzle taken from a newspaper.

   Hint: You will need the `uniq` predicate used for the Sudoku problem for the rows and for the columns. It will also be convenient to define two auxiliary predicates, sub and div, where $sub(x, y, z)$ holds when either $z = x - y$ or $z = y - x$, and $div(x, y, z)$ holds when either $z = x \div y$ or $z = y \div x$.

6. The answers submitted by five students to a true/false quiz are as follows:

   Teresa: true, true, false, true, false
   Tim: false, true, true, true, false
   Tania: true, false, true, true, false
   Tom: false, true, true, false, true
   Tony: true, false, true, false, true

Tania got more answers right than Teresa did. Tom got more right than Tim. Tony did not get all the answers right, nor did he get them all wrong. Write a Prolog program to find the correct answers to the quiz.

Hint: Write a predicate $\text{grade}(s_1, s_2, s_3, s_4, s_5, a_1, a_2, a_3, a_4, a_5, n)$ that holds when n is the number of correct answers when a student submits the s_i, and the correct answers are the a_i. (So grade counts the matches between the s_i and a_i.)

7. Consider a course timetable for a Fine Arts student at a mythical university. The student wants to take a course in art, music, film, and dance, and each of these has three hours of classes a week. To accommodate a variety of timing constraints, some courses offer two sections at different times.

   - There are two possible sections for art. One is offered MWF10, and the other, MWF11.

   - There is a single section of dance: Friday 1–4.

   - Music can be taken either Monday at 11, Wednesday at 3, and Friday at 3, or Monday at 2, Wednesday at 2, and Friday at 11.

   - There are two sections of film: one on Monday at 11, Wednesday at 11, and Friday at noon, and one on Monday at noon, Wednesday at noon, and Wednesday at 3.

In addition, the student wants a free hour for lunch each day at noon or at 1. Write a Prolog program that generates a timetable for the student.

* 6   Case Study: Interpreting Visual Scenes

The previous chapter gave examples of the sort of thinking required to solve certain puzzles. This type of thinking does have some distinctive features when done by people. It requires concentration and effort; memory aids (like pencil and paper) are usually helpful; some people are much better at it than others; and some people see no fun in the activity at all.

In this chapter, the idea of constraint satisfaction is applied to a form of thinking that seems much more natural and relaxed: *visual interpretation*. This is a type of thinking that everyone can do to some extent, typically with a lot less conscious effort than puzzles require.

The first section briefly considers the concept of vision and its connection to thinking. The following sections examine a sampling of three visual interpretation tasks: the interpretation of an image of a two-dimensional terrain as seen from above (section 2); the interpretation of the edges in an image of three-dimensional polyhedral objects (section 3); and recognizing objects of interest in an image (section 4).

6.1   The thinking part of vision

What is vision? In its simplest terms, it is the process of identifying the physical objects around us by interpreting the patterns of light that reflect off them. Digitizing the problem somewhat, one can rephrase it as follows. Imagine that a certain number of times per second, our eyes are presented with an *image*, that is, a two-dimensional grid of picture elements (or *pixels*). The job of vision is to respond to these images with something like "German shepherd puppy" or "Jackson Pollock painting" or "delivery truck coming straight for me." The exact details of the image and the desired responses need not concern us.

Figure 6.1.   A mystery picture

Much of what happens during vision does not seem to depend on what we know about the world, and so by the definition given previously, does not involve thinking. Our eyes and brains have evolved to be able to very quickly group together regions of pixels in an image that have similar features (like brightness, color, or texture) and to locate discontinuities in these features that are potential edges or contours of objects.

But not all of vision is like this. Consider the picture in figure 6.1, courtesy of Antonio Torralba. Part of it has been blacked out and only an out-of-focus blob at the bottom right is visible. Even if we stare at this blob long and hard, we cannot readily identify what it is supposed to be. However, in the right-hand picture of figure 6.2, it is quite easily identifiable as a car.

Why do we see the blob as a car, and not as an eagle or a biscuit or a person's face? The rest of the picture by itself does not say "car" any more than it says "biscuit." But despite the fact that the picture is out of focus, there is enough information in it for us to identify houses, sky, and road. And once we have made that identification, we can *use what we know* to constrain the possible interpretations of the blob: cars are physical objects of this size and shape on a road beside houses. This is thinking!

This chapter is concerned with using what is known in this way to interpret images. It does not deal with arrays of pixels directly but only with a list of *image components*, such as the regions or edges that appear in an image. It does not work from precise numeric values for these regions or edges but only from qualitative descriptions of their properties, such as the relative sizes of the regions or which edges meet at which vertices. Then, based on knowledge about how an actual scene can appear in

Figure 6.2. The mystery picture revealed

Figure 6.3. An aerial sketch map

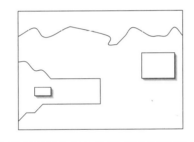

An aerial sketch map is depicted on the left. The interpretation task is to identify each region of the image as one of grass, water, pavement, a house, or a vehicle.

an image, the job is to *interpret* the image components, that is, to identify (at some level) what the regions or edges actually represent in the scene.

This visual interpretation can be formulated as a constraint satisfaction problem. However, considerably more knowledge of the world will have to be applied than for the problems of chapter 5.

6.2 Aerial sketch maps

Imagine looking down from an airplane passing over a terrain and seeing the image represented by the sketch in figure 6.3. The job is to identify the various regions in the image. Here is the background knowledge one might expect to use to help identify these regions:

- A region cannot border or be surrounded by a region of the same type.
- Houses cannot be next to or surrounded by water.
- Vehicles must be next to or surrounded by pavement.
- Pavement cannot be completely inside any other region.
- Houses, vehicles, and pavement have regular shapes (with straight edges); grass and water have irregular shapes.
- Vehicles are small; the other regions are large.

These statements constrain the permissible interpretations of regions that appear in images in terms of size (large or small), shape (regular or irregular), borders (what is next to what), and containment (what is surrounded by what). In reality, of course, there are many exceptions to these rules (like houseboats that are on water, and paved tennis courts that are surrounded by grass), but these are ignored for now.

A Prolog program that captures these facts appears in figure 6.4. It describes what is *permissible* in an image of this sort. For example, the query border(pavement,grass) returns *success*. This does not mean that an image must have a region of pavement next to a region of grass but only that it could. The query border(water,vehicle), on the other hand, returns *failure*, which means that an image cannot portray a region of water next to a vehicle.

6.2.1   Constraints on image regions

With this background knowledge about the scene, the image can now be interpreted. Start with a list of regions, along with the properties they have in the image, as in figure 6.5. Approach the visual interpretation task as a constraint satisfaction problem:

- The variables are the regions of the image: R1, R2, R3, R4, R5.
- Each variable must take a value from one of the region types: grass, water, pavement, house, and vehicle.
- The constraints that need to be satisfied are the image properties listed in figure 6.5, in conjunction with the background knowledge about the permissible interpretations of region types.

Figure 6.4. The types of regions and their properties　　　　　　　`regions.pl`

```
% The five types of regions that can appear in an image
region(grass).   region(water).   region(pavement).
region(house).   region(vehicle).

% small(X) holds when region X can be small in an image.
small(vehicle).

% regular(X) holds when region X can be regular in an image.
regular(pavement).  regular(house).  regular(vehicle).

% border(X,Y) holds when region X can border region Y.
border(X,Y) :- \+ bad_border(X,Y), \+ bad_border(Y,X).

    % Unacceptable borders
    bad_border(X,X).
    bad_border(house,water).
    bad_border(vehicle,X) :- \+ X=pavement.

% inside(X,Y) holds when region X can be surrounded by Y.
inside(X,Y) :- \+ bad_inside(X,Y).

    % Unacceptable containment
    bad_inside(X,X).
    bad_inside(house,water).
    bad_inside(vehicle,X) :- \+ X=pavement.
    bad_inside(pavement,_).
```

Figure 6.5. The image regions and their properties

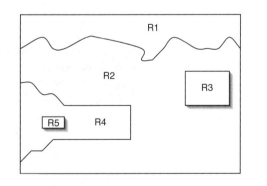

- Region R5 is small; the others are large.

- Region R3 and R5 are regular; R1 and R2 are irregular; R4 could go either way.

- Region R1 borders on R2; R2 borders on R4.

- Region R3 is inside R2; R5 is inside R4.

This leads to the `solution` predicate in Prolog that appears in figure 6.6. Loading this program together with the one in figure 6.4 produces this behavior:

Figure 6.6.   The sketch map interpretation   sketch.pl

```
solution(R1,R2,R3,R4,R5) :-
   region(R1), region(R2), region(R3), region(R4), region(R5),
   % Size constraints
      \+ small(R1), \+ small(R2), \+ small(R3),
      \+ small(R4), small(R5),
   % Regularity constraints (none for R4)
      regular(R3), regular(R5), \+ regular(R2), \+ regular(R1),
   % Border constraints
      border(R1,R2), border(R2,R4),
   % Containment constraints
      inside(R3,R2), inside(R5,R4).
% The definitions of region, small, border, etc. are elsewhere.
```

```
?- solution(R1,R2,R3,R4,R5).
R1 = water,   R2 = grass,   R3 = house,
R4 = pavement,   R5 = vehicle
```

This is the only visual interpretation that satisfies all the constraints. Note how the interpretations for some regions help to disambiguate others. For example, R4 is large, so it cannot be a vehicle. But it is not clear whether it should be seen as regular or irregular. However, it clearly surrounds region R5, and once it is determined that R5 is a vehicle, background knowledge leads to the conclusion that R4 must be pavement. On a much smaller scale, this is precisely the sort of thinking that took place to interpret the blob as a car in figure 6.2!

Also note that the constraints work together to identify the regions and that there can be redundancy. For example, if the \+ small(R3) constraint is eliminated from the solution predicate, one still gets a unique interpretation of the image as before. This is why it was not necessary to specify whether region R4 was regular or irregular in the image. On the other hand, if the small(R5) constraint were eliminated instead, there would be two interpretations: the previous one and a second one where R5 is a house. Of course, if the constraint \+ small(R1) were replaced by small(R1), the image would have no interpretation at all.

6.3   Polyhedral objects

Figure 6.7 shows a very different type of image, a three-dimensional, L-shaped, block-like object (or *polyhedron*). At first, it is not clear that any interpretation is needed here.

Figure 6.7. A polyhedral object and its labels

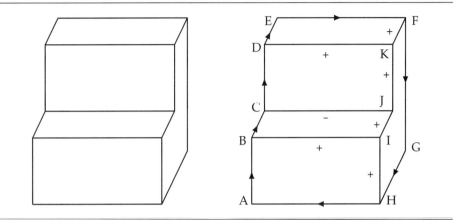

But consider the five horizontal lines that appear in the image. Part of making sense of this image is realizing that these lines do not all mean the same thing:

- The top horizontal line is a boundary of the object. The viewer understands that just below the line is a face of the object, and just above the line is empty space (unless the object is up against a wall).

- The bottom horizontal line is also a boundary of the object. But this time the space just above the line is part of the object, and just below the line is empty space (unless the object is on top of another).

- The middle horizontal line represents the intersection of two faces of the object. Moreover, the intersection is *concave* (or hinged inward, like the letter V as seen from above).

- The two remaining horizontal lines also represent the intersection of two faces of the object. In these cases, however, the intersection is *convex* (or hinged outward, like the letter V as seen from below).

Interpreting an image of a polyhedral object involves labeling each edge in this way. The image at the right in figure 6.7 shows the vertices named and the edges labeled: + for a convex edge, - for a concave edge, and an arrow for a boundary edge with a surface to the right relative to its direction. The edge AH is labeled < meaning that in going from A to H the surface is to the left. Of course, there is nothing inherently directional in the edges of an image. So the reverse edge HA should be understood

Figure 6.8.   The four vertex types

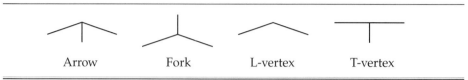

Arrow   Fork   L-vertex   T-vertex

as labeled >, since in going from H to A the surface is to the right. (The + and – labels will be the same for either direction of the edge.)

6.3.1   Constraints on vertices and edges

What kind of background knowledge is expected in order to interpret edges in an image like this? The answer has to do with the *vertices*, where the edges meet. Only four types of vertices are expected in such an image, as shown in figure 6.8. (All but the T-vertex appear in figure 6.7: E, A, and G are L-vertices; C, K, and I are forks; the rest are arrows.) Furthermore, in any polyhedral image, only some combinations of edge types can meet at a vertex.

Consider, for example, the L-vertex of figure 6.8. Suppose that both edges meeting at the vertex were labeled +. Then because of the surfaces below each edge, there would need to be an extra edge where they meet, making the vertex into an arrow. The conclusion: two edges labeled + *cannot meet* at an L-vertex.

The full range of possibilities for the edges at each type of vertex are shown in figure 6.9. These facts can be encoded in Prolog in a straightforward way, as is done in figure 6.10. In all cases, the edges are understood as leaving the vertex. The `reverse` predicate is used to relate the label of an edge to the label of the same edge in the reverse direction.

With this background knowledge, the visual interpretation of a polyhedral image can proceed. Given is a list of vertices, their types, and the edges that leave each vertex. The job is to assign labels to each edge; this is approached as a constraint satisfaction problem:

- The variables are the edges in the image.

- Each variable takes a value from one of the four labels: >, <, +, and –.

- The constraints are that each vertex in the image must connect edges with labels that are in accordance with the rules shown in figure 6.9.

Figure 6.9. Permissible vertices in polyhedral images

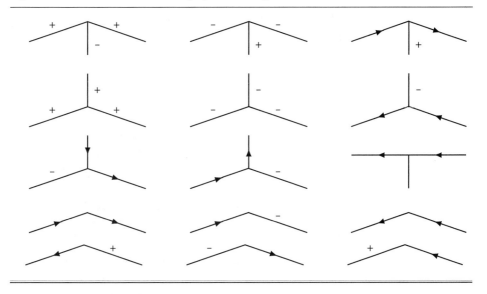

Figure 6.10. Permissible vertices in Prolog   polyrules.pl

```
% All edges are assumed to leave the vertex in question.

% arrow(left,bottom,right)
arrow('+','-','+').  arrow('-','+','-').  arrow('<','+','>').

% fork(left,top,right)
fork('+','+','+').  fork('-','-','-').  fork('>','-','<').
fork('-','<','>').  fork('<','>','-').

% tvertex(left,bottom,right)
tvertex('>',_,'<').

% lvertex(left,right)
lvertex('<','>').  lvertex('<','-').   lvertex('>','<').
lvertex('>','+').  lvertex('-','>').   lvertex('+','<').

% Reversing the direction of an edge: only < and > change.
reverse('+','+').        reverse('-','-').
reverse('<','>').        reverse('>','<').
```

For the L-shaped object of figure 6.7, the solution predicate is shown in figure 6.11. There are fifteen arguments, corresponding to the fifteen edges in the image. The first eleven atoms in the body correspond to the eleven vertices in the image. Note

Figure 6.11.   Interpreting the edges in figure 6.7   `polyinterp.pl`

```
solution(AB,BC,CD,DE,EF,FG,GH,HA,HI,IB,IJ,JC,JK,KD,KF) :-
    lvertex(AH,AB), arrow(BA,BI,BC), fork(CB,CD,CJ),
    arrow(DC,DK,DE), lvertex(ED,EF), arrow(FE,FK,FG),
    lvertex(GF,GH), arrow(HG,HI,HA), fork(IH,IB,IJ),
    arrow(JK,JC,JI), fork(KD,KF,KJ),

    reverse(AB,BA), reverse(BC,CB), reverse(CD,DC),
    reverse(DE,ED), reverse(EF,FE), reverse(FG,GF),
    reverse(GH,HG), reverse(HA,AH), reverse(HI,IH),
    reverse(IB,BI), reverse(IJ,JI), reverse(JC,CJ),
    reverse(JK,KJ), reverse(KD,DK), reverse(KF,FK).

print_lshape_interpretation :-
    solution(AB,BC,CD,DE,EF,FG,GH,HA,HI,IB,IJ,JC,JK,KD,KF), nl,
    write(AB), write(BC), write(CD), write(DE), write(EF),
    write(FG), write(GH), write(HA), write(HI), write(IB),
    write(IJ), write(JC), write(JK), write(KD), write(KF).
```

that in each case the edge leaving the vertex is used. For vertex A, for example, `lvertex(AH,AB)` is used, and not `lvertex(HA,AB)` or `lvertex(AH,BA)`. (Since an edge connects two vertices, each direction of the edge will be used exactly once in the eleven atoms.) Loading this program together with the one in figure 6.10 produces the following behavior:

```
?- print_lshape_interpretation.
>>>>>>>>+++-+++  ;
>>>>--->>+++-+++  ;
---->>>>+++-+++  ;
>>>>>>--+++-+++  ;
No
```

So four visual interpretations are found. These are shown graphically in figure 6.12. They all agree on the internal edges HI, IB, IJ, JC, JK, KD, and KF. The first interpretation (top left of figure 6.12) is the one depicted in figure 6.7, where all the remaining edges are boundaries. In the next interpretation (top right of figure 6.12), the object is seen as up against a wall (or another object) behind it, with EF and FG as concave edges between two surfaces. In the third interpretation (bottom right), the object is seen as against a wall on the left, with AB, BC, CD, and DE as concave. Finally, in the last interpretation (bottom left), the object is seen as resting on another, with GH and HA as concave. Note that if the edge BC is concave (as in figure 6.12, bottom right), the edges AB, CD, and DE cannot be boundaries; they, too, must be concave. Note

Figure 6.12. The four interpretations of the polyhedral object

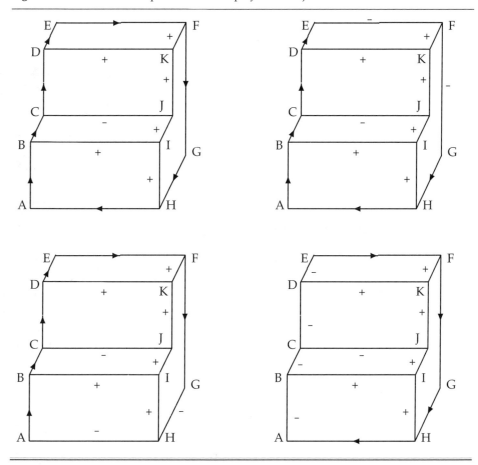

also that there is no interpretation where the object is against a wall behind it *and* to the left, as this would require vertex E to be a fork.

The object depicted in figure 6.7 is *almost* unambiguous. Once the boundaries of the object are determined, which a low-level visual process may be able to do based on differences in color or brightness between the object and the background, everything else falls into place. But this still depends on putting all the constraints together. For example, if you cover the top and right parts of the figure, you can (with a bit of effort) come to see the surface CDKJ as being closer than ABIH, where the edge CJ is now convex. Globally, however, this interpretation is unsustainable.

Figure 6.13. A polyhedral object and an impossible variant

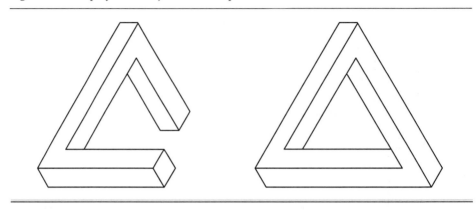

6.3.2   Impossible objects

This idea of images having only local interpretations is at the root of so-called *impossible objects*. Consider figure 6.13. The image on the left is somewhat unusual but can be interpreted as an object with two 90° turns. The one on the right (due to Roger Penrose), however, cannot be interpreted as a polyhedral object at all. By covering parts of the figure it is possible to interpret the rest of the figure in one way or another. In doing visual interpretation, however, it is necessary to look for local cues and to try to assemble a global interpretation that accounts for everything that is seen.

6.4   Object recognition

Given an image of some sort, the task of object recognition is to determine whether the image contains a depiction of a particular object, say, a door that is an exit, or a banquet table with food on it, or a parcel to pick up for delivery. This is the sort of perceptual task that we do all the time, and it is absolutely crucial when we arrive at a new location. It is also somewhat different from the visual interpretation discussed in the previous sections. Rather than interpreting all the image elements, the goal is to pick out elements in the image corresponding to the kind of object being sought.

Here is a simple case. The image given is like the one in figure 6.14 and the job is to see if there is a *cuboid* (a rectangular-shaped block) in the image. As shown in the figure, a list of vertices in the image is given (of the four types mentioned in the previous section) together with the vertices to which they connect. The predicates from

Figure 6.14. An image with a cuboid and a wedge

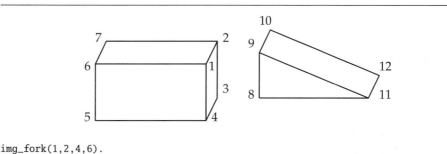

```
img_fork(1,2,4,6).
img_arr(6,5,1,7).    img_arr(2,7,1,3).    img_arr(4,3,1,5).
img_arr(9,8,11,10).  img_arr(11,12,9,8).
img_lv(3,2,4).       img_lv(5,4,6).       img_lv(7,6,2).
img_lv(8,11,9).      img_lv(10,9,12).     img_lv(12,10,11).
```

Figure 6.15. Finding a cuboid in an image   cuboid.pl

```
% A 3D view of a cuboid (seven vertices)
cuboid(A,B,C,D,E,F,G) :-
    calc_arr(A,F,G,B), calc_lv(B,A,C), calc_arr(C,B,G,D),
    calc_lv(D,C,E), calc_arr(E,D,G,F), calc_lv(F,E,A),
    calc_fork(G,A,C,E).

% Vertex V, then left, mid, and right vertices
calc_arr(V,V1,V2,V3) :- img_arr(V,V1,V2,V3).

% Vertex V, then left and right vertices
calc_lv(V,V1,V2) :- img_lv(V,V1,V2).

% Vertex V, then the vertices in clockwise order
calc_fork(V,V1,V2,V3) :- img_fork(V,V1,V2,V3).
calc_fork(V,V1,V2,V3) :- img_fork(V,V3,V1,V2).
calc_fork(V,V1,V2,V3) :- img_fork(V,V2,V3,V1).
```

the image `img_lv`, `img_arr`, `img_fork`, and `img_tv` represent an L-vertex, an arrow, a fork, and a T-vertex, respectively. For example, `img_arr(9,8,11,10)` indicates that vertex 9 in the image is an arrow vertex, with vertex 8 on its left branch, vertex 11 on its middle branch, and vertex 10 on the right. The task is to locate a cuboid within this collection of vertices.

What the cuboid predicate needs to do is to find a pattern of vertices that connect in a certain way. The Prolog code for this appears in figure 6.15. (The predicates calc_arr, calc_lv, and calc_fork are used rather than the img predicates directly, since they will be refined later.) Loading this program and including the image data from figure 6.14 produces

```
?- cuboid(A,B,C,D,E,F,G).
A = 6,   B = 7,   C = 2,   D = 3,   E = 4,   F = 5,   G = 1 ;
A = 2,   B = 3,   C = 4,   D = 5,   E = 6,   F = 7,   G = 1 ;
A = 4,   B = 5,   C = 6,   D = 7,   E = 2,   F = 3,   G = 1 ;
No
```

The program finds three cuboids in the scene, which are actually just three ways of looking at the same seven vertices. (Since there is no orientation information in the image, there is no reason to prefer one view over the others.)

Of course, this predicate would be unable to find a cuboid that was positioned in such a way that some of its vertices were hidden. Moreover, the only given information is about the connectivity of the vertices. The wedge in figure 6.14 does not contain the cuboid pattern of vertices, but a *truncated* version of it would. To disambiguate between a cuboid and a truncated wedge, one would need image information about the relative orientation of the edges (in particular, which edges are *parallel*). If there were also image information about the relative lengths of the edges, one could go further and find objects like a *cube* in the image.

∗ 6.4.1   Handling occlusion

One interesting extension of this analysis concerns occlusion. Consider the two cuboids in figure 6.16. Neither would be recognized by the previous cuboid predicate. This is because the cuboid on the right occludes part of the cuboid on the left. So, for example, both vertex 8 and vertex 2 connect to T-vertices (vertices 3 and 10, respectively). These T-vertices are the signal that occlusion is taking place, and the identification cannot be handled by the current cuboid definition.

Consider the occluding cuboid on the right. The goal would be to say that this is a cuboid over vertices 8, 9, 15, 12, 13, 14, 11 and to simply bypass any intervening T-vertices. To do so, it is necessary to extend the definition of the predicates calc_lv and calc_arr. For calc_lv, instead of having

```
calc_lv(V,V1,V2) :- img_lv(V,V1,V2).
```

the following is used:

```
calc_lv(V,V1,V2) :-
    img_lv(V,X,Y), ltv_seq(V,X,V1), rtv_seq(V,Y,V2).
```

Figure 6.16. Two cuboids with occlusion

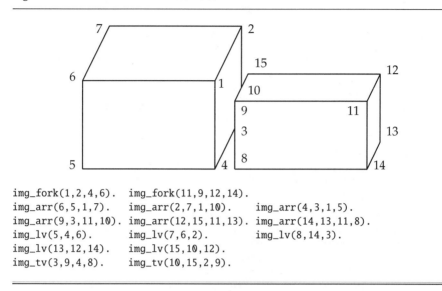

```
img_fork(1,2,4,6).   img_fork(11,9,12,14).
img_arr(6,5,1,7).    img_arr(2,7,1,10).     img_arr(4,3,1,5).
img_arr(9,3,11,10).  img_arr(12,15,11,13).  img_arr(14,13,11,8).
img_lv(5,4,6).       img_lv(7,6,2).         img_lv(8,14,3).
img_lv(13,12,14).    img_lv(15,10,12).
img_tv(3,9,4,8).     img_tv(10,15,2,9).
```

where the query `rtv_seq(V,Y,V2)` looks for zero or more T-vertices between the `Y` and `V2`, aligned with `V` on the right. (The predicates `rtv_seq` and `ltv_seq` are defined in figure 6.17.) With this change, the query `calc_lv(8,14,9)` will now return *success*, as desired, despite the fact that `img_lv(8,14,3)` is what actually appears in the image.

Recognizing a partially occluded cuboid like the one on the left in figure 6.16 is much more problematic. Start by assuming that there is a unique L-vertex that is hidden, so the cuboid is over vertices 5, 6, 7, 2, occ, 4, 1, where occ is the hidden vertex. First, `calc_lv` and `calc_arr` need to be extended to deal with a hidden vertex:

$$\texttt{calc\_arr(V,V1,V2,occ) :- img\_tv(V3,\_,V,\_), calc\_arr(V,V1,V2,V3).}$$

This says that an arrow vertex V connects to a hidden vertex on its right branch if in the image it actually connects to a T-vertex that has V on its middle branch. With this, the query `calc_arr(2,7,1,occ)` will return *success* even though what appears in the image is `img_arr(2,7,1,10)`. This is done for the left branch of the arrow also, and for both branches of an L-vertex.

Finally, the occluded L-vertex itself must be described. Given what little information there is in the image, maybe the best one can do is to say that the hidden vertex might connect to *any* pair of vertices that are at the ends of the middle branches of T-vertices:

Figure 6.17.   Finding vertices with occlusion   `occlusion.pl`

```
calc_arr(V,V1,V2,V3) :-
    img_arr(V,X,V2,Y), ltv_seq(V,X,V1), rtv_seq(V,Y,V3).
calc_arr(V,V1,V2,occ) :- img_tv(V3,_,V,_), calc_arr(V,V1,V2,V3).
calc_arr(V,occ,V2,V3) :- img_tv(V1,_,V,_), calc_arr(V,V1,V2,V3).

calc_lv(V,V1,V2) :-
    img_lv(V,X,Y), ltv_seq(V,X,V1), rtv_seq(V,Y,V2).
calc_lv(V,V1,occ) :- img_tv(V2,_,V,_), calc_lv(V,V1,V2).
calc_lv(V,occ,V2) :- img_tv(V1,_,V,_), calc_lv(V,V1,V2).
calc_lv(occ,V1,V2) :- img_tv(_,_,V1,_), img_tv(_,_,V2,_), \+ V1=V2.

% ltv_seq(V,X,Y): V X ... Y via T-vertices left to right
ltv_seq(_,X,X).
ltv_seq(V,X,Y) :- img_tv(X,V,_,Z), ltv_seq(X,Z,Y).

% rtv_seq(V,X,Y): V X ... Y via T-vertices right to left
rtv_seq(_,X,X).
rtv_seq(V,X,Y) :- img_tv(X,Z,_,V), rtv_seq(X,Z,Y).
```

```
calc_lv(occ,V1,V2) :-
    img_tv(_,_,V1,_), img_tv(_,_,V2,_), \+ V1=V2.
```

This is a very permissive rule, as there could be many T-vertices in an image. But it does allow `calc_lv(occ,2,4)` to return *success* for this image, as desired. And with all the other constraints in place for a cuboid, it will be sufficient. (If there were additional image properties, one could be more selective.)

With all the pieces together for `calc_arr` and `calc_lv`, the occlusion program is shown in figure 6.17. This will also handle the nonoccluded vertices as a special case. If it is combined with the earlier definitions of `cuboid` and `calc_fork` from figure 6.15 and run on the image in figure 6.16, the result is

```
?- cuboid(A,B,C,D,E,F,G).
A = 6,   B = 7,   C = 2,   D = occ, E = 4,   F = 5,   G = 1 ;
A = 9,   B = 15,  C = 12,  D = 13,  E = 14,  F = 8,   G = 11 ;
A = 12,  B = 13,  C = 14,  D = 8,   E = 9,   F = 15,  G = 11 ;
A = 14,  B = 8,   C = 9,   D = 15,  E = 12,  F = 13,  G = 11 ;
A = 2,   B = occ, C = 4,   D = 5,   E = 6,   F = 7,   G = 1 ;
A = 4,   B = 5,   C = 6,   D = 7,   E = 2,   F = occ, G = 1 ;
No
```

So the final program is able to tease apart the two objects and find all three views of the occluding cuboid and all three views of the occluded cuboid.

Want to read more?

This chapter was about interpreting visual scenes; it showed how thinking played a fundamental role in that process. (The picture in Figure 6.2 is taken from [35].) The aerial sketch map interpretation of section 6.2 was inspired by the work of Reiter and Mackworth [34], and the object recognition task of section 6.4 has appeared in many guises and is the subject of a textbook by Grimson [32]. Other studies of knowledge-based vision include the early work of Badler [29] and Tsotsos [36], concerning motion in visual scenes. Another related area is reasoning about space and how shapes occupy it (see, for example, [30]). For a retrospective on the problem of visual interpretation as a whole, including some of the challenges faced by researchers in the field, see [31]. From a more artistic point of view, the idea of impossible objects and visual ambiguity is exploited to great effect in the work of M. C. Escher (see, for example, his *Relativity*).

However, much of what happens when we view the world around us appears to take place without any knowledge of the world, and therefore (by the account here) without any thinking. For example, we do not have to know what we are looking at to spot something yellow in a large field of red. Pylyshyn [33] has written a book explaining how this part of the visual process is very different from thinking. The subarea of AI called *computer vision* is currently dominated by research on "early vision" of this sort.

The polyhedral scene labeling considered in section 6.3 is an interesting intermediate case. It comes out of the work of Waltz [37] in the 1970s and was one of the first tasks formulated as a constraint satisfaction problem. However, it is not necessary to know very much about the world to perform this task. There are vertex types and line labels but no open-ended class of objects like vehicles or houses or banquet tables. For this reason, Pylyshyn prefers to categorize this task as not depending on thinking at all, but rather as embodying what he calls "natural constraints."

If you reflect on what it actually feels like to look at visual scenes, you might be tempted to conclude that the thinking is really quite unlike constraint satisfaction. It seems like visual interpretations come to you without any mental effort—nothing at all like solving a Sudoku puzzle, for instance. Part of this feeling is due to the fact that your eyes are able to quickly dart back and forth over a scene, too quickly to register how you are using what you know. To get a better sense of how a visual interpretation is assembled, imagine that you cannot move your eyes in this way. Simulate this by cutting a small hole in a sheet of paper, looking at an image like figure 6.2 through the hole only, and then slowly moving the paper to take in the entire scene.

7   Lists in Prolog

Before moving on to consider bigger and better varieties of thinking, this chapter brings the programming skills learned so far up to the next level.

The Prolog symbols in previous chapters were single atomic units: constants, variables, numbers. This chapter considers larger *symbolic structures* called lists, and some predicates that assemble them and take them apart.

Lists are essential to the sorts of thinking studied in the chapters to follow. Chapter 8, for example, deals with thinking about sentences and phrases of English, and these end up being *lists of words*. Chapter 9 surveys thinking about plans to achieve goals, and these end up being *lists of actions* to perform.

The first section of this chapter introduces lists and the two notations in Prolog that are used for them. Section 2 considers how to write the clauses for predicates that take lists as arguments, allowing properties over groups of objects to be expressed very succinctly. Section 3 explains how to use two very useful built-in list predicates, member and append, and reformulates in a clear and concise way the blocks-world program from section 4.2.

7.1   Lists

A problem that comes up again and again in Prolog is writing clauses for predicates that are very similar except for the number of arguments they take. Consider, for example, the predicates used in chapter 5 to ensure that individuals in a group were all distinct:

```
uniq_person3(X,Y,Z) :- ...          % For three people
uniq_person5(X,Y,Z,U,V) :- ...      % For five people
```

The uniq_digits predicate in figure 5.8 handles eight digits and has $(8 \times 7)/2 = 28$ inequalities in it. If there were eighteen people, one would need a predicate like this:

```
uniq_person18(A,B,C,D,E,F,G,H,I,J,K,L,M,N,O,P,Q,R) :- ...
```

where the body would contain $(18 \times 17)/2 = 153$ inequalities. It would clearly be much better to be able to write just one predicate, like this:

```
uniq_people(L) :- ...            % For any number of people
```

This predicate would have to work for any *collection* L of people, no matter how big or small. Prolog provides such a collection, and it is called a list.

A Prolog *list* is a sequence of objects that are called its *elements*. Here are some examples:

- [anna,karenina]
  A two-element list whose first element is the constant anna and whose second element is the constant karenina.

- [john,paul,george,ringo,zeppo]
  A five-element list.

- [1,2,3,3,2,1]
  Lists may have repeated elements.

- []
  A list with no elements: the *empty list*.

Lists may contain other lists as elements:

- [[john,23],[mary,14],[hello]]
  A list whose three elements are also lists.

- [8,john,['199y',john]]
  Another three-element list.

- [[]]
  A one-element list whose single element is the empty list.

Note that a one-element list is different from the element itself:

[anna] is different from anna;

[[]] is different from [].

The first element of a nonempty list is called the *head* of the list. The list that is formed by removing that first element (and the comma that follows it, if there is one) is called the *tail* of the list. Here are some examples:

- [a,b,c,d] has head a and tail [b,c,d];

- [[a],b,[c]] has head [a] and tail [b,[c]];

- [a,[b,c]] has head a and tail [[b,c]];

- [[a,b]] has head [a,b] and tail [];
- [] has neither head nor tail.

The head of a nonempty list can be *anything*, but the tail is always a *list*. This turns out to be a very convenient property when it comes to recursion.

7.1.1   Lists as Prolog terms

The review of the Prolog language in figure 3.10 can now be extended to say that a Prolog <u>term</u> is a constant, variable, number, or list. Prolog provides two ways of writing lists as terms:

1. A left square parenthesis, followed by a sequence of terms separated by commas, and terminated by a right square parenthesis, for example,

   [1,-4,[a,X,'b 2'],joe]

2. A left square parenthesis, followed by a nonempty sequence of terms separated by commas, followed by a *vertical bar* |, followed by a term denoting a list, and terminated by a right square parenthesis. For example, the list [1,X,3] can be written as

   [1|[X,3]]   or
   [1,X|[3]]   or
   [1,X,3|[]].

While the first notation focuses on the elements of a list, the second notation focuses on the head and tail of a list. The list [X|Y] is the list whose head is X and whose tail is Y; the list [X,Y|Z] is the list whose head is X and whose tail is the list whose head is Y and whose tail is Z. So, for example, the list [1|[X,3]] is the list whose head is 1 and whose tail is [X,3], which is just another way of describing the list [1,X,3].

7.1.2   Unification with lists

Much of the power of lists in Prolog has to do with the fact that variables can appear within a list term. But this also brings up concern about which pairs of lists *unify* (as needed for back-chaining). The basic rule is this:

- Two lists without variables are considered to unify when they are identical, element for element.

- Two lists with distinct variables are considered to unify when the variables can be given values that make the two lists identical, element for element.

Here are some examples of pairs of lists that do unify:

```
[] and []
[a,b,c] and [a,b,c]
[X] and [a] with X=a
[a,b,X] and [Y,b,Y] with X=a, Y=a
[X,X] and [[Y,a,c],[b,a,c]] with X=[b,a,c], Y=b
[[X]] and [Y] with X=_G237, Y=[_G237]

[a,b,c] and [a|[b,c]]
[a,b,c] and [a|[b|[c]]]
[X|Y] and [a] with X=a, Y=[]
[a|[b,c]] and [a,X,Y] with X=b, Y=c
[a,b,c] and [X|Y] with X=a, Y=[b,c]
[X,Y|Y] and [a,[b,c],b,c] with X=a, Y=[b,c]
```

Lists will not unify if they have different numbers of elements or if at least one corresponding element does not unify. Here are some nonunifying pairs:

```
[a] and []
[a,b,c] and [a,a,c]
[] and [[]]
[X,Y] and [U,V,W]
[a,b,c] and [X,b,X]
[X|Y] and []
```

Here are some useful conclusions to draw from these examples:

X matches anything, including any list.
[X] matches any list with exactly one element.
[X|Y] matches any list with at least one element.
[X,Y] matches any list with exactly two elements.

7.2   Writing programs that use lists

Programs that go through lists usually end up being *recursive*, since it may not be known in advance how many elements are involved. Each list will have *some number* n of elements. This is just like the recursion discussed in section 4.3, where a block that is above another has *some number* of intermediate blocks. As in that section, writing recursive programs is a two-step operation:

- Write clauses to handle the $n = 0$ case. This means writing clauses to handle the empty list with no elements.

- Write clauses to handle the $(n + 1)$ case, on the assumption that the n case is already taken care of.

  This is where the [H|T] notation comes in very handy. Clauses that handle a list [H|T] with $(n + 1)$ elements are written under the assumption that there are already clauses to take care of the list T with n elements.

7.2.1 Some example list predicates

The following four examples of recursive predicates over lists illustrate this two-step operation.

Example 1: List of people

Suppose there already is a predicate $person(x)$ that holds when x is a person. To be defined is another predicate $person\_list(z)$, that holds when z is a list whose elements are all people. So the desired behavior is this:

```
?- person_list([john,sue,george,harry]).
Yes

?- person_list([john,5,harry]).
No
```

This predicate will need to go through and check each element of the list. Therefore it needs to be a recursive predicate.

1. Write clause(s) to handle the empty list. The list with no elements is trivially a list whose elements are all people:

   ```
   % The empty list is a (trivial) list of people.
   person_list([]).
   ```

2. Write clauses to handle the list [H|T], assuming that the predicate already works for the list T.

   The elements of the list [H|T] are all people if the head H is a person and all the remaining elements in T are people. Assume that person_list(T) will correctly determine whether the elements in T are all people.

Figure 7.1. A trace of a list predicate

```
?- person_list([john,sue]).
 Call: (7) person_list([john, sue])
 Call: (8) person(john)
 Exit: (8) person(john)
 Call: (8) person_list([sue])
 Call: (9) person(sue)
 Exit: (9) person(sue)
 Call: (9) person_list([])      % This is where the first
 Exit: (9) person_list([])      % clause is used.
 Exit: (8) person_list([sue])
 Exit: (7) person_list([john, sue])
```

```
% If H is a person and T is a list of people,
% then [H|T] is also a list of people.
person_list([H|T]) :- person(H), person_list(T).
```

These two clauses complete the definition. A trace of a query appears in figure 7.1. Here is how unification works with the two clauses during back-chaining:

1. [john,sue] does not unify with [] in the first clause, but it does unify with [H|T] in the second clause for H=john and T=[sue].

2. [sue] does not unify with [], but it does unify with [H|T] for H=sue and T=[].

3. [] unifies with [], and the predicate succeeds immediately.

Note how the two notations for lists work together.

Example 2: Membership in a list

Define a predicate elem that will determine whether something is an element of a list. This is the desired behavior:

```
?- elem(b,[a,b,c,d]).
Yes

?- elem(f,[a,b,c,d]).
No
```

Prolog systems provide a predefined predicate, member, with exactly this behavior, but the following defines a version as a recursive predicate:

1. Write clauses for the empty list. There is nothing to write here since the query elem(X,[]) should always fail.

2. Write clauses to handle the list [H|T], assuming the list T is already taken care of. The query elem(X,[H|T]) should succeed if X is equal to H, or if X is an element of list T. So two clauses are needed:

```
% X is an element of any list whose head is X.
elem(X,[X|_]).
```

```
% If X is an element of a list L,
% then it is an element of any list whose tail is L.
elem(X,[_|L]) :- elem(X,L).
```

Note the use of the anonymous variable. In the first clause, the query succeeds no matter what the tail is; in the second clause, the query succeeds no matter what the head is.

We can follow the behavior in a trace:

```
?- elem(c,[a,b,c,d]).
 Call: (7) elem(c,[a,b,c,d])
 Call: (8) elem(c,[b,c,d])
 Call: (9) elem(c,[c,d])      % Here the first clause is used and
 Exit: (9) elem(c,[c,d])      % succeeds immediately.
 Exit: (8) elem(c,[b,c,d])
 Exit: (7) elem(c,[a,b,c,d])
```

Example 3: List of unique people

The member predicate (or the elem predicate just defined) can be used to write the clauses for a predicate uniq_people(z) that holds when z is any list of people that are all distinct, as needed for many constraint satisfaction problems. As before, assume that a predicate person is already defined. The uniq_people predicate will once again be recursive:

1. The empty list [] is a (trivial) list of unique people.

2. For the list [P|L], if P is a person, L is a list of unique people, and in addition, P is *not* an element of L, then [P|L] is also a list of unique people.

This gives a definition of the predicate with the following two clauses:

```
uniq_people([]).
uniq_people([P|L]) :- uniq_people(L), person(P), \+ member(P,L).
```

This recursive predicate will work properly for lists of any size. Note how succinct and elegant this definition is compared to the long sequences of inequalities written in chapter 5 for each constraint satisfaction problem.

* *Example 4: Joining two lists*

Here is a more advanced example. Define a predicate `join` that concatenates two lists:

```
?- join([a,b,c,d],[e,f,g],L).
L=[a,b,c,d,e,f,g]
Yes

?- join([],[a,b,c,d],L).
L=[a,b,c,d]
Yes
```

Prolog systems provide a predefined predicate, **append**, with exactly this behavior, but again a version is defined here as a recursive predicate.

The predicate `join` needs to determine what the third argument (the answer) should be for any two lists. The first list can be empty or nonempty, and the second list can also be empty or nonempty. However, it turns out that it is sufficient to do recursion on the *first argument* only:

1. Write clauses to handle the case where the first argument is [] and the second argument is any list L;

2. Write clauses to handle the case where the first argument is [H|T] and the second argument is any list L (assuming that `join` already works when the first argument is T and the second argument is L).

This leads to the following two clauses:

```
% Joining [] and any list L produces L itself.
join([],L,L).

% If joining T and L produces the list Z,
% then joining [H|T] and L produces the list [H|Z].
join([H|T],L,[H|Z]) :- join(T,L,Z).
```

The head of the second clause is quite complex. Much of the work of `join` is done by unification with this head.

A trace is shown in figure 7.2. As the query succeeds at each level, new elements are added to the third argument, building the final concatenated list. Here is how the unification works:

1. The top-level query is `join([a,b,c,d],[e,f],R)`.

2. This does not unify with `join([],L,L)`, but it unifies with `join([H|T],L,[H|Z])` for the following values: H=a, T=[b,c,d], L=[e,f], and R=[a|Z].

Figure 7.2. Another trace of a list predicate

```
?- join([a,b,c,d],[e,f],R).
 Call: (3) join([a,b,c,d],[e,f],_G306)
 Call: (4) join([b,c,d],[e,f],_G378)
 Call: (5) join([c,d],[e,f],_G381)
 Call: (6) join([d],[e,f],_G384)
 Call: (7) join([],[e,f],_G387)       % Now the first clause is used.
 Exit: (7) join([],[e,f],[e,f])       % It succeeds immediately.
 Exit: (6) join([d],[e,f],[d,e,f])
 Exit: (5) join([c,d],[e,f],[c,d,e,f])
 Exit: (4) join([b,c,d],[e,f],[b,c,d,e,f])
 Exit: (3) join([a,b,c,d],[e,f],[a,b,c,d,e,f])
R = [a,b,c,d,e,f]
Yes
```

3. The new query is then join(T,L,Z), that is, join([b,c,d],[e,f],Z).

4. This subquery does not unify with the head of the first clause, but it does unify with the head of the second clause.

5. Eventually, this subquery succeeds with Z=[b,c,d,e,f].

6. Then the top-level query succeeds with R=[a|Z], that is, R=[a,b,c,d,e,f].

7.3 Using the member and append predicates

From now on, the built-in Prolog predicates member and append (which behave like elem and join) are used in the examples. One very useful application of member is to generate the elements of a list:

```
?- member(X,[a,b,c]).
X = a   ;
X = b   ;
X = c   ;
No
```

This means that queries (or bodies of clauses) can be written that go through the elements of a list looking for one that satisfies some condition:

```
... member(X,L), p(X), ...
```

If L is a nonempty list, and the variable X is not instantiated, the member(X,L) query will succeed, with X getting the head of the list as its value. If the query p(X) then fails, the program will backtrack, and X will be assigned to the next element of the list, and so on, until an element of L is found for which p(X) succeeds. Here is an example of this generate-and-test in a query:

```
?- member(N,[1,2,3,-3,5,-5,7]), N < 0.
N = -3 ;        % The first element that is < 0
N = -5 ;        % The second element that is < 0
No
```

However, when using list predicates to generate values in this way, one must be careful not to generate an *infinite* set of candidates. Consider the following:

```
?- member(3,L).              % What list has 3 as an element?
L = [3|_G214]          ;     % Any list whose first element is 3,
L = [_G213, 3|_G217]   ;     % any list whose second element is 3,
L = [_G213, _G216, 3|_G220]  % and so on.
Yes

?- member(3,L), 1=2.
ERROR: Out of global stack   % This query causes an error.
```

In the second query, each time the subquery 1=2, fails, the program backtracks to try to find a new value for L. Since there will always be another value to consider (that is, a bigger list), the process runs until L gets so large that it causes an error. This caveat aside, variables can be used in either argument of the member predicate:

```
?- member(a,[X,b,Y]).
X = a,      Y = _G163   ;
X = _G157,  Y = a       ;
No

?- L=[a,X,b], member(3,L).
L = [a, 3, b],  X = 3   ;
No

?- L=[X,b,Y], member(a,L), member(X,[b,c]).
L = [b, b, a],  X = b,  Y = a   ;
L = [c, b, a],  X = c,  Y = a   ;
No
```

So unlike numbers, variables that are not instantiated can be used within lists. Prolog finds their values when it needs to.

The append predicate can also be used to generate lists:

```
% What pairs of lists when joined give [a,b,c]?
?- append(X,Y,[a,b,c]).
X = [],            Y = [a, b, c]    ;
X = [a],           Y = [b, c]       ;
X = [a, b],        Y = [c]          ;
X = [a, b, c],     Y = []           ;
No
```

Using append to generate a pair of lists in this way is a very useful technique. (In chapter 8, it is used to break up a list of words into phrases.) Variables can also be used freely within the arguments to append:

```
% [a,b] joined to what list L gives [a,b,c,d,e,f]?
?- append([a,b],L,[a,b,c,d,e,f]).
L = [c, d, e, f]
% Solve for the variables X, Y, and L.
?- append([X,b],[d|L],[a,_,Y,e,f]).
X = a,   L = [e, f], Y = d
```

The append predicate is quite powerful, and a number of additional predicates can be defined with it. Here are some one-line examples:

- The predicate front(L1,L2) holds if the list L1 is the start of list L2:

    ```
    front(L1,L2) :- append(L1,_,L2).
    ```

- The predicate last(E,L) holds if E is the last element of list L:

    ```
    last(E,L) :- append(_,[E],L).
    ```

- Yet another version of the member predicate:

    ```
    elem2(E,L) :- append(_,[E|_],L).
    ```

This definition of elem2 says that E is an element of list L if L is the result of joining something (the first _) with a list whose head is E and whose tail is something (the second _). In other words, E is an element of L if L is a list that has some number of elements, then E, then some number of other elements.

As with the member predicate, one needs to be careful not to generate an infinite set of candidate values. Consider this version of a predicate that determines whether one element appears *before* another in a list:

```
% A first version
before(X,Y,L) :- append(_,[X|_],Z), append(Z,[Y|_],L).
```

Figure 7.3.   The blocks-world program redone   `blocks2.pl`

```
% This is a list-based version of the blocks-world program.

% X appears before Y in list L.
before(X,Y,L) :- append(Z,[Y|_],L), append(_,[X|_],Z).

% The given blocks-world scene: three stacks of blocks
scene([[b1,b2],[b3,b4,b5,b6],[b7]]).

% above(X,Y) means that block X is somewhere above block Y.
above(X,Y) :- scene(L), member(Stack,L), before(X,Y,Stack).

% left(X,Y) means that block X is somewhere left of block Y.
left(X,Y) :- scene(L), before(Stack1,Stack2,L),
             member(X,Stack1), member(Y,Stack2).

right(Y,X) :- left(X,Y).
```

This says that X appears before Y in list L if there is a list Z such that X appears somewhere in Z, and joining Z to a list whose head is Y results in L.

This almost does the right thing:

```
?- before(2,4,[1,2,3,4,5]).
Yes

?- before(8,4,[1,2,3,4,5]).
ERROR: Out of global stack
```

The problem is the first atom in the body, append(_,[X|_],Z). There are infinitely many lists Z that contain X, and it may turn out that none of them satisfy the second query. The solution is to change the order of the queries so that Z is generated as a sublist of L:

```
% A better version
before(X,Y,L) :- append(Z,[Y|_],L), append(_,[X|_],Z).
```

This results in the desired behavior:

```
?- before(2,4,[1,2,3,4,5]).
Yes

?- before(8,4,[1,2,3,4,5]).
No
```

Figure 7.4.   Using the list version of the blocks world program

```
?- left(b1,b7).
 Call: (7) left(b1, b7)
 Call: (8) scene(_L205)                      % Get the scene.
 Exit: (8) scene([[b1, b2], [b3, b4, b5, b6], [b7]])
 % Generate a first pair of stacks.
 Call: (8) before(_L206, _L207, ...)
 Exit: (8) before([b1, b2], [b3, b4, b5, b6],...)
 Call: (8) member(b1, [b1, b2])              % Test if X is in the first.
 Exit: (8) member(b1, [b1, b2])              %      YES
 Call: (8) member(b7, [b3, b4, b5, b6])      % Test if Y is in the second.
 Fail: (8) member(b7, [b3, b4, b5, b6])      %      NO
 Redo: (8) member(b1, [b1, b2])
 Fail: (8) member(b1, [b1, b2])
 % Generate another pair of stacks.
 Redo: (8) before(_L206, _L207, ...)
 Exit: (8) before([b1, b2], [b7], ...)
 Call: (8) member(b1, [b1, b2])              % Test if X is in the first.
 Exit: (8) member(b1, [b1, b2])              %      YES
 Call: (8) member(b7, [b7])                  % Test if Y is in the second.
 Exit: (8) member(b7, [b7])                  %      YES
 Exit: (7) left(b1, b7)                      % The second pair works.
Yes
```

7.3.1   The blocks world revisited

The predicates member and append can be used to define a much more succinct version of the blocks-world program (see section 4.2).

Here is the idea. An entire blocks-world *scene* can be represented by a left-to-right list of stacks, where a *stack* is represented by a top-to-bottom list of blocks. So the scene depicted in figure 4.1 is represented by the following list:

> [[b1,b2],[b3,b4,b5,b6],[b7]]

The predicates above and left can then be defined using the before predicate:

- A block X is above a block Y in the scene if there is a stack in the scene where X appears before Y in the stack.

- A block X is somewhere to the left of a block Y if there is a stack in the scene that contains X that is before a stack in the scene that contains Y.

The full blocks-world program is shown in figure 7.3. A trace of the left predicate is shown in figure 7.4.

Want to read more?

This chapter considered programming in Prolog, concentrating on programs that deal with lists. This type of list processing, which involves dealing with collections of symbols as single larger units, has a long history. The first truly symbolic (that is, non-numerical) programming language, called IPL, was also the first to provide explicit facilities for dealing with lists. A more influential and still quite popular programming language of this sort is LISP [38] and its direct descendant, Scheme [53]. Both LISP and Scheme take list processing as their central focus.

A few simple examples of list-processing predicates were reviewed in this chapter. The blocks-world program was rewritten using lists, and many other programs in previous chapters could be redone more clearly using lists. It takes time and practice to master this type of programming, however. A typical second-year or third-year undergraduate computer science course might involve writing predicates that are similar to append but perhaps more complex (for example, a predicate that returns every second element of a list, or a predicate that sorts a list of numbers into ascending order). Any programming textbook on Prolog (such as those mentioned at the end of chapter 4) will cover writing predicates like these.

It turns out, however, there are even more advanced list-processing techniques that can be employed in Prolog but that do not fit well in other programming languages. In particular, the fact that an uninstantiated variable can be an element of a list allows certain operations to be performed very elegantly in Prolog, by building a list but leaving parts of it unspecified at first. These techniques and many more are covered in the more advanced Prolog textbooks such as [39].

Exercises

1. The text defined a predicate $\text{elem}(x, y)$ that held when x was an element of the list y. Consider the following variant:

   ```
   elem3(X,[X]).
   elem3(X,[_|L]) :- elem3(X,L).
   ```

   Give an example of an x and a y such that $\text{elem}(x, y)$ holds but where $\text{elem3}(x, y)$ does not hold. Describe in English when the predicate $\text{elem3}(x, y)$ holds in general.

2. Consider the mystery predicates p and q defined by the following three clauses:

```
p(X) :- q(X,[],X).
q([],Y,Y).
q([E|L],Y,Z) :- q(L,[E|Y],Z).
```

Describe in English the lists x for which the predicate p(x) holds.

3. Explain informally why [X,[1,X,3]] does not unify with [Y,Y]. It turns out that Prolog thinks these two lists *do* unify: it creates a *cyclic term*, which in this case is a list that contains itself as an element.

4. Use the append predicate to define a predicate just_before(x, y, z) that holds when x appears just before y as an element of list z. So, for example,

```
?- just_before(3,4,[1,2,3,4,5,6]).
Yes

?- just_before(3,5,[1,2,3,4,5,6]).
No
```

Hint: This can be done with one clause. Look at how elem2 is defined.

5. The list version of the blocks world gave short definitions of the above and left predicates. Define the on predicate using the just_before predicate.

6. Write Prolog clauses that define each of the following predicates:

   a. exactly_3(x) is true if x is a list with exactly three elements.

   b. at_least_3(x) is true if x is a list with at least three elements.

   c. at_most_3(x) is true if x is list with at most three elements.
   Hint: Use four clauses.

   d. intersect(x, y) is true if x and y are lists with an element in common.

      intersect([1,2,3,4],[5,4,1,6]) holds, but
      intersect([1,2,3,4],[5,6]) does not hold.

   Hint: Use member but no recursion.

   e. all_intersect(z, y) is true if every element of list z is a list x such that intersect(x, y) holds.

      all_intersect([[1,2,3],[5,4,6]],[3,4]) holds, and
      all_intersect([],[3,4]) holds, but
      all_intersect([[1,2,3],[1,2,5],[5,4,6]],[3,4]) does not hold.

   Hint: Use intersect and recursion.

8 Case Study: Understanding Natural Language

This chapter turns attention to the sort of thinking required to make sense of expressions in a *natural language*, that is, a language like English or Italian or Swahili that is spoken naturally by people.

When it comes to tasks that require thinking, understanding language holds a position of honor. One of the features that distinguishes humans from all other living creatures is our ability to communicate using a system as rich as a natural language. And to deal with this richness, we need to be able to think. A speaker can say words like "the American President during the Civil War" and expect that under normal circumstances a hearer will use what she knows to make a connection with Abraham Lincoln. This need for thinking was displayed in a very simple but pure form in chapter 1 in resolving the pronoun *it* in the trophy-suitcase sentences.

But the connection between thinking and language goes even deeper. It is not just that thinking supports our ability to use language; the converse is also true: language feeds our thinking. As emphasized throughout, thinking is using what we know, and much of what we know is due to language. We find out about the world and the people around us to a large extent not from personal experience but by being *told*: people talk to us, we attend lectures, we listen to weather reports and to the dialogue in movies, and we read: text messages, recipes, sport scores, mystery novels, and so on. What we know and use in our thinking is a staggering amount of language-mediated material. We pass on to our descendants much more of this information in written form than all of the genetic information in our DNA. Given this dependence on language, it is not surprising that thinking often feels like using a language, talking to ourselves in some sort of inner voice.

This chapter only scratches the surface of the truly remarkable story of how language can both depend on thinking and provide the raw material for it. Section 1 explains how language is usually studied in terms of syntax and semantics. Section 2 focuses on the noun phrases of English and how they can be used to refer to known individuals and objects. Section 3 examines how these noun phrases can be put to work in answering yes/no questions written in English and in adding to what is known using English declarative sentences. (To do so, a new feature of Prolog is introduced: *dynamic predicates*.) Section 4 briefly discusses how the utility of noun phrases actually is even more extensive.

8.1   Analyzing the syntax of a language

Although the expressions of a written language are nothing more than sequences of words and punctuation, what those sequences are and how they can be used is phenomenally complex. The study of natural language in general is called *linguistics*, and it analyzes language at a variety of levels:

- Morphology: What are the roots of words, the prefixes and suffixes?

  ran = run + PAST
  children = child + PLURAL

- Syntax: How do the words group together?

  Mary kicked the boy in the knee.
  Mary kicked the boy in the first row.

- Semantics: What do the words mean?

  The astronomer spotted a star.
  The astronomer married a star.

  The trophy would not fit into the brown suitcase
  because it was too small.
  because it was too big.

- Pragmatics: What are the words being used for?

  Can you juggle?
  Can you pass the salt?

(There are additional levels for *spoken* language, such as phonology and prosodics.) This chapter concentrates mainly on the syntax of written English, with some excursions into semantics.

A syntactic analysis of a language looks at how words group together into phrases, sentences, and even larger units like paragraphs and stories. For example, consider the following phrase:

  the boy in the park with the red bench

Clearly the intention is to group words in this phrase as follows:

(*the boy in* (*the park with* (*the red bench*)))

Now, consider the following instead:

the boy in the park with the gray sweater

In this case, the words would be grouped differently, perhaps as follows:

(*the boy in* (*the park*) *with* (*the gray sweater*))

The main point of these groupings is that in the first case, the phrase *with the red bench* is understood as being connected to *the park*; in the second case, *with the gray sweater* is understood as being connected to *the boy*. It might not be obvious on first reading what should be grouped with what. For example,

The cat the dog the boy next door owns chases sleeps all day.

may only be resolved with some difficulty to a grouping like the following:

(*The cat* (*the dog* (*the boy next door owns*) *chases*) *sleeps all day*).

Knowing how the words in a phrase or sentence should be grouped together is not the same thing as understanding what they mean (which is the subject of semantics). In particular, there can be sentences of English that are syntactically well formed but do not mean anything. Here is a famous example (due to Noam Chomsky):

Colorless green ideas sleep furiously.

The pattern and the grouping of these words are familiar even if the sentence is odd semantically. Similarly, there can be meaningful groups of words that are odd syntactically:

Accident car passenger hospital.

Even though this is not a well-formed sentence of English, one can still extract at least part of its meaning.

8.1.1 Lexicon

The starting point for the syntactic analysis of a language is a *lexicon*. This specifies the word categories of the language and the vocabulary in each category:

- Articles: *a, the*

- Adjectives: *fat, rich, happy, oldest, orange, . . .*

- Proper nouns: *Mary, John, Toronto, Great Britain, . . .*

- Common nouns: *boy, sweater, park, milk, justice, . . .*

- Transitive verbs: *kick, love, throw, make, ...*

- Intransitive verbs: *walk, sleep, die, listen, ...*

- Copula verbs: *be, seem, ...*

- Prepositions: *in, on, from, beside, ...*

- Others (pronouns, adverbs, interjections, ...)

Note that words can appear in more than one category. For example, the word *run* in English is both a noun and a verb; the word *fat* is both a noun and an adjective.

8.1.2   Grammar

A *grammar* of a language is a specification of how the various types of words can be grouped in the language. These word groups are called the syntactic *categories*. A distinction is made between the following:

- Lexical or *terminal* categories, like an article or a transitive verb. These will be written in lowercase.

- Group or *nonterminal* categories, like a phrase or a sentence. These will be written in uppercase. (It is customary in linguistics to name the nonterminal categories of a language using short, cryptic abbreviations like NP for noun phrase.)

Usually grammars are specified by a collection of *rules* (similar to Prolog clauses) describing how each type of word group is formed from other word groups. For present purposes, a grammar rule will have the following form:

$$category \rightarrow category_1\ category_2\ \ldots\ category_n$$

where the category on the left must be nonterminal, and the categories on the right (if any) can be terminal or nonterminal. For example, the grammar rule

    PP   →   preposition NP

says that in English a prepositional phrase (PP) can be made up of a preposition followed by a noun phrase (NP).

Figure 8.1 shows a grammar for some declarative sentences of English. Starting at the top, the rule says that a sentence S can be made from a noun phrase NP followed by a verb phrase VP. Note that this grammar does not include many features of English, such as pronouns or clauses. Note also that the grammar is *recursive*: the category Mods (modifiers), for instance, is made up of zero or more of the PP category. This allows stacking the modifiers, as in the following noun phrase: *the boy from France in the library on the phone with the gray sweater.*

Figure 8.1. A grammar for declarative sentences

```
   S   →   NP VP
  VP   →   copula_verb Mods
  VP   →   transitive_verb NP Mods
  VP   →   intransitive_verb Mods
Mods   →
Mods   →   PP Mods
  PP   →   preposition NP
  NP   →   proper_noun
  NP   →   article NP2
 NP2   →   adjective NP2
 NP2   →   common_noun Mods
```

Figure 8.2. A sample parse tree

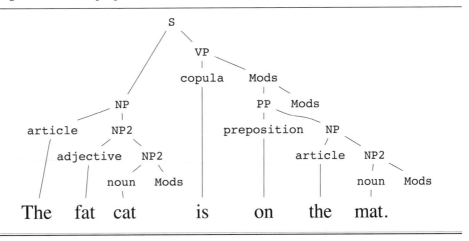

8.1.3 Parsing and ambiguity

The process of taking a sequence of words and determining how they are structured by the rules of a grammar is called *parsing*. This is done by producing a *parse tree*, with the sequence of words at the leaves (usually at the bottom) and the desired nonterminal category at the root (usually at the top). A sample parse tree appears in figure 8.2. For any of the categories that appear in the tree, the leaves below them are

Figure 8.3.   A sequence of words with two parse trees

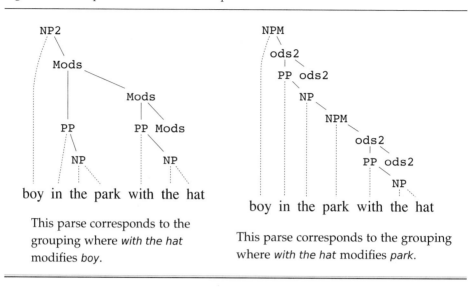

This parse corresponds to the grouping where *with the hat* modifies *boy*.

This parse corresponds to the grouping where *with the hat* modifies *park*.

the words that make up that category. For example, the sequence *on the mat* is a PP, while the sequence *is on the mat* is a VP.

A grammar is said to be *ambiguous* if there is a sequence of words with two distinct parse trees. An example appears in figure 8.3. (The dashed lines indicate details that are missing from the diagram.) According to the grammar, the noun phrase *with the hat* can be attached as a modifier either to the NP2 that has the head noun *boy* (on the left in the figure) or to the NP2 that has the head noun *park* (on the right). It is only when *semantics* are taken into account that the ambiguity disappears. Prior knowledge provides the fact that boys, not parks, have hats. This is precisely the sort of thinking that is described, beginning in the next section.

8.2   Interpreting noun phrases

The goal in this section is to develop a Prolog program that does simple syntactic and semantic processing of noun phrases written in English. This involves two things:

- Parsing the noun phrases according to a given grammar
- Determining what is being referred to by the noun phrases

To accomplish this, the knowledge base in Prolog has three distinct pieces:

1. A world model. These are clauses that represent what is known about the relevant world: what the objects are, who the people are, where they are located, what they are wearing, and so on. *Nothing in the world model is intended to be language-specific.*

2. A lexicon. These are clauses that describe the English words used in the noun phrases. They also link these words to their meanings in the predicates and constants of the world model. *Nothing in the lexicon depends on the grammar.*

3. A parser/interpreter. These are clauses that define the grammar. They also use information provided by the lexicon and the world model to decide what individual is being referred to by the noun phrases.

8.2.1   Writing a world model

The world model is actually the easiest part of the Prolog program to write since it really has nothing to do with English. All that is needed is a collection of clauses about some world of interest, for example, the family world (figure 3.1) or the blocks world (figure 4.2). To provide a wider range of individuals than those worlds contain, a new world is invented:

> There are people, parks, trees, and hats to talk about. The people are either male or female, the hats are either red or blue, and every person, tree, and hat is either small or big. In addition, the people and trees are in the parks, and the hats are on the people. Finally, some of the people are beside others.

A Prolog program with these facts is shown in figure 8.4. This represents the background knowledge that will be used in thinking about expressions in English. (All the clauses happen to be atomic, but this is not essential.)

8.2.2   Writing a lexicon

The lexicon needs to describe all the English words to be used and how they relate to the predicates and constants in the world model. The lexicon here is restricted to articles, common nouns, adjectives, proper nouns, and prepositions using the following predicates: `article`, `common_noun`, `adjective`, `proper_noun`, and `preposition`. These predicates take one, two, or three arguments (the first of which will always be an English word). A sample lexicon of this form is shown in figure 8.5. Here is a description:

Figure 8.4.   A world of people, parks, trees, hats   nldb.pl

```
person(john). person(george). person(mary). person(linda).
park(kew_beach). park(queens_park).
tree(tree01). tree(tree02).  tree(tree03).
hat(hat01).   hat(hat02).  hat(hat03).  hat(hat04).

sex(john,male).    sex(george,male).
sex(mary,female).  sex(linda,female).

color(hat01,red).    color(hat02,blue).
color(hat03,red).    color(hat04,blue).

in(john,kew_beach).      in(george,kew_beach).
in(linda,queens_park).   in(mary,queens_park).
in(tree01,queens_park).  in(tree02,queens_park).
in(tree03,kew_beach).

beside(mary,linda). beside(linda,mary).

on(hat01,john). on(hat02,mary). on(hat03,linda). on(hat04,george).

size(john,small).    size(george,big).
size(mary,small).    size(linda,small).
size(hat01,small).   size(hat02,small).
size(hat03,big).     size(hat04,big).
size(tree01,big).    size(tree02,small).  size(tree03,small).
```

- The predicate article(w) holds if the word w is an article.

- The predicate common_noun(w, x) holds when the common noun w can be used to refer to the object x in the world model. So, for example, this clause is in the lexicon:

    ```
    common_noun(man,X) :- person(X), sex(X,male).
    ```

    This says that if X is a person whose sex is male (in the world model), then X can be what is referred to when using the common noun *man*. (This is intended to represent what is known about the meaning of the word *man*.)

- The predicate adjective(w, x) holds when the adjective w can be used to describe the object x in the world model. This clause is in the lexicon:

    ```
    adjective(red,X) :- color(X,red).
    ```

    This says that if X has the color red (in the world model), then X can be what is referred to when using the adjective *red*.

Figure 8.5. A lexicon in Prolog `lexicon.pl`

```
article(a).  article(the).

common_noun(park,X) :- park(X).
common_noun(tree,X) :- tree(X).
common_noun(hat,X)  :- hat(X).
common_noun(man,X)  :- person(X), sex(X,male).
common_noun(woman,X) :- person(X), sex(X,female).

adjective(big,X) :- size(X,big).
adjective(small,X) :- size(X,small).
adjective(red,X) :- color(X,red).
adjective(blue,X) :- color(X,blue).

preposition(on,X,Y) :- on(X,Y).
preposition(in,X,Y) :- in(X,Y).
preposition(beside,X,Y) :- beside(X,Y).
% The preposition 'with' is flexible in how it is used.
preposition(with,X,Y) :- on(Y,X).      % Y can be on X
preposition(with,X,Y) :- in(Y,X).      % Y can be in X
preposition(with,X,Y) :- beside(Y,X).  % Y can be beside X

% Any word that is not in one of the four categories above.
proper_noun(X,X) :- \+ article(X), \+ adjective(X,_),
                    \+ common_noun(X,_), \+ preposition(X,_,_).
```

- The predicate $\text{preposition}(w, x, y)$ holds when the preposition w can be used to describe the relation between the objects x and y in the world model. So, for example, this clause is in the lexicon:

  ```
  preposition(with,X,Y) :- on(Y,X).
  ```

  This says that if object Y is on object X (in the world model), then that relation can be what is described when using the preposition *with*.

- Finally, the predicate $\text{proper\_noun}(w, x)$ holds when the word w is a name for the object x in the world model. There are two simplifying assumptions here:

  - Any word that does not belong to the other categories is a proper noun.

  - The constants in the world model like `john` and `tree02` are proper names.

One thing to notice is that the words in the lexicon are sometimes the same as the predicates and constants in the world model:

```
common_noun(hat,X)  :- hat(X).
adjective(small,X) :- size(X,small).
preposition(in,X,Y) :- in(X,Y).
```

But the lexicon and the world model have very different purposes:

- The lexicon describes the words being used (like the English *word hat*).

- The world model describes the facts in the world (like the *concept* of a hat).

The world model itself is intended to be language-neutral. Constants and predicates like `red` and `size` are used in it, but just for convenience. As mentioned, Prolog would work the same on these if they were named `property19` and `concept42`. But the lexicon is about the *actual words*, so there it is important to use constants that correspond exactly to English (as the first argument to the lexicon predicates).

As a general rule, it is a good idea to distinguish between the world model and the lexicon for these two reasons:

- Different words may be used for the same concept, as in the following:

  - Synonyms

    ```
    common_noun(cap,X) :- hat(X).
    common_noun(bonnet,X) :- hat(X).
    ```

  - Other languages

    ```
    common_noun(chapeau,X) :- hat(X).     % French
    common_noun(cappello,X) :- hat(X).    % Italian
    ```

- The same word may be used for different concepts, as in the following:

  ```
  common_noun(cap,X) :- hat(X).
  common_noun(cap,X) :- bottle_top(X).
  common_noun(cap,X) :- regulated_maximum(X).
  ```

How does the lexicon work? It will be used by a *parser* to identify word categories and locate objects in the world model. For example, parsing the noun phrase *a red hat* will use the lexicon and end up with the query

```
color(X,red), hat(X).
```

for which there are two answers in the world model, X=hat01 and X=hat03. Parsing the noun phrase *a red hat on a man* will result in the query

```
color(X,red), hat(X), on(X,Y), person(Y), sex(Y,male).
```

which has a unique answer, X=hat01. Note that the predicate `preposition` here deals with two objects: the X is the object that is *on* the other (namely, the hat), and the Y is the object that has something on it (namely, the man).

Figure 8.6.   A parser of noun phrases in Prolog   np.pl

```
np([Name],X) :- proper_noun(Name,X).
np([Art|Rest],X) :- article(Art), np2(Rest,X).

np2([Adj|Rest],X) :- adjective(Adj,X), np2(Rest,X).
np2([Noun|Rest],X) :- common_noun(Noun,X), mods(Rest,X).

mods([],_).
mods(Words,X) :-
    append(Start,End,Words),    % Break the words into two pieces.
    pp(Start,X),                % The first part is a PP.
    mods(End,X).                % The last part is a Mods again.

pp([Prep|Rest],X) :- preposition(Prep,X,Y), np(Rest,Y).
```

8.2.3   Writing a parser

In writing a parser of noun phrases, the idea is that each *nonterminal* category in the grammar will have its own predicate in the parser. (The terminal categories are already defined in the lexicon.) Each such predicate takes two arguments:

- A *list* of words to be parsed
- An object in the world model

The lists studied in chapter 7 are now used to represent *sequences of words*. Each predicate in the parser will hold if the sequence of words is both of the category stated by the predicate and can be used to refer to the object according to the facts in the world model.

The parser corresponding to the grammar for noun phrases shown in figure 8.1 appears in figure 8.6. Note how closely this Prolog program follows the grammar. Each rule (in the noun phrase portion of the grammar) becomes a clause in Prolog.

Typically each predicate in the parser uses list notation to extract the first word in the sequence (the head of the list) and the remaining words (the tail of the list). For example, the first clause for np2 says that the head can be an adjective and the tail can be another np2, both describing the same object X in the world model. (The parser uses Prolog variables with descriptive names like Adj and Noun instead of A and N, but this is just to help keep track of what is being looked for.)

The rule for a pp is similar. The first word must be a preposition, and the remaining words must form an np. In this case, however, there are two objects in the world model to consider. The prepositional phrase can be used to refer to an object X only if the embedded noun phrase can be used to refer to another object Y, where the X and

Figure 8.7.   A first trace of the noun phrase parser

```
?- np([a,big,tree],X).
 Call: (7) np([a, big, tree], _G322)
 Call: (8) article(a)
 Exit: (8) article(a)
 Call: (8) np2([big, tree], _G322)
 Call: (9) adjective(big, _G322)
 Call: (10) size(_G322, big)
 Exit: (10) size(george, big)          % George is big.
 Exit: (9) adjective(big, george)
 Call: (9) np2([tree], george)

   ... this fails, but then eventually ...

 Redo: (10) size(_G322, big)
 Exit: (10) size(tree01, big)           % Tree01 is big.
 Exit: (9) adjective(big, tree01)
 Call: (9) np2([tree], tree01)
 Call: (10) common_noun(tree, tree01)
 Exit: (10) common_noun(tree, tree01)   % Tree01 is a tree.
 Call: (10) mods([], tree01)
 Exit: (10) mods([], tree01)
 Exit: (9) np2([tree], tree01)
 Exit: (8) np2([big, tree], tree01)
 Exit: (7) np([a, big, tree], tree01)
X = tree01
```

---

the Y stand in the appropriate relation for the preposition word (as determined by the `preposition` predicate in the lexicon).

The exception to this pattern in the parser of extracting the first word from a list occurs with the predicate `mods`. Instead of just working on the head and on the tail of a list of words, it uses `append` to break the list into two pieces: the first piece must be a pp, and the second piece must be another `mods`. This allows breaking apart a list such as `[in,the,park,with,a,red,hat]` into two lists: `[in,the,park]` and `[with,a,red,hat]`. (See section 7.3 on append.)

8.2.4   Putting the pieces together

After a world model, a lexicon, and a parser have been loaded into Prolog, the program is ready to parse and interpret noun phrases. To do this, the `np` predicate is queried with a list of words as the first argument and a variable as the second. Prolog attempts to locate an object from the world model described by the noun phrase.

Figure 8.8. A second trace of the noun phrase parser

```
?- np2([woman,beside,mary],W).
 Call: (9) np2([woman, beside, mary], _G313)
 Call: (10) common_noun(woman, _G313)
 Exit: (10) common_noun(woman, mary)      % The first woman: mary
 Call: (10) mods([beside, mary], mary)
 ... this fails and then ...
 Redo: (10) common_noun(woman, _G313)
 Exit: (10) common_noun(woman, linda)     % The second woman: linda
 Call: (10) mods([beside, mary], linda)   % Break into two pieces:
 Call: (11) pp([], linda)                 % [] and [beside,mary]? No.
 Call: (11) pp([beside], linda)           % [beside] and [mary]?  No.
 Call: (11) pp([beside, mary], linda)     % [beside,mary] and []?
 Call: (12) preposition(beside, linda, _L720)
 Exit: (12) preposition(beside, linda, mary)
 Call: (12) np([mary], mary)              % This succeeds.
 Call: (11) mods([], linda),              % This succeeds, too.
 ... and eventually ...
 Exit: (9) np2([woman, beside, mary], linda)

W = linda
```

A partial trace for the words [a,big,tree] is shown in figure 8.7. Observe that np2 must locate something that is big and that is also a tree. In looking for something big (via adjective and then size), it first locates george, but then eventually backtracks and settles on tree01, which passes the remaining test.

A more complex trace for the words [woman,beside,mary] as an np2 appears in figure 8.8. The process is the same, but there are many more steps. In looking for a woman, the parser first comes up with Mary. But Mary is not beside Mary, so the rest of the parse fails. It then backtracks and finds Linda. At this point, mods needs to use append to break up the sequence of words [beside,mary] into a pp followed by another mods, as required by the grammar. Here is what happens:

1. The parser uses append to split the list into [] and [beside,mary], but [] is not a pp, so it backtracks and reconsiders.

2. It tries [beside] and [mary], but [beside] is not a pp either.

3. It gets to [beside,mary] and [], where [beside,mary] is the pp
   (that correctly describes Linda) and [] is the remaining mods.

This show how append can be used to divide a list of words into syntactic groups.

Figure 8.9.   Handling ambiguity in noun phrases

```
Call: (7) np2([man,in,the,park,with,a,tree],_G334)
Call: (8) common_noun(man,_G334)
Exit: (8) common_noun(man,john)
Call: (8) mods([in,the,park,with,a,tree],john)
Call: (9) pp([],john)
Call: (9) pp([in],john)
Call: (9) pp([in,the],john)
Call: (9) pp([in,the,park],john)
Exit: (9) pp([in,the,park],john)                    % Part 1: yes.
Call: (9) mods([with,a,tree],john)
Fail: (9) mods([with,a,tree],john)                  % Part 2: no.
Fail: (9) pp([in,the,park],john)
Call: (9) pp([in,the,park,with],john)
Call: (9) pp([in,the,park,with,a],john)
Call: (9) pp([in,the,park,with,a,tree],john)        % A better split.
Call: (10) preposition(in,john,_G335)
Exit: (10) preposition(in,john,kew_beach)
Call: (10) np([the,park,with,a,tree],kew_beach)
Exit: (10) np([the,park,with,a,tree],kew_beach)
Exit: (9) pp([in,the,park,with,a,tree],john)
Exit: (8) mods([in,the,park,with,a,tree],john)
Exit: (7) np2([man,in,the,park,with,a,tree],john)
```

Although this parser deals mainly with syntactic structure, it is also able to disambiguate certain phrases using the world model. Consider the trace in figure 8.9. The English noun phrase in question is the ambiguous *a man in the park with a tree*. Once np2 decides that the man is John, it must confirm using mods that [in,the,park,with,a,tree] describes John. The parser needs to break this into some number of prepositional phrases (again using append) that each describe John. Here is what is seen in the trace:

- One possibility is that there are two modifying phrases [in,the,park] and [with,a,tree]. However, while the first one can be used to describe John, the second one, [with,a,tree] cannot. So this parse is rejected.

- The second possibility is that the entire sequence of words is a single modifying phrase. For this to work, [the,park,with,a,tree] must be a noun phrase that refers to kew_beach, since that is where John is located. This works out.

So while the English phrase is ambiguous as to whether *with a tree* modifies *man* or *park*, the parser uses *semantic* considerations to reject the first of these interpretations.

Figure 8.10. Connecting a partial trace to a parse tree

```
np2([man,in,the,park,with,a,tree],_)

common_noun(man,_),
    mods([in,the,park,with,a,tree],_)

mods([in,the,park,with,a,tree],_)

pp([in,the,park,with,a,tree],_),
mods([],_)

preposition(in,_,_),
    np([the,park,with,a,tree],_)

np([the,park,with,a,tree],_)

article(the), np2([park,with,a,tree],_)

np2([park,with,a,tree],_)

common_noun(park,_), mods([with,a,tree],_)

mods([with,a,tree],_)

pp([with,a,tree],_), mods([],_)

preposition(with,_,_), np([a,tree],_)

np([a,tree],_)

article(a), np2([tree],_)

np2([tree],_)

common_noun(tree,_), mods([],_)
```

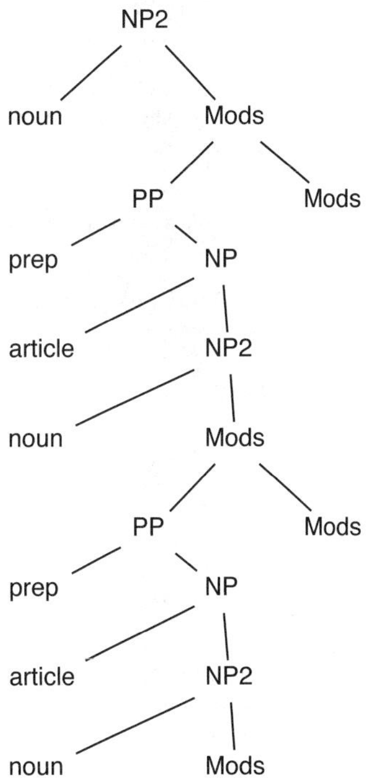

So the thinking here is not only about the words and the grammar, but also about what the words mean.

* Reconstructing parse trees

There is a close connection between these traces and parse trees. It is possible with some effort to reconstruct a parse tree from the trace of a successful query to the parser. Look at figure 8.10. On the left-hand side of the figure are the Call parts of a successful trace of an np2; on the right, is the corresponding parse tree.

Some additional queries

Some additional queries and their answers are shown in figure 8.11. Note that noun phrases can be used to identify hats as easily as people, as the second query shows.

Figure 8.11.   More queries over noun phrases

```
?- np([a,man,with,a,big,hat],X).
X = george    ;
No

?- np([the,hat,on,george],X).
X = hat04     ;
No

?- np([a,man,in,a,park,with,a,big,tree],X).
No

?- np([a,woman,in,a,park,with,a,big,tree],X).
X = mary      ;
X = linda     ;
No

?- np([a,woman,in,a,park,with,a,big,red,hat],X).
X = linda     ;
No

?- np([a,woman,beside,a,woman,with,a,blue,hat],X).
X = mary      ;    % This is not the obvious reading.
X = linda     ;    % This is the obvious reading.
No

?-  np([a,woman,with,a,blue,hat,beside,a,woman],X).
X = mary      ;
No
```

The third and fourth queries reveal that there are no men in a park with a big tree, but there are two women there. The fifth query brings the result that Linda is the only woman in a park with a big red hat.

Given this information, observe in the sixth query the handling of the noun phrase *a woman beside a woman with a blue hat*. This phrase is ambiguous, although the more common interpretation is to attach *a blue hat* to the second woman mentioned, in which case the entire phrase refers to Linda (who is wearing a red hat). If one wanted to attach both prepositional phrases to the first woman, one would normally use a noun phrase like *a woman with a blue hat beside a woman* (as in the final query), which can only refer to Mary.

Generating noun phrases

Figure 8.12 shows what happens with the np predicate when variables are put into the noun phrase part of the query:

Figure 8.12. Some other uses of noun phrases

```
?- np([the,Word,on,john], hat01).
Word = hat  ;
No

?- L=[_,_,_,_,_], np(L,linda), \+ member(the,L).
L = [a, small, small, small, woman]     ;
L = [a, small, woman, in, queens_park]  ;
L = [a, small, woman, beside, mary]     ;
L = [a, small, woman, with, hat03]      ;
L = [a, small, woman, with, mary]       ;
L = [a, woman, in, a, park]             ;
L = [a, woman, beside, a, woman]        ;
L = [a, woman, with, a, hat]            ;
L = [a, woman, with, a, woman]          ;
No

?- np(L,linda).
L = [linda]    ;
ERROR: Out of local stack      % Making 'a small small small ...'
```

1. The first query looks for a single missing word within a given phrase such that the entire phrase would refer to hat01. The word is hat.

2. The second query asks for a noun phrase L with five words that refers to Linda and does not contain the word the. There are nine such phrases. (Note that *a small small small woman* means the same thing here as *a small woman*.)

3. The third query asks for a noun phrase L that refers to Linda without any further restrictions. It generates the first answer, which is the proper noun linda. But after this, it must generate an article followed by an NP2. The first clause of the np2 predicate is recursive, since an NP2 can be an adjective followed by another NP2. Unfortunately, the program gets stuck in a loop here, attempting to generate a sequence of adjectives describing Linda, never making it to the second clause of the np2 predicate, where a common noun is required.

The third query is an example of trying to go through an infinite set of candidates, which can be problematic (see the discussion of member and append in section 7.3).

Figure 8.13.   A grammar for questions

WH	$\rightarrow$	wh_word copula_verb NP
		Who is the woman with Linda?
		What is the hat on the man in the park?
WH	$\rightarrow$	wh_word copula_verb PP
		What is in Queen's Park?
		Who is beside a man with a small hat?
YN	$\rightarrow$	copula_verb NP NP
		Is the man with the blue hat John?
		Is Mary the woman beside Linda?
YN	$\rightarrow$	copula_verb NP PP
		Is John beside a woman with a blue hat?
		Is the big red hat on George?

8.3   Interpreting sentences

With a parser/interpreter for noun phrases in place, some simple forms of English *sentences* can now be considered. Sentences will be treated as lists of words, just as was done for noun phrases. However, for convenience, a special predicate split_words(*string, list*) is used to break a quoted string into a list of words:

```
?- split_words('the quality of mercy',X).
X = [the, quality, of, mercy]
Yes
```

This predicate is part of the package wordUtils.pl mentioned in appendix A. This predicate has nothing to do with thinking about the words, but it does make the Prolog queries look more natural.

8.3.1   Yes/no questions

First, consider English sentences that are *questions*. Figure 8.13 shows a grammar for simple *wh* and yes/no questions. There are two rules for each as well as example sentences. Parsing yes/no questions requires a predicate yn(z) that holds when z is a

Figure 8.14. A parser for yes/no questions   yesno.pl

```
yes_no(String) :-
    split_words(String,Words),   % Get the list of words.
    yn(Words).                    % Use yn on the words.

yn([Verb|Rest]) :-
    Verb=is,                      % The first word must be "is".
    append(W1,W2,Rest),           % Break the rest into two parts.
    np(W1,Ref),                   % The first part must be an NP.
    np_or_pp(W2,Ref).             % The second part must be an NP or a PP.

np_or_pp(W,Ref) :- np(W,Ref).
np_or_pp(W,Ref) :- pp(W,Ref).
```

list of words that forms a yes/no question and whose answer is yes. (A predicate for *wh* questions is not discussed here.)

A Prolog program for the yn predicate is shown in figure 8.14. It uses append to split the list of words after the word is into two groups, where the first must be a noun phrase, and the second is either a noun phrase or a prepositional phrase. It works by finding a referent for the first group and checking that it can also be a referent for the second group. The yes_no predicate is similar, except that it takes a quoted string as its argument. Here are some examples of its use:

```
?- yes_no('is mary in a park with linda').
Yes

?- yes_no('is the man with the blue hat john').
No

?- yes_no('is the big red hat on the woman beside mary').
Yes

?- yes_no('is a red with a woman hat').    % Ungrammatical
No
```

Note that this predicate returns *success* only if the object described by the first noun phrase is the same as the object described by the second (noun or prepositional) phrase. So with this predicate one cannot distinguish between a *failure* (a question that is ungrammatical or where no referent can be found) and a well-formed question to which the answer happens to be no.

8.3.2   Dynamic predicates in Prolog

Section 8.3.3 deals with declarative sentences. There, instead of being used to *query* the world model, a declarative sentence is used to *update* it. In other words, a declarative sentence is interpreted as providing *new information* that needs to be incorporated into the world model.

Prolog allows the clauses associated with some of the predicates to be changed by a program itself. These are called *dynamic* predicates. For example, suppose a predicate my_pred(x,y,z) takes three arguments. To make that predicate dynamic, a special Prolog declaration `dynamic` is used. The line

```
:- dynamic my_pred/3.
```

is included in the program file before my_pred is used. The clauses in the file can then define my_pred as usual, but there are also two special Prolog operations, `assert` and `retract`, which can be used in queries or in the bodies of clauses:

- assert(*atom*)
  This query always succeeds; it has the effect of adding the atom as a clause to Prolog's knowledge base.

- retract(*atom*)
  This query has the effect of removing the first clause in Prolog's knowledge base that matches the atom. It fails if there is no match.

So Prolog programs can be written as follows:

```
get_married(X) :-
    retract(single(X)),    % X is no longer single.
    assert(married(X)).    % X is now married.
```

Predicates like this can be used to keep a model of a changing world up-to-date. So for example, if a program with this predicate is loaded together with a world model that contains the fact that John is single, the following behavior results:

```
?- single(john).
Yes

?- get_married(john).
Yes

?- single(john).
No

?- married(john).
Yes
```

This change to John's status happens only within the Prolog session. The file with the world model remains unchanged. This means that if the programmer exits, restarts Prolog, and then reloads the file, John's status will again show as single. To keep John's married status as a permanent part of the world model, the knowledge base of clauses would have to be saved to a new file, which the program could then run.

8.3.3   Simple declarative sentences

For simplicity, consider declarative sentences described by the following single grammar rule:

SD   →   NP copula_verb preposition NP

This is a special case of the sentences described by the S category of the grammar in figure 8.1. An example sentence of this form is the following:

The man with the red hat is in the park with the big tree.

Parsing sentences like these requires a predicate sd(z) that holds when z is a list of words that forms a simple declarative sentence. In addition, the parser should find the objects corresponding to the two noun phrases, and update the world model. For the example sentence shown here, it should assert in(john,queens_park).

To parse and interpret declaratives in this way, prepositions must be used dynamically, not just to locate objects in the world model. The simplest way to do this is to extend the lexicon to include a predicate add_for_preposition that states how new information for each preposition should be handled:

```
add_for_preposition(on,X,Y) :- assert(on(X,Y)).
add_for_preposition(in,X,Y) :- assert(in(X,Y)).
add_for_preposition(beside,X,Y) :-
    assert(beside(X,Y)), assert(beside(Y,X)).
```

Note that the assertions for beside give both orders of arguments, since that is the convention in the world model (for example, for Linda and Mary). Note also that there is no clause for the preposition with. This is because of its ambiguity: given the statement X is with Y, it is not clear what relation should be updated.

With clauses like these in the lexicon, simple declarative sentences can be handled using the program in figure 8.15. The split_words predicate is used to break a quoted string into a list of words. The sd predicate takes this list of words and uses append to break it into a noun phrase, the constant is, a single word Prep (which must be a preposition), and a second noun phrase. The predicate np is used to find each referent, and the predicate add_for_preposition is used to change the world model.

Figure 8.15.   A parser for declaratives   `declarative.pl`

```
simple_declarative(String) :-
    split_words(String,Words),      % Get words from string.
    sd(Words).                      % Use sd on the words.
sd(Words) :-
    append(NP1,[is,Prep|NP2],Words),  % Split words.
    np(NP1,X),                        % Find referent for first NP.
    np(NP2,Y),                        % Find referent for second NP.
    add_for_preposition(Prep,X,Y).    % Add new atom to database.
```

No attempt is made here to ensure that the new information is *reasonable*, however. (As it stands, for example, people could end up being located at more than one place.)

8.4   Nonreferential noun phrases

The sort of natural language processing described in this chapter is really just the start. What makes language so interesting is that it can be used in ways that are much more versatile than hinted at here.

For both the interrogative and declarative sentences that have been examined, noun phrases were used to refer to some known individual in the world model. But not all noun phrases are *referential* in this sense.

Consider the following: *a man without a hat*. This is like previous noun phrases using the preposition *without*. However, in this example, the noun phrase *a hat* is *not* used referentially; it would be a mistake to look in the world model for the hat that is being referred to. Indeed, the reference is to a man for whom there is no such hat. (The program clearly needs to be redesigned with respect to prepositional phrases that start with the word *without*.)

Similarly, for the sentence *Mary eats an apple every day*, one should not look for the object referred to by the noun phrase *an apple*. There is no single object that Mary eats over and over; each day it is a different one. The following sentence, on the other hand, is semantically ambiguous: *John wants to marry a rich lawyer*. The phrase *a rich lawyer* may be referential in designating somebody (say, Susan) whom John wants to marry and who happens to be a rich lawyer. Or it may be nonreferential in that there is no particular individual that John has in mind: whoever it will turn out to be, however, he wants her to be both rich and a lawyer.

Want to read more?

This chapter looked at the thinking behind parsing and interpreting expressions in a natural language.

While there is a long tradition of studying grammar and parsing in classrooms, it is primarily in the work of Noam Chomsky on what is called *transformational grammar* starting in the late 1950s that the study of syntax took on a new mathematical precision and generality of description [41]. Chomsky is also well known for having first proposed a solution to the puzzle of how young children could learn the language of their parents after being exposed to so few sentences. His proposal is that we are actually born with a *universal grammar* that allows us to adapt very quickly to the actual grammar of the sentences we first hear.

The approach to semantics in this chapter, which seeks to query or update a separate knowledge base of facts about the world, owes much to the work of the computer scientist Terry Winograd. His doctoral thesis [43] at MIT in the early 1970s was a much more elaborate version of what was considered here, in a world of blocks. To get a glimpse of the major developments in computational linguistics since then, consult the textbook by Jurafsky and Martin [42].

It needs to be emphasized that the discussion in this chapter only scratches the surface of how natural language can be used and the kind of thinking that goes on behind it. The few examples presented here may have given the impression that the primary purpose of language is to provide information or to request it. In fact, even a casual study of how people actually use language will reveal that this is but a small part of the overall picture.

It was the philosopher John Austin in the 1950s who first observed that the important thing about language is that people perform language *actions* (informing, warning, lying, threatening, promising, and so on) to further their goals [40]. Sometimes these goals involve information, but often they are quite different. A speaker might be interested, for example, in having a door closed. One way of achieving that is to get up and close it; another way, in the right circumstances, is to utter some words like, "Can you close the door?" (clearly not expecting a yes/no answer) or even "Door, please." This suggests that the thinking behind language actually has much in common with the thinking about how to achieve goals using actions, which is the topic of chapter 9.

Figure 8.16.   A robot arm and some blocks

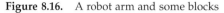

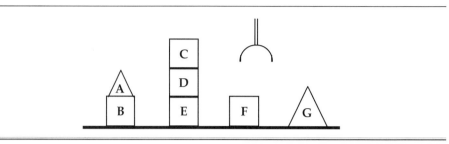

However, even if language is about using words to achieve goals, it is sometimes far from clear what those goals are, or how the words contribute to achieving them. Consider a conversation like this:

> "Hey! How is it going?"
> "Not bad. Not bad. How about you?"
> "Oh, could be worse. I can't wait for winter to be over."
> "You and me both!"

This kind of chit-chat could be ignored if it didn't make up such a large part of language behavior. What is going on here appears to have little to do with details about the weather (or the sport scores, or the latest celebrity scandal). It's much more like a dance where the two parties exchange stylized moves and indicate a willingness to act together. From an evolutionary point of view, it seems that language behavior arose out of a strong desire for social interaction of this sort and that all the rest of it (beyond the chit-chat) is more like an interesting offshoot.

Exercises

These exercises put what you have learned about natural language into practice in a new domain. Imagine a robot that is capable of picking up and moving blocks located on a table in front of it, as in figure 8.16.

The goal is to tell the robot what to do using ordinary English imperative sentences like, "Pick up the pyramid beside the small green cube and put it directly in front of the yellow block." To interpret English sentences like these, you need to construct a *world model* of facts about this world, a *lexicon* with all the necessary English vocabulary, and a *parser/interpreter* to process the English expressions.

Before using English words, you will need to build a simple world model of facts about this blocks world in Prolog. Each block can be assumed to have a color, a size, and a certain shape (a cube, a pyramid, a wedge, ...). Also, each block is located somewhere in the scene. To simplify matters, suppose that the robot lives in a two-dimensional world with these properties:

- A block is located either on the table or on another block.

- Each block is on at most one other block (which must be a cube) and has at most one other block directly on it.

- The surface of the table is divided into some number (say, 5) of contiguous areas, ordered from left to right.

- Each block on the table is located in exactly one of these areas, and each table area has at most one block directly on it.

With these assumptions, the locations of blocks can then be represented using a Prolog predicate `located_on`(*block*,*location*), where *block* is a block and *location* is either a cube or one of the table areas. Then a second Prolog predicate `area_left_of`(*area*$_1$,*area*$_2$) is used to state that *area*$_1$ is the area on the table immediately to the left of *area*$_2$.

1. Build a world model that expresses basic facts about colors, sizes, shapes, and locations of some blocks in a scene. Include within your documentation a drawing of the blocks-world scene that corresponds to that world model.

2. Write clauses defining the predicates `beside`(x,y), which holds when block x and y are both on the table in two adjacent areas, and `above`(x,y), which holds when block x is somewhere above block y.

3. Show that your world model works properly by getting Prolog to answer some queries about it. (These queries should *not* use English noun phrases.)

Once your world model is working satisfactorily, you are ready to consider English noun phrases and the blocks they refer to in your scene. Here are some example queries using English noun phrases:

- `np([a,wedge],B).`

- `np([any,small,green,block],B).`

- `np([a,pyramid,on,a,big,cube],B).`

- `np([a,cube,beside,the,orange,wedge],B).`

- `np([a,cube,below,an,orange,wedge,on,a,red,block],B).`
  (This is ambiguous: is it the cube or the wedge that is on the red block?)

```
    - np([a,green,wedge,above,a,block,
                beside,the,small,red,pyramid],B).
```

4. Build a Prolog lexicon of articles, adjectives, common nouns, and prepositions, including all the words in the six example noun phrases. The word *any* should be treated as an article.

5. Copy the Prolog parser/interpreter for noun phrases presented in the chapter (or write your own). Then test the np predicate on a variety of noun phrases to show that it is capable of identifying the blocks being referred to in your scene.

To model moving a block within your blocks world, suppose there is a predicate put_on($block_1, block_2$) that uses the Prolog assert and retract operations to change the location of a block. This predicate should fail if the move action would be impossible, that is, if there is a block on either $block_1$ or $block_2$, or if $block_2$ is not a cube. Otherwise, put_on should retract the located_on fact involving $block_1$, and assert that it is now on $block_2$.

6. Write clauses defining the put_on predicate, and test it on a variety of move operations. After each operation, include a sketch of what the new scene looks like, and have your program answer some queries involving that new scene.

7. Extend your parser/interpreter from exercise 5 to handle simple imperative sentences of the form "Put NP on NP" where NP is a noun phrase. For example, the following are syntactically well-formed imperative sentences:

    Put a green pyramid on the small red cube.
    Put an orange wedge on the block beside a red cube.
    Put any small block on a green cube on the big red cube.

    The effect of parsing and interpreting sentences such as these should be to update the scene using the put_on predicate from exercise 6.

8. Test your parser on a variety of imperative sentences like those in exercise 7, including some that are syntactically well formed but impossible to execute.

9. Show that your grammar for imperative sentences is *ambiguous* by drawing two parse trees for the third example sentence in exercise 7. Also show that your parser can sometimes disambiguate a sentence using facts about the current scene.

10. Handle the article *the* properly. The idea here is that a noun phrase like "the red pyramid" should only succeed in naming a block if there is a *unique* block of the appropriate kind.

9 Case Study: Planning Courses of Action

Intelligent behavior is made intelligent by the application of knowledge. We are able to act intelligently because we know a lot about the world around us and are able to bring this knowledge to bear on our decisions about what to do. In particular, we make decisions not just by *reacting* to what we see, hear, or smell around us but by *deliberating* about what we want and how to achieve it. For example, instead of heading toward a file cabinet that contains something we want, we might first think about it and decide to move in a completely opposite direction (if we need to get the key that will unlock it). As another example, consider the deliberations involved in a (traditional) wedding: the invitations, the ceremony, the dinner, the reception. Hundreds, even thousands of decisions are pondered well in advance of the wedding day itself. Nobody would call this sort of thinking intellectual, like playing chess or discussing Schopenhauer, but it is clearly intelligent behavior of the highest order.

So what is the thinking that underlies these sorts of deliberations? In its simplest form it is *planning*, contemplating various possible courses of actions, until we find one that we believe will achieve what we want. This is the sort of thinking that is investigated in this chapter.

To plan, we need to be able to think about the actions we can take, and imagine what the world would be like if we took them. Unlocking a file cabinet will allow a drawer to be opened if the right key is available. Contacting a property manager will allow a wedding planner to discover if a hall can be rented for a reception. Planning is not just thinking about the way the world *is* but about the way it *can be*. This requires thinking about the *state* of the world and how that state is affected by what we (and others) do. It is a major intellectual achievement of humans (and no doubt other animals, too) to be able to step back from the world in this manner and imagine it as being quite different from the way it is.

This chapter has four sections. Section 1 discusses two simple but very different planning problems and how the planning process is really the same for both of them. Section 2 considers a general planning program in Prolog, and applies it to three planning problems. The final two sections consider how planning changes as the

Figure 9.1.   The three-coins problem at the outset

scope gets larger, first in terms of how the thinking should proceed and then in terms of how the knowledge itself should be represented.

9.1   Planning problems

Once it is determined how to represent knowledge about the states of the world and how they change as the result of actions, the planning will always be the same.

9.1.1   A first example: The three coins

Consider this very simple puzzle:

> Imagine coins arranged with heads and tails as shown in figure 9.1. Make them all the same (that is, either all heads or all tails) using exactly three moves. A move here means turning over one of the coins (so that a head becomes a tail, or a tail becomes a head).

This is not a very hard problem, and a moment's thought will reveal many possible ways of solving it:

- Flip the middle coin, then flip the right one, then flip the middle one again.
- Flip the left coin twice, then flip the right one.
- Flip the right coin three times. . . .

In all cases, a solution will end up with three heads, and here is why. After one move, there will be an even number of tails; after two moves, an odd number of tails; after three moves, an even number of tails; and if all three coins are to be the same, that even number must be zero. Furthermore, all the solutions involve either moving the right coin three times, or moving it once and moving one of the other coins twice.

Figure 9.2. The monkey and bananas problem at the outset

9.1.2 A second example: The monkey and bananas

Now consider a second problem, first suggested by John McCarthy:

> A monkey is in a room where a bunch of bananas is hanging from the ceiling, too high to reach. In the corner of the room is a box, which is not under the bananas. The box is sturdy enough to support the monkey if he climbs on it, and light enough so that he can move it easily. If the box is under the bananas, and the monkey is on the box, he will be high enough to reach the bananas.

The initial setup for this problem is sketched in figure 9.2. In this case, the moves available to the monkey are described informally. The monkey can do the following:

- Go to anywhere in the room (provided the monkey is not on the box).
- Climb on the box (provided the monkey is at the box but not on it).
- Climb off the box (provided the monkey is on the box).
- Push the box anywhere (provided the monkey is at the box but not on it).
- Grab the bananas (provided the monkey is on the box under the bananas).

Note the provisos for these actions. In thinking about how to solve this problem, one needs to realize that the monkey cannot push the box after he has climbed on it, for instance. Here is what the monkey needs to do to solve the problem:

1. Go to where the box is.
2. Push it under the bananas.

3. Climb on the box.

4. Grab the bananas.

This is not the only way to get the bananas, but it is the most direct.

9.1.3   States and operators

In general, the planning problems in this chapter are characterized by their states and operators, as follows:

- The *states* of a planning problem are snapshots of the world that are passed through while solving the problem. For the two examples, the states are
  - the sides of the three coins that are showing;
  - the location of the monkey, the box, and the bananas.
- The *operators* (or *moves* or *actions*) of a planning problem are the ways of going from one state to another. For the two examples, the operators are
  - turning over one of the three coins;
  - climbing on the box (among others).
- The *initial state* of a planning problem is the state of the problem at the outset. For the two examples, the initial states are
  - HHT;
  - as shown in figure 9.2.
- The *goal state* of a planning problem is the desired state (or states) of the problem at the end. For the two examples, the goal states are
  - HHH or TTT;
  - any state where the monkey has the bananas.

The planning problems considered in this chapter are always the same: find a way of going from the initial state of the problem to a goal state by applying a sequence of operators.

The solution to a planning problem is a *plan*: a sequence of moves performed in order, starting from an initial state, and ending at a goal state. In any state along the way it must be possible to apply the current move *legally*, that is, without violating any of the given provisos for the move.

9.2 Generating plans

To solve a planning problem using Prolog, the general idea is this:

- Represent the initial state, the goal state(s), and the operators of the problem.
- The Prolog program will then find a way of getting from the initial state to a goal state using those operators.

How will it do this? By *thinking* about the problem, of course! The thoughts will be like this:

If I am in state S and I do move M, that will take me to state S'.
From S' if I now do move M', that will take me to S''. ...

The programmer tells Prolog where to start (that is, the initial state) and where it should end (the goal state). Along the way, the program will need to keep track of all the moves it is considering and assemble them into a working plan at the end.

9.2.1 A general planning program

A plan is a sequence of moves from an initial state to a goal state. So the main thing in planning is knowing how to go from one state S_1 to another state S_2 using a sequence of legal moves L. (Bigger planning problems will present much more to think about.) The state S_2 is said to be _reachable_ from S_1 using L, which is written this way:

$$S_1 \xrightarrow{L} S_2$$

There are only two principles to know about this reachability:

- S is reachable from S (trivially) using no moves: $S \xrightarrow{\langle\rangle} S$.
- If there is a legal move M_0 that goes from state S_1 to state S_2, and S_3 is reachable from S_2 using moves $\langle M_1, \ldots, M_n \rangle$, then S_3 is also reachable from S_1 using moves $\langle M_0, M_1, \ldots, M_n \rangle$. This is represented as follows:

$$\text{If } S_1 \xrightarrow{M_0} S_2 \text{ and } S_2 \xrightarrow{\langle M_1, \ldots, M_n \rangle} \ldots \rightarrow S_3, \text{ then } S_1 \xrightarrow{\langle M_0, M_1, \ldots, M_n \rangle} \ldots \rightarrow S_3$$

A planner can be defined in Prolog by encoding these two reachability principles directly, as shown in figure 9.3. To solve a planning problem, the plan predicate is used to generate a list of moves L such that a goal state G is reachable from the initial state I using L.

Figure 9.3. A general planner in Prolog   plan.pl

```
% This general planner needs the predicates below to be defined:
%      - legal_move(BeforeState,Move,AfterState)
%      - initial_state(State)
%      - goal_state(State)

% plan(L): L is a list of moves from the initial state to a goal state.
plan(L) :- initial_state(I), goal_state(G), reachable(I,L,G).

% reachable(S1,L,S2): S2 is reachable from S1 using moves L.
reachable(S,[],S).
reachable(S1,[M|L],S3) :- legal_move(S1,M,S2), reachable(S2,L,S3).
```

Figure 9.4. The three-coins problem in Prolog   coins.pl

```
% The three-coins problem formulated for the general planner.
initial_state([h,h,t]).

goal_state([h,h,h]).
goal_state([t,t,t]).

% The three possible moves. Each changes one of the coins.
legal_move([X,Y,Z],flip_left,[X1,Y,Z]) :- opposite(X,X1).
legal_move([X,Y,Z],flip_middle,[X,Y1,Z]) :- opposite(Y,Y1).
legal_move([X,Y,Z],flip_right,[X,Y,Z1]) :- opposite(Z,Z1).

opposite(h,t).                  % Flipping a head gives a tail.
opposite(t,h).                  % Flipping a tail gives a head.
```

This is what is called a *general* planner. For each specific planning problem to be solved, one must provide clauses that define the initial_state, goal_state, and legal_move predicates for that problem.

9.2.2   Solving the three-coins problem

To solve a planning problem like the three-coins problem, the first thing to determine is how to represent the states of the problem symbolically. In this case, a state is determined by which sides of the coins are showing. So a state of the problem can be represented using a list with three elements $[x,y,z]$, where the x, y, and z are either h (for heads) or t (for tails). (There are eight states in total.)

The full program based on this representation is shown in figure 9.4. Note the single initial state and the two possible goal states. The next three clauses define the legal_move predicate. There are three possible moves: turning over the left, the

Figure 9.5.   Generating three-coins plans

```
?- plan([M1,M2,M3]).
M1 = flip_left
M2 = flip_left
M3 = flip_right    ;

M1 = flip_left
M2 = flip_right
M3 = flip_left
```

---

middle, or the right coins. The first clause says, If I start in any state of the world $[x,y,z]$ and flip the leftmost coin, I will end up in a state $[x',y,z]$ that is the same as before except that x' will be the opposite of x (where opposite is defined by the last two clauses). The other two flips are analogous.

Now load both the general planner (figure 9.3) and the three-coins program (figure 9.4) into Prolog. Figure 9.5 shows a query to the plan predicate asking for a plan with precisely three moves. It also shows the first two solutions found by the general planner.

9.2.3   Atoms as terms in Prolog

This section takes a small digression to consider a feature of Prolog that has not been studied yet but that will simplify matters considerably.

So far, Prolog terms have been identified as variables, numbers, lists, or constants. But, in fact, Prolog terms are variables, numbers, lists, or *atoms*. A constant as a term is merely a special case of an atom where the predicate has no arguments and no parentheses. (This aspect of Prolog was not discussed earlier, but at this stage the distinction is no longer necessary.) So queries can be the following:

```
?- X=p, Y=q(a).              % X is a constant, but Y is an atom.
X = p,   Y = q(a)

?- Y=p(a), Z=[a,Y,b].        % Atoms can appear in lists.
Y = p(a),   Z = [a, p(a), b]

?- Y=p(W,W), p(a,_)=Y, Z=q(Y)      % Atoms can be nested.
Y = p(a,a),   W = a,   Z = q(p(a,a))
```

This feature of Prolog is used for moves. To previous moves like flip_middle one can now add moves represented by atoms like go(loc2).

9.2.4   Solving the monkey and bananas problem

The states in the monkey and bananas problem are more complex than for the three-coins problem. Each state must specify the location of the monkey, bananas and box, and also whether the monkey is on the box, and whether the monkey has the bananas. This suggests using a five-element list $[b,m,l,o,h]$, as follows:

- b, m, and l are the locations of the bananas, monkey, and box, respectively.

- o is either y or n according to whether the monkey is on the box. (The monkey can be at the same location as the box but not on it.)

- h is either y or n according to whether the monkey has the bananas.

For locations, the easiest thing to do is to name the initial locations of the bananas, monkey, and box as loc1, loc2, and loc3. So, for example, the initial state will be [loc1,loc2,loc3,n,n]. No other location needs to have a name. A goal state will be a five-element list whose last element is y.

The moves available to the monkey are the following:

- climb_on (climbing on the box)

- climb_off (climbing off the box)

- grab (grabbing the bananas)

- go(X) (going to location X)

- push(X) (pushing the box to location X)

Clauses for legal_move must be written for each of these operators, just as was done for the operators of the three-coins problem. These clauses should say how a *before state* is transformed to an *after state* by the operator in question. The clauses should fail if the operator in question cannot be used in the before state.

Consider climb_on. It takes a state $[b,m,l,o,h]$ to another state just like it except $o = $ y. But this move is only legal when the monkey is at the same location as the box ($m = l$) and when the monkey is not already on the box ($o = $ n):

```
legal_move([B,M,L,O,H],climb_on,[B1,M1,L1,O1,H1]) :-
    M=L, O=n,                       % Provisos on the old state
    B1=B, M1=M, L1=L, O1=y, H1=H.   % Values for the new state
```

This can be written more succinctly as

```
legal_move([B,M,M,n,H],climb_on,[B,M,M,y,H]).
```

The climb_off and grab operators will be similar.

Figure 9.6. The monkey and bananas problem in Prolog   monkey.pl

```
% This is the monkey and bananas as a planning problem.
% The bananas, monkey, and box are at different locations.
% The monkey is not on the box and has no bananas.
initial_state([loc1,loc2,loc3,n,n]).

% The goal is any state where the monkey has the bananas.
goal_state([_,_,_,_,y]).

% Climbing on the box causes the monkey to be on the box.
legal_move([B,M,M,n,H],climb_on,[B,M,M,y,H]).
% Climbing off the box causes the monkey to be off the box.
legal_move([B,M,M,y,H],climb_off,[B,M,M,n,H]).
% Grabbing the bananas causes the monkey to have the bananas.
legal_move([B,B,B,y,n],grab,[B,B,B,y,y]).
% Pushing the box changes where the monkey and the box are.
legal_move([B,M,M,n,H],push(X),[B,X,X,n,H]).
% Going to a location changes where the monkey is.
legal_move([B,_,L,n,H],go(X),[B,X,L,n,H]).
```

Now consider the push(X) operator. The effect will be to move to a state where the monkey and the box are both at location X. In other words, performing push(loc2) will result in a state where $m = l = \text{loc2}$. However, this operator is only legal in states where climb_on would also be legal. This leads to

```
legal_move([B,M,M,n,H],push(X),[B,X,X,n,H]).
```

The clause for go(X) will be similar. Note how the atom push(X) is used as an argument of the predicate legal_move. Using atoms as terms avoids having to write separate operators for each location: push_loc1, push_loc2, push_loc3, ..., and similarly for the go operators.

The complete monkey and bananas program is shown in figure 9.6. Running this program together with the general planner will give the results shown in figure 9.7. The planner finds the desired four-step plan, and it is unique. There are no three-step plans for this problem, but there is a five-step plan: simply go somewhere in the first step and then apply a four-step plan. The last query in figure 9.7 shows that in any five-step plan, the first move must be a go action.

9.2.5 Bounding plan length

The plan queries so far have always specified how many moves a plan should have. If a plan for the monkey did not specify the number of steps, the result would be

Figure 9.7.   Generating plans for the monkey

```
?- plan([M1,M2,M3,M4]).        % Is there a four-step plan?
M1 = go(loc3)
M2 = push(loc1)
M3 = climb_on
M4 = grab          ;           % Are there any others?
No

?- plan([M1,M2,M3]).           % Is there a three-step plan?
No

?- plan([M1,M2,M3,M4,M5]).     % Is there a five-step plan?
M1 = go(_G325)                 % First go to any location.
M2 = go(loc3)                  % Then proceed as above.
M3 = push(loc1)
M4 = climb_on
M5 = grab
?- plan([M1,M2,M3,M4,M5]), \+ M1 = go(_).
No
```

```
?- plan(L).
ERROR: Out of global stack
```

The reason for this is that `reachable` looks for a path from an initial state S_0 to a goal state G. A trace of the query would show the following:

1. The first action is a go action from state S_0 to a state S_1, so the planner needs to find a path from S_1 to G.

2. The next action is a go action from state S_1 to a state S_2, so the planner needs to find a path from S_2 to G. . . .

In the end, the planner would look for ever longer sequences of go actions and never get to the other moves. On the other hand, if the sequence were *bounded* in advance, for instance, if the planner looked only for plans with four steps, then after four go actions, the `reachable` predicate would fail, and the planner would be forced to backtrack and consider other actions.

   This suggests that it is useful to have a version of the general planner that first tries [], then [_], then [_,_], then [_,_,_], and so on, until it finds a plan. There are a few ways to do this, but perhaps the simplest is shown in figure 9.8. The new general planner is called `bplan`. Its predicate `tryplan`(x, y) holds if y is a successful plan and is like x but possibly with some additional elements at the front. This predicate works

Figure 9.8. A general but bounded planner   bplan.pl

```
% This looks for plans, short ones first, using the plan predicate.
% bplan(L) holds if L is a plan.
bplan(L) :- tryplan([],L).

% tryplan(X,L): L is a plan and has X as its final elements.
tryplan(L,L) :- plan(L).
tryplan(X,L) :- tryplan([_|X],L).
```

Figure 9.9. A trace of the bplan predicate

```
?- bplan(L).
 Call: (9) bplan(_G210)
 Call: (10) tryplan([], _G210)
 Call: (11) plan([])
    %% plan fails. Details omitted.
 Redo: (10) tryplan([], _G210)
 Call: (11) tryplan([_G301], _G210)
 Call: (12) plan([_G301])
    %% plan fails. Details omitted.
 Redo: (11) tryplan([_G301], _G210)
 Call: (12) tryplan([_G304, _G301], _G210)
 Call: (13) plan([_G304, _G301])
    %% plan fails. Details omitted.
 Redo: (12) tryplan([_G304, _G301], _G210)
 Call: (13) tryplan([_G307, _G304, _G301], _G210)
 Call: (14) plan([_G307, _G304, _G301])
    %% plan fails. Details omitted.
 Redo: (13) tryplan([_G307, _G304, _G301], _G210)
 Call: (14) tryplan([_G310, _G307, _G304, _G301], _G210)
 Call: (15) plan([_G310, _G307, _G304, _G301])
    %% This is where plan is finally successful.
 Exit: (15) plan([go(loc3), push(loc1), climb_on, grab])
 Exit: (14) tryplan([go(loc3), ...], [go(loc3), ...])
 Exit: (13) tryplan([push(loc1), climb_on, grab], [go(loc3), ...])
 Exit: (12) tryplan([climb_on, grab], [go(loc3), ...])
 Exit: (11) tryplan([grab], [go(loc3), ...])
 Exit: (10) tryplan([], [go(loc3), ...])
 Exit: (9) bplan([go(loc3), push(loc1), climb_on, grab])
L = [go(loc3), push(loc1), climb_on, grab]
```

because the number of elements in *x* is always known during the back-chaining and so can be used with the existing plan predicate as is.

Figure 9.10.   The 15-puzzle

1	6	3	8
10	2	7	15
13	5	4	
9	14	11	12

$\Longrightarrow$

1	2	3	4
5	6	7	8
9	10	11	12
13	14	15	

initial state   goal state

A partial trace of the `bplan` predicate in action on the monkey and bananas problem is shown in figure 9.9. Note that if a planning problem cannot be solved, that is, if there is no sequence of moves that go from the initial state to a goal state, the `bplan` predicate (like the `plan` predicate) will continue searching indefinitely for ever longer sequences of moves.

9.2.6   A third example: The 15-puzzle

This section considers a more substantial planning problem, the 15-puzzle, attributed to Noyes Chapman (and sometimes to Sam Loyd). It is a puzzle that consists of a 4×4 frame containing tiles numbered 1 to 15 placed in random order (with one space empty). The object of the puzzle is to place the tiles in numerical order by making sliding moves that use the empty space. Figure 9.10 shows one possible initial state and the desired final state.

A state of the puzzle can be represented with a sixteen-element list $[p_1, p_2, \ldots, p_{16}]$, where each p_i is a number from 0 to 15 indicating which tile is in position i (and where 0 means that position i is empty). For the puzzle in figure 9.10,

- the initial state is `[1,6,3,8,10,2,7,15,13,5,4,0,9,14,11,12]`;

- the goal state is `[1,2,3,4,5,6,7,8,9,10,11,12,13,14,15,0]`.

The available moves involve sliding a tile up, down, left, or right, according to the position of the empty space. The corresponding operators are `up(X)`, `down(X)`, `left(X)`, and `right(X)`, where X is a tile.

The easiest way to write `legal_move` for the up operator is to write a clause for each of the twelve locations of the empty square where a tile can go up. For example, to handle a tile X moving up when the empty space is in position 3, one would write the following:

Figure 9.11.   A 2×3 version of the 15-puzzle   puzzle2x3.pl

```
% This is a 2x3 version of the 15 puzzle.          %%%%%%%%%
initial_state([0,1,5,4,3,2]).     %--------------------->  %  1 5 %
goal_state([1,2,3,4,5,0]).                          % 4 3 2 %
legal_move([0,B,C, X,E,F],up(X),[X,B,C, 0,E,F]).    %%%%%%%%%
legal_move([A,0,C, D,X,F],up(X),[A,X,C, D,0,F]).
legal_move([A,B,0, D,E,X],up(X),[A,B,X, D,E,0]).
legal_move(S1,down(X),S2) :- legal_move(S2,up(X),S1).

legal_move([0,X,C, D,E,F],left(X),[X,0,C, D,E,F]).
legal_move([A,0,X, D,E,F],left(X),[A,X,0, D,E,F]).
legal_move([A,B,C, 0,X,F],left(X),[A,B,C, X,0,F]).
legal_move([A,B,C, D,0,X],left(X),[A,B,C, D,X,0]).
legal_move(S1,right(X),S2) :- legal_move(S2,left(X),S1).
```

```
        legal_move(S1,up(X),S2) :-
            S1=[A,B,0,D, E,F,X,H, I,J,K,L, M,N,O,P],
            S2=[A,B,X,D, E,F,0,H, I,J,K,L, M,N,O,P].
```

Note that nothing changes between the two states except at positions 3 and 7, where the empty space and tile X are interchanged. There will be twelve such clauses for each of the four operators. Writing these is both tedious and error-prone. (This issue is discussed in section 9.4.) However, there is a shortcut because up and down are *inverses* (as are the left and right operators). Once the necessary clauses for up have been written, a single clause for down will suffice:

```
        legal_move(S1,down(X),S2) :- legal_move(S2,up(X),S1).
```

A complete program for the 2 × 3 version of the puzzle is shown in figure 9.11. Running it gives the following result:

```
        ?- bplan(L).
        L = [left(1), up(3), left(2), down(5), right(3), up(2), left(5)]
```

9.3   Scaling up: The search problem

For small planning problems like the three puzzles just considered, the thinking works fine. But for more realistic domains, the planning will have to be done in a different way. This section reconsiders the thinking process itself; the next section, reconsiders how to better represent the states of a changing world.

In the search for a path from an initial state to a goal state, only the moves that are legal in each state need to be considered. Nonetheless it is not hard to see that the number of paths is *exponential* in the length of the path.

For example, consider the 15-puzzle. Suppose there are exactly three legal moves possible from any state. (Some states have four legal moves, and when the empty space is in a corner, there are only two legal moves.) This means that from a starting state there are three paths that have just one move; from each of these final states (not necessarily distinct), there are three new states, meaning there are nine paths that contain two moves; similarly, there are twenty-seven paths with three moves. In general, there are 3^n paths with n moves.

This means that to find a path with twenty moves in the 15-puzzle, there might be as many as 10^9 paths. This is perhaps manageable, but twenty moves are not very many. For thirty moves, there might be 10^{14} paths, and for forty moves, as many as 10^{19} paths. Even with something as simple as the 15-puzzle, finding a plan with one hundred moves will be well outside the reach of a simple planner.

This is similar to the exponential growth that occurred in solving constraint satisfaction problems (see section 5.2.3). As with constraint satisfaction problems, to deal with this issue, the planning must be more sophisticated.

9.3.1   Knowledge-based planning

For many planning problems, thinking (that is, using what is known about the problem) focuses on those actions that actively contribute to achieving a goal. To get to a grocery store to buy food, for example, one would usually not spend any time contemplating actions like packing a suitcase. It might be perfectly legal to pack a suitcase on a Saturday morning, but we have knowledge from experience that this legal action is not part of an effective plan to achieve the grocery store goal.

Considerations like these suggest that planning should go beyond merely looking for a sequence of legal moves from a start to a goal state. Perhaps the simplest way to accommodate more knowledge into the process is to assume that each planning problem will come with an additional predicate acceptable(a,s) that tells the general planner when a legal action a should be considered in a state s as part of a plan to achieve the current goal. Instead of

```
reachable(S1,[M|L],S3) :- legal_move(S1,M,S2), reachable(S2,L,S3).
```

the general planner would now say

```
reachable(S1,[M|L],S3) :-
        legal_move(S1,M,S2), acceptable(M,S1), reachable(S2,L,S3).
```

It would then be up to the programmer of each individual planning problem to specify which actions are acceptable for the goal in question and which should be filtered. If it so happens that absolutely nothing is known about how to plan for the goal, the clause

```
acceptable(_,_).    % No filter, so anything goes.
```

can be included in the problem specification, and the resulting planning behavior is the same as before.

For the 15-puzzle, imagine that in a current state tiles 1, 2, 3, and 4 are in their correct positions in the first row, and that the empty space is below tile 2 (in position 6). While it is perfectly legal to move tile 2 down next, experience says that this is not a good idea: once the first row is in place, it should not be disturbed. A simple first step toward using this knowledge in planning would be to filter that action in a program for the 15-puzzle, as follows:

```
acceptable(down(X),S) :- \+ row1_done(X,S).
row1_done(X,S) :- member(X,[1,2,3,4]), S=[1,2,3,4|_].
```

This would prevent the program from wasting its time considering plans that disturb the first row once it is in place.

Decomposing a problem

This idea of not disturbing some parts of a goal that have been solved is a general one. Many planning problems have the following property: they are made of subproblems that can be solved *independently* and then combined.

How does this help? Imagine there is a problem that can be solved using twenty-five moves. Assume there are three legal moves at each state; this means that there might be 3^{25}, or about 10^{12}, paths to a goal state.

But suppose that this problem can be broken down into two independent pieces, A and B, where the A part can be solved in ten steps, and the B part can be solved in the remaining fifteen steps. To solve A, there might be as many as 3^{10} paths, and to solve B, 3^{15} paths, so that in total, there might be $(3^{10} + 3^{15})$, or about 10^7, paths to a goal state. But this is much less than 10^{12} paths. Similarly, if the problem can be broken down into five independent pieces, each requiring five steps (for a total of twenty-five), there might be only $5 \cdot 3^5$, or about 10^3, paths. In general, solving a problem that can be broken down into independent subproblems requires dealing with the *sum* of their search spaces, not the *product*, an enormous difference.

Many natural problems have this decomposition structure allowing them to be handled effectively. Consider the 15-puzzle again. The goal of getting all the tiles in

Figure 9.12.   Decomposing the 15-puzzle

1	2	3	4
5	-	-	-
9	-	-	-
13	-	-	-

first goal

6	7	8
10	-	-
14	-	-

second goal

11	12
15	

third goal

place breaks down into independent subgoals, as shown in figure 9.12. The first goal is to get the top row and left column of tiles in place without regard for the placement of any of the others. Once this first goal is achieved, the tiles in the top row and left column are not disturbed, and the second goal can be considered as a 3 × 3 puzzle. The second goal involves getting what is left of the second row and second column in place, again without regard for the other three tiles. Once this second goal is achieved, the third goal, with the remaining three tiles, is handled as a 2 × 2 puzzle. Note that each of the goals can be solved independently, as required. Moreover, the first goal itself can be broken down into two independent goals: getting the first row into place and then getting the remaining three tiles of the first column into place.

* *Problem decomposition in Prolog*

One way to encode this type of problem decomposition in Prolog is to assume that the general planner is given a set of *stages* that it must pass through to solve a problem. If there is no knowledge at all about how to decompose the problem, there would be exactly two stages: an initial one (applying to every state of the problem) and a final one (applying to just the goal states). Other problems would have additional intermediate stages. For example, for the 15-puzzle, the intermediate stages might be one that applies to every state where the first row is in place, another where both the first row and first column are in place, and a third where the first two rows and two columns are in place. Note that these stages are ordered and that each stage applies to all states of the subsequent stages. This guarantees that as the planner passes through each stage, it moves ever closer to the final goal.

A Prolog program that plans in stages is shown in figure 9.13. It uses the predicate `legal_move` and `initial_state` as before. But instead of a predicate for `goal_state`, it expects to see two predicates: `stages`, which provides a list of the names of the

Figure 9.13. A staged planner in Prolog splan.pl

```
% This staged planner needs the predicates below to be defined:
%      - legal_move(BeforeState,Move,AfterState)
%      - initial_state(State)
%      - stages(ListofStages)
%      - goal_stage(Stage,State)
% plan(L): L is a list of moves through a list of goal stages.
plan(L) :- initial_state(I), stages([G|GL]), plan_all(G,I,L,GL).

% plan_all(G,S,L,GL): L passes from G through each stage in GL.
plan_all(_,_,[],[]).
plan_all(G1,S1,L,[G2|GL]) :-
    append(L1,L2,L), reach(G1,S1,L1,G2,S2), plan_all(G2,S2,L2,GL).

% reach(G1,S1,L,G2,S2): L moves from S1 in stage G1 to S2 in G2.
reach(_,S,[],G2,S) :- goal_stage(G2,S).        % S attains stage G2.
reach(G1,S1,[M|L],G2,S3) :-                     % Move from S1 to S2.
    legal_move(S1,M,S2), goal_stage(G1,S2), reach(G1,S2,L,G2,S3).
```

stages that the planner must pass through, and goal_stage(g, s), which holds when the stage named g applies to state s. The 15-puzzle might include these clauses:

```
stages([init,r1,r1c1,r12c12,goal]).
goal_stage(init,_).
goal_stage(r1,[1,2,3,4|_]).
goal_stage(r1c1,[1,2,3,4,5,_,_,_,9,_,_,_,13,_,_,_]).
goal_stage(r12c12,[1,2,3,4,5,6,7,8,9,10,_,_,13,14,_,_]).
goal_stage(goal,[1,2,3,4,5,6,7,8,9,10,11,12,13,14,15,0]).
```

The way the planner works is to (use append to) break the sequence of moves into parts that will proceed from stage to stage until all the stages have been attained and the problem is solved. Whenever it considers a legal move (within the reach predicate), it checks that the current stage applies to the state that results from doing the move. This automatically guarantees that the moves within a stage will not compromise a subgoal that was previously achieved. (This was handled manually using the acceptable predicate.)

* 9.3.2 Best-first search

Once it has been determined that the best one can do is to search for a path from some start state to an end state, there are other ways of searching that can be much more effective than those used so far. One obvious thing to do is to avoid *loops* that

Figure 9.14.   The best-first search procedure

To find a path from an initial state S_0 to a goal state G:

1. Maintain a list of states L to explore, starting with $L = [S_0]$.

2. If L is empty, then return failure.

3. Otherwise, select from L the state S that is *estimated* to be closest to the goal G.

4. If $S = G$, then return *success* (and the saved path to S_0).

5. Otherwise, remove S from L, and add to L all states S' for which there is a legal move from S to S' (and remember the move involved).

6. Go to step 2.

---

produce a sequence of actions that go back from a current state to a start state. (See exercise 8 at the end of this chapter.)

But there are even more radical changes that can be made. Consider how the `reachable` predicate works to find a path from a start state to a goal state. Suppose there are two legal moves from a starting state S, call them S_1 and S_2. Also, there is a short path from S_2 to the goal, but there is no path at all from S_1 to the goal. Here is what happens with `reachable`:

1. Generate the state S_1 using `legal_move`.

2. Recursively look for a path from S_1 to the goal, eventually failing.

3. Backtrack and generate the next state S_2 using `legal_move`.

4. Recursively look for a path from S_2 to the goal, quickly succeeding.

Observe that state S_2 is considered only after all the options from S_1 have been explored. This is called *depth-first search*, since the program looks as deeply as it can for the goal from S_1 before it fails and backtracks to consider S_2. If the search from S_1 is large, this could take a lot of time, even if S_2 is very close to the goal state.

To do better, suppose that for any state, one can *estimate* how far it is from the goal. This allows a new way of searching, called *best-first search*, summarized in figure 9.14. At any given point, this search finds the state estimated to be the closest to the goal and considers legal moves from there. This avoids the problem of searching for the goal for a long time from state S_1 even though state S_2 is very close to the goal.

Of course, for this to work, the programmer must be able to estimate how far a state is from a goal. The estimate does not have to be exact, since it is just a guide to what state should be explored next.

In the case of the 15-puzzle, there is a natural estimate of how far a state is from the goal. In the initial state in figure 9.10, tiles 1 and 3 are in their correct position, but tile 6 has to be moved down one position. Tile 4 has to go up two and right one. The horizontal or vertical distance is known as a *Manhattan distance* (by analogy with the grid of streets in Manhattan). So tile 1 has a Manhattan distance of 0 from its home, tile 6 has a Manhattan distance of 1 from its home, and tile 4 has a Manhattan distance of $2 + 1 = 3$ from its home. In general, one can estimate how far a state is from the goal by summing the Manhattan distances of every tile from its home. So the goal state in figure 9.10 has a distance of 0 from the goal (since every tile is at its home), and the initial state in figure 9.10 has a distance of

$$0 + 1 + 0 + 1 + 2 + 1 + 0 + 3 + 1 + 2 + 3 + 1 + 0 + 1 + 1 = 17$$

from the goal. Note that this estimate has the nice property that it is a *lower bound* on the number of moves required to get to a goal state: at the very least, each tile has to do that number of horizontal or vertical moves to get it to its home. The actual number of moves to get to a goal state will typically be much larger, since the tiles get in each other's way.

9.4 Scaling up: The representation problem

For planning problems like the three small puzzles considered up to now, the method of representing a state worked just fine. A state was represented as a list whose elements were the various aspects of the problem, such as the visible side of a coin, the location of the monkey, or the position of a tile in a rectangular frame. But for more realistic domains, it becomes very awkward to deal with lists that include *all* the relevant aspects of that domain.

For example, imagine a world with 1,000 boxes that can be moved independently. Representing this state requires a list like $[loc_1, loc_2, loc_3, \ldots, loc_{1000}]$. Then 1,000 clauses would be needed to describe the legal_move predicate, one for each box in the list. The clause would change the location of that box and leave the values of all the others unchanged, using 999 Prolog variables.

This is not just a problem with locations. In general, even in domains with many aspects, each action will change only a few of them. Pushing a box under the bananas will change the location of the monkey and the box, but it will *not* affect the location of the bananas, the color of the bananas, any other objects in the room, whether or not doors are open, the temperature in the room, the weather outside, the students enrolled at a nearby university, the price of tea in China, and so on.

What is needed is a representation of the state of the world that is more explicit about what aspects of the world are affected by what actions. The dynamic predicates considered in section 8.3.2 had this desirable property. One could start with single(john) in the knowledge base, for example, then use the predicate get_married(john) in a query, and end up with married(john), quite independently of any other predicates. Unfortunately, dynamic predicates cannot be used as is for planning. They allow changing the state by changing the knowledge base, but they do not yield sentences that talk about the before and after states *simultaneously*, which is what is needed for legal_move.

This section considers a new way to represent the state of the world that is suitable for planning but makes it possible to talk explicitly about changing aspects of the world, like the marital status of John or the location of the box.

9.4.1 Situations and fluents

The purpose of a state in planning is to keep track of the relevant aspects of the world and how these are affected by actions. Instead of representing these aspects in a big list, another approach is to make a list of all the *actions* that have been performed, and then to *calculate* from this list any relevant aspect.

For example, suppose there is a list of all the actions performed in the monkey and bananas world, and one wants to calculate the location of the box from this list. The thinking can go as follows:

- If there is no push action in the list, then the box will be located wherever it was in the initial state.

- If there are push actions in the list, and the *most recent* one performed is push(loc6), then the box will be located at loc6.

So the location of the box is fully determined by a history of all the actions performed, which is called a situation.

A *situation* is an ordered list of actions used to represent a state of the world. The actions will appear in this list most recent ones first. For example,

- [] is the *initial situation*, before any action has been performed;

- [*a*] is the situation after the single action *a* has been performed;

- [b,a,a] is the situation where action *a* was performed twice and then action *b* was performed, *b* being the most recent action.

Note that the situation [a,b] is not the same situation as [b,a]; it might make a difference which action is done first. For example, it is quite different to climb on the box before grabbing the bananas than to grab for the bananas before climbing on the box.

Using Prolog notation, performing action A in situation S (which must be a list of actions) always results in the situation [A|S], since the most recent action is listed at the head of the list.

With this representation of a state, the various relevant aspects in our world are represented as predicates that take a situation as an argument. Such predicates are called *fluents*. (By convention, the situation is the final argument of the fluent.) So instead of using a predicate like location(x,l), a final argument is added to make it location(x,l,s), which is read as "item x is at location l in situation s." Informally, all the following sentences involving this fluent should work out to be true:

- location(box,loc3,[])   (the initial location of the box)

- location(box,loc3,[go(loc3)])

- location(box,loc5,[push(loc5),go(loc3)])

- location(box,loc5,[go(loc1),push(loc5),go(loc3)])

- location(box,loc5,[go(loc7),
                      go(loc1),push(loc5),go(loc3)])

- location(box,loc5,[go(loc5),go(loc7)
                      go(loc1),push(loc5),go(loc3)])

- location(box,loc4,[push(loc4),go(loc5),go(loc7)
                      go(loc1),push(loc5),go(loc3)])

- location(box,loc4,[go(loc2),push(loc4),go(loc5),go(loc7)
                      go(loc1),push(loc5),go(loc3)])

Note how the most recent push action in the situation determines where the box is located (from loc3 to loc5 to loc4). After a push, the location of the box stays where it is as other actions are performed (here, they are all go actions, but they could be anything), until another push changes it again. The job is to write clauses for the location fluent so that all these queries succeed.

Initial and successor state clauses

The easiest way to characterize a fluent in a program is to do it in two steps:

1. State what holds in the initial situation, []. This is writing what are called the *initial state clauses* for the fluent.

2. State what holds in a noninitial situation, [A|S]. This is writing what are called the *successor state clauses* for the fluent. Typically, there are cases involved depending on the action A and according to whether

   a. A makes the fluent true;

   b. A makes the fluent false;

   c. A leaves the fluent unchanged, as it was in situation S.

Here are the three clauses that characterize the location of the box in any situation:

```
location(box,loc3,[]).
location(box,L,[push(L)|_]).
location(box,L,[A|S]) :- \+ A=push(_), location(box,L,S).
```

- The first clause is the initial state clause stating that the box is initially located at loc3. (The remaining clauses are the successor state clauses.)

- The second clause states that if the most recent action in a situation is pushing the box to L, then the location of the box is L, no matter what the previous actions in the situation are. Note that it is not the job of the successor state axiom to ensure that the push is *legal*.

- The third clause states that if the location of the box in a situation S is L, then the location of the box in situation [A|S] (in other words, after doing action A) is also L, provided A is not a push action. Note that this provides a *recursive* definition of location: to calculate the location of the box in situation [A|S], one may need to calculate the location of the box in situation S.

It is not hard to see that these three clauses will allow all the previous location sentences to succeed as queries.

This pattern can be applied to other fluents in the monkey and bananas world. For example, one would want a fluent on_box to indicate whether or not the monkey is on the box. Climbing on the box makes it true; climbing off the box makes it false; all the other actions leave this fluent unchanged. In other words,

```
on_box([climb_on|_]).
on_box([A|S]) :- \+ A=climb_off, on_box(S).
```

The monkey is on the box if it has just climbed on the box or if it was already on it and did not just climb off. To characterize a person as being married or single, the pattern will be exactly the same except that getting married makes being married true, and getting divorced makes it false:

```
married(X,[get_married(X)|_]).
married(X,[A|S]) :- \+ A=get_divorced(X), married(X,S).
```

There might be a fluent that can be made true and then stays true thereafter. For example, there was no action in this world for the monkey to dispose of the bananas after grabbing them. So the following successor state clauses apply:

```
has_bananas([grab|_]).
has_bananas([_|S]) :- has_bananas(S).
```

Once the monkey has performed a grab action, it has the bananas and will continue to have them no matter what action is performed next. Similarly, in this world, the location of the bananas is unaffected by any action:

```
location(bananas,loc1,[]).    % The initial location
location(bananas,L,[_|S]) :- location(bananas,L,S).
```

More concisely, the location of the bananas can be characterized as being the same as the initial location in all situations:

```
location(bananas,loc1,_).
```

The final fluent needed is the location of the monkey. This is just like the location of the box, except that it is affected by both push and go actions:

```
location(monkey,loc2,[]).
location(monkey,L,[push(L)|_]).
location(monkey,L,[go(L)|_]).
location(monkey,L,[A|S]) :-
    \+ A=push(_), \+ A=go(_), location(monkey,L,S).
```

In other words, the monkey is at a location if it just went or pushed the box there, or if it was already there and did not just go or push the box to somewhere else.

Action precondition clauses

The only thing left to do to fully characterize a world in terms of situations and fluents is to state the conditions under which it is possible to perform an action. This was done implicitly in the legal_move predicate, but here it is useful to state these properties separately using a special predicate poss(a,s), which is interpreted as saying that a is a possible action to perform in situation s.

Here are the clauses for poss in the monkey and bananas world:

```
poss(climb_off,S) :- on_box(S).
poss(go(_),S) :- \+ on_box(S).
poss(grab,S) :-
    on_box(S), location(box,L,S), location(bananas,L,S).
poss(push(_),S) :- poss(climb_on,S).
poss(climb_on,S) :-
    \+ on_box(S), location(box,L,S), location(monkey,L,S).
```

Clauses like these are called *action precondition clauses*. Note how they use the fluents to state when it is possible to perform an action. For example, the monkey can climb on the box only when it is located at the same place as the box and is not already on it. A push action is only possible under the same conditions.

This completes the representation of the monkeys and bananas world using situations and fluents.

9.4.2 Planning with situations and fluents

After all the initial state, successor state, and action precondition clauses for some world have been written, the planning can begin. Recall that for the plan (or bplan) predicate, one must provide three problem-specific predicates: initial_state, goal_state, and legal_move. With situations and fluents, this is very easy:

```
initial_state([]).
legal_move(S,A,[A|S]) :- poss(A,S).
goal_state(S) :- has_bananas(S).
```

The initial state is always the same for any problem: it is the initial situation, the empty list. Similarly, the legal_move clause is always the same: one can move from situation S to situation [A|S] for any action A for which poss holds. Only the goal state varies from problem to problem; for the monkey and bananas, it is any situation where the monkey has the bananas.

So if these three clauses are added to the characterization of the monkey and bananas world in terms of situations and fluents, the plan predicate can be used to find the four-step plan as before.

9.4.3 Why is this representation useful?

Representing the monkeys and bananas world using situations and fluents might seem like a lot of effort for very little benefit. There was already a less verbose and quite workable characterization of this world for planning (figure 9.6). So why bother? The answer is that, in general, a representation in terms of situations and fluents has one significant advantage:

> *A representation in terms of situations and fluents allows characterizing part of a world without having to know in advance all the other actions and fluents.*

Consider again the fluent on_box, for example. Once the actions affecting this fluent are identified, one can write the successor state clauses:

```
on_box([climb_on|_]).
on_box([A|S]) :- \+ A=climb_off, on_box(S).
```

Even if it later becomes important to keep track of a new aspect, say, the color of the box, with a new action paint_box that changes the color, the successor state clause for the on_box predicate will not be affected. It continues to work as is.

So a representation in terms of situations and fluents has the advantage of making a very complex state with a large number of properties and actions more manageable.

9.4.4 Other kinds of actions

It is worth noting some of the complications that arise in planning when other kinds of actions are included, such as the following.

Durative actions

So far the planning has been done as if the actions (or moves) under consideration were *instantaneous*, like turning on a light. But some actions, like filling a bathtub, take time. This means that plans with a smaller number of actions may take longer to complete. Among other things, such actions compel us to consider plans where more than one action is performed simultaneously.

Exogenous actions

In the real world, the actions that one person takes are not the only things that change the state of the world. Other agents can be performing actions completely outside of an individual's control, and natural processes like the weather can unfold without anybody doing anything. Finding a plan to achieve a goal becomes much more challenging in the presence of such exogenous actions by other agents.

Sensing actions

Ordinary actions (the kind considered so far) change the state of the world. But sensing actions, such as reading a thermometer or listening to a message, are not used to change the world but to change what is *known* about the world. In many cases of planning, information is available to achieve the goal, but that information only becomes available via sensing actions after execution of the plan has begun.

Want to read more?

This chapter was about planning, a form of thinking that is fundamental to intelligent behavior. The first research paper that can be clearly said to be about artificial intelligence deals with this topic [47]. This seminal paper by John McCarthy (parts of which date back to 1958) discusses reasoning about how to achieve goals using actions, and introduces the monkey and bananas problem. It also presents for the first time a representation based on situations and fluents.

Since the time of McCarthy's paper, researchers in the area of AI planning have sought to expand the boundaries of what could be effectively handled by automated planning. Part of this involved using *less expressive* representation formalisms that appear to have better computational properties. But some of the research involved using *more expressive* representations to capture a wider range of planning problems. The state of the art of this research is well covered in a graduate-level textbook by Ghallab, Nau, and Traverso [45]. The idea of using knowledge to filter the actions considered at each step of the planning process is explored in a technical paper by Bacchus and Kabanza [44].

While planning clearly plays an important role in our own intelligent behavior, it seems implausible to imagine that we would constantly be planning from first principles each time we need to act. So the question concerning what exactly a thinking agent in a dynamic environment should be thinking about is what is studied in the area of *cognitive robotics* [46]. Planning is involved, no doubt, but thinking about action and change clearly needs to go beyond this, as discussed in the outstanding (but technically demanding) book by Reiter [48].

The problem of how to think in general about what is and is not affected by an action in a complex setting is called the *frame problem*. The solution outlined here (in terms of successor-state clauses and the like) is due to Reiter [48].

Exercises

1. The version of the monkey and bananas problem in section 9.2.4 did not consider what happened *after* the monkey grabbed the bananas. Imagine that there is a very clever monkey who wants to trick the scientists studying him (while they are out having coffee) by obtaining the bananas as before, but then restoring everything else as it was, so that it looks like the box has not even been touched.

   Suppose you want to use the `plan` predicate to solve this new version of the problem. The states and operators will be exactly the same as before. The initial state will also be the same, but some of the definitions of legal moves will have to change. In particular, if the monkey has the bananas and goes somewhere, the location of the bananas should change as well.

   a. What is the new goal state?

   b. Explain why the `legal_move` clauses for `climb_on`, `climb_off`, and `grab` do not need to be changed from those in section 9.2.4.

   c. Write a clause for the `legal_move` predicate for the go action for those initial states where the monkey does *not* have the bananas.

   d. Write a clause for the `legal_move` predicate for the go action for those initial states where the monkey has the bananas.

   e. Repeat the exercise for the push action (two clauses required).

   f. Use the `plan` predicate to find a solution. How many steps are now needed to solve the problem?

2. Suppose the `plan` predicate from figure 9.3 had been defined by

   ```
   plan(L) :- initial_state(I), reachable(I,L,G), goal_state(G).
   ```

   Are there planning problems where this might work better than the previous version? Are there problems where it might do worse?

3. Consider a more ambitious version of the monkey and bananas problem. In this version, the monkey cannot reach the bananas even if he is on the box. However, there is a big stick located in a corner of the room that can be used to knock the bananas down when the monkey has the stick and is on the box under the bananas. The monkey can pick up or drop the stick, and can climb on the box while holding the stick. But the stick is bulky, and he can only push the box if he is not carrying the stick.

In this variant, a state can be represented using a list $[b,m,l,o,h,s,c]$, which has two more components than the list in section 9.2.4: s stands for the current location of the stick, and c is y or n according to whether or not the monkey is carrying the stick. The actions available are climb_on, climb_off, go(x), and push(x), as before, and three new actions involving the stick: pick_up_stick, drop_stick, and swing_stick. (The grab action is omitted, since it no longer accomplishes anything.)

Formulate this version of the problem in Prolog and use the plan predicate to find a seven-step sequence of actions the monkey can do to get the bananas. You will need to write clauses for the initial state and goal state, as well as legal_move clauses for each of the actions. For the first four actions, you can adapt the solution presented in section 9.2.4, but note that you now have to worry about the state of the stick. For example, going to a location changes the location of the stick if the monkey happens to be carrying it.

4. Consider the following well-known problem:

   In his yard, a farmer has a fox, a hen, and a bushel of grain. The farmer must transfer all these things to a stall at the market, using only a cart which can carry at most one of them (plus himself) at a time. The problem is that if the farmer leaves the fox unattended with the hen, it will eat the hen. Similarly, if the hen is left unattended with the grain, it will eat the grain.

   Is there a way for the farmer (without helpers) to transfer all three items to market without any of them getting eaten?

   Use Prolog to solve this as a planning problem using the plan predicate. A state can be represented by a list with four elements, [*fox, hen, grain, cart*], where each of these elements is a location: either yard or market. (Assume that the farmer is always with the cart.) A move is either go_alone(loc) or go_with$(item, loc)$ where *loc* is a location and *item* is one of fox, hen, or grain. A move should not be legal if something will get eaten in the resulting state.

   a. Define a predicate safe_state(s) that holds whenever s is a state where nothing will be eaten. So [yard,yard,market,yard] is considered to be a safe state, but [yard,market,market,yard] is not because the hen is with the grain unattended.

   b. Define the predicate legal_move using the safe_state predicate.

   c. Define initial_state and goal_state, and use the plan predicate to find a seven-step solution.

Figure 9.15. A planning problem with blocks

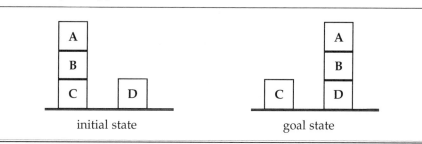

initial state   goal state

5. Consider the `reachable` predicate defined in figure 9.3. Suppose the second clause had been this:

```
reachable(S1,[M|L],S3) :-
    reachable(S2,L,S3), legal_move(S1,M,S2).
```

Are there problems where this might work better than the previous version? Are there problems where it might do worse?

6. The `bplan` predicate presented in figure 9.8 can run forever, looking for longer and longer plans, if it happens that there is no way to achieve the goal. Modify the predicate so that it takes an extra argument *n* and will eventually stop with failure if there is no plan of length *n* or less.

7. This exercise returns to a blocks world similar to the one shown in figure 8.16.

Imagine that there is a group of blocks (cubes, for simplicity) arranged in some configuration on a table in front of a robot, and you would like the robot to rearrange them without having to tell it how to do so. Assume that there is a single type of action, *moving a block to a location*, where a location is either an area on the table or on top of another block. This action can only be performed by the robot if there is nothing on the blocks and nothing at the desired location.

For the example problem shown in figure 9.15, an acceptable plan is this: move block A to area 5 (on the table), move block B onto block D, and move block A onto block B.

Use situations and fluents as the representation of the states in this blocks world. For example, after performing the actions in this plan, the final situation would be [move(a,b),move(b,d),move(a,area5)]. You will only need to use one fluent, located_on(*b,l,s*), which should hold when block *b* is at location *l* in situation *s*.

a. Write the initial state clauses for the fluent located_on for the initial situation in figure 9.15. (As you test your program with different initial situations, you will need to vary these clauses.)

b. Write the successor state clauses for the fluent located_on. You need to decide for each action a how located_on$(b, l, [a|s])$ depends on a and what holds in situation s. Show that your located_on works properly by testing it on a variety of situations.

c. Write a clause for the goal state in figure 9.15. (As you test your program with different goals, you will need to vary this clause.)

d. Define the poss predicate for your move action, using located_on.

e. Show that the planning problem in figure 9.15 can be solved with plan.

f. Show that your program works on other small problems of your choosing.

8. As noted in section 9.3.2, the reachable predicate defined in figure 9.3 allows for *loops*, where a sequence of moves passes through a state and later returns to exactly the same state. For example, in the monkey and bananas problem where the monkey starts at location 2, a sequence of go moves that ends with go(loc2) returns the monkey to the initial state. The presence of such loops can only slow down the process of searching for a reachable goal state.

Write clauses to define a new predicate reachable_uniq(s, l, s') that is just like reachable except that the moves in l do not pass through the same state twice.

Hint: Define an auxiliary predicate reachable_list(s, l, x, s') that holds when l is a list $[m_1, \ldots, m_n]$ of n moves (as before), and x is a list of $n + 1$ states in reverse order $[s_n, \ldots, s_0]$ with no repetitions, such that $s = s_0$, $s' = s_n$, and for every i from 1 to n, there is a legal move m_i from state s_{i-1} to state s_i.

9. Consider the following, called the jealous husband problem:

> Three married couples find themselves on one bank of a river wanting to get to the other side using a boat that can only hold two people at a time. However, each husband insists on being with his wife whenever there are other men present.

The shortest solution involves eleven boat crossings, too many to solve comfortably using the reachable predicate. Use reachable_uniq from exercise 8 to solve it. (Not to take this example too seriously or anything, but we might prefer a solution where the jealous husbands all end up on one side of the river without a boat, and the women have all gone off to find better husbands!)

10   Case Study: Playing Strategic Games

One of the main complications that can arise in planning is that *other agents* may be performing actions at the same time as you are, which can interfere with what you are doing. In a sense, this is what is involved in playing a game like chess. The object of the game is simple enough, to capture the other player's king. But a plan to achieve that goal cannot be a *sequence of moves* like the plans in chapter 9. Instead, each time you make a move, your opponent gets a turn to play and will make a move to try to stop you from attaining your goal. You must then decide what to do next, and the process iterates. Ideally, you will figure out a strategy that will eventually lead to your goal no matter what your opponent does along the way. The thinking that is required to do this is the subject matter of this chapter.

Why should we care about games like this? The answer is that playing a strategic game like chess is considered to be a major intellectual challenge. We are awed by the prodigies who can play well at an early age, and we see chess champions as demonstrating remarkable prowess—not physical but mental prowess: clear, unadulterated thinking at its very finest.

Of course, this chapter is not about chess itself but about playing games in general. The ideas explored here apply to a wide variety of games, although not to everything that is called a game. The focus in this chapter is on games with the following characteristics:

- Discrete-move and turn-taking. This excludes games where the players are continuously moving at the same time, such as physical games, and many first-person video games.

- Deterministic. This excludes games where chance is involved, such as Monopoly or backgammon.

- Two-person. This excludes solitaire and multiplayer games like Clue.

- Perfect-information. This excludes games where part of the state of the game is hidden from the other player, as in Scrabble or Battleship.

Figure 10.1.   A problem in tic-tac-toe

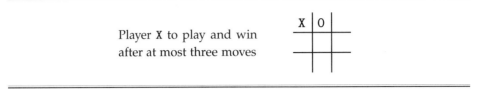

Player **X** to play and win
after at most three moves

- Zero-sum. This means that the players in the game are always in complete opposition: what is good for one player is bad for the other, and vice versa. This is total war!

Chess and checkers both fit this description, and so do much simpler games like Othello (Reversi) and tic-tac-toe.

This chapter has three sections. The first section explores how game problems of this sort are similar to, and different from, the planning problems of chapter 9, and how the rules of a game can be encoded in Prolog. The second section develops a general game player in Prolog, analogous to the general planning program of chapter 9. The third section considers how the thinking has to adapt for more complex games like chess.

10.1   Games as problems

To see how playing a game is related to planning, consider the problem posed in figure 10.1 for the well-known game of tic-tac-toe. Here is an example of *faulty reasoning* applied to this problem:

> Player **X** can move to position 9 (bottom left). At this point, player 0 can move to position 3 (top right), after which player **X** can move to position 5 (center), thereby winning the game.

The reason this is faulty is clear. After player **X** moves to position 9, player 0 is free to make any legal move. If instead of going to position 3, player 0 chooses to move to position 5, then player **X** is no longer guaranteed a win. Instead, the game would probably end in a tie. (Section 10.2.4 looks at the thinking behind tic-tac-toe in detail.)

10.1.1   How a game can be defined

It is the fact that one player does not control the moves of the other player that makes games different from planning. Nonetheless, there are some clear similarities. A game (whether very complex like chess or very simple like tic-tac-toe) can be characterized by the following:

- There are two *players*. One of them moves first.

- There is a space of *states* in the game. One of them is the *initial state* of the game. There is also a *final state* of the game, where the game is over and one of the two players is the winner (or there is a tie).

- In any state that is not a final state of the game, there is a set of *legal moves*, that go from one game state to another. Throughout the game, players take turns choosing a move that is legal in the current state.

For any given game, the *rules of the game* characterize it in these terms. Note that the rules of the game always tell how to play the game, but they do not tell how to play it *well* (see section 10.2).

In the previous chapter, three predicates were used to characterize any planning problem in Prolog: `initial_state`, `goal_state`, and `legal_move`. It will be similar for games except that there are four predicates:

- `player`(*player*). This says that *player* is one of the two players in the game.

- `initial_state`(*state, player*). This says that the game starts in *state* and that *player* moves first.

- `game_over`(*state, player, winner*). This says that when it is the turn of *player* in *state*, then the game is over and *winner* wins. The *winner* is either one of the two players, or the special constant `neither` when there is a tie.

- `legal_move`(*state₁, player, move, state₂*). This says that when it is the turn of *player* in *state₁*, then *move* is legal and the game goes to *state₂*, where it will be the turn of the other player.

These four predicates are used to define each of the games considered in this chapter.

10.1.2   A first example: Race to 21

Race to 21 is an even simpler game than tic-tac-toe:

There are 21 chips on a table. Players take turns removing either one or two chips. The player removing the last chip wins.

Figure 10.2.   A Prolog program for Race to 21   raceto21.pl

```
% This is the Prolog definition of the game Race to 21.
player(max).  player(min).       % The two players.
initial_state(21,max).           % Player Max goes first.
game_over(0,max,min).            % If it is Max's turn to play,
game_over(0,min,max).            % then Min wins, and vice versa.
legal_move(OldState,_,Move,NewState) :-
    small_number(Move),          % A move is a small number.
    OldState >= Move,
    NewState is OldState - Move.
small_number(1).                 % A small number is either
small_number(2).                 % the number 1 or 2.
```

To characterize this game using the four predicates, the programmer has to decide how to represent the *states* and the *moves*, just as was done for planning.

A state in this game is a number between 0 and 21, representing how many chips are left on the table:

- The initial state is 21.

- The final state is 0. The player whose turn it is to move loses. (In Race to 21, there is never a tie.)

A move in Race to 21 is a number, either 1 or 2. A move is legal provided there are at least that many chips remaining on the table. (A player cannot remove two chips in a state where there is only one chip remaining.) The new state after making a move is the *difference* between the current state and the move. As shown in figure 10.2, this can be encoded directly in a Prolog program, for two players called Max and Min, where Max plays first. (See section 10.3.1 for the reason the players have the names Max and Min.) This defines the game and how it is played according to the rules.

The next section turns to the issue of playing games well.

10.2   Finding the best move

To see how to play a game well, no matter what game it is, observe the following:

- A player will not need to find a list of moves from an initial to a final state. The player must find the *best next move*, wait for the opponent to make a move, then find the best next move again, and so on, until the game is over.

- The best next move for a player must take into account the *responses* available to the opponent. The responses from the opponent will also take into account the possible counterresponses from the player, which should take into account the possible counter-counterresponses, and so on.

- The best next move for a player should not rely on the opponent's making a *mistake*. If an opponent plays poorly, so much the better. Ideally, however, a player will find a move that is a first step toward winning even when the opponent is playing at her very best.

10.2.1 Game trees

To see how players can take into account all the possible responses, the counterresponses and so on, it is useful to look at a structure called a *game tree*, whose nodes correspond to states of the game:

- The root node of the tree (usually at the top) is the initial state of the game.

- Each leaf node of the tree (usually at the bottom) is a final state of the game, where according to the rules, one of the players has won or there is a tie.

- Each non-leaf node has as children (below it) all the game states that can be reached by making legal moves according to the rules.

Figure 10.3 shows a game tree for an anonymous game between two players, Max and Min. In this game, in the initial state (level 0), Max has two moves available to him (move 1 and move 2). In the two states to which these moves lead at level 1, Min has three legal moves available to her, leading to six states at level 2. From there, Max has either two or three moves available to him, which either lead to the game's being over at level 3, or Min's moving one final time from level 3 to level 4. The tree depicts all possible unfoldings of this game, ending with final states where either Max wins (labeled W) or Min wins (labeled L). The tree does not display what the states or the moves of the game are. Nonetheless, the rules of the game determine the entire structure of this game tree, from the start to the end.

The main observation is that just by looking at how the game unfolds according to the tree, one can determine whether Max should choose move 1 or move 2 as his first move. To figure this out, every node on the tree is *labeled* as either a winning position for Max (W) or a winning position for Min (L).

Figure 10.3.   An example game tree

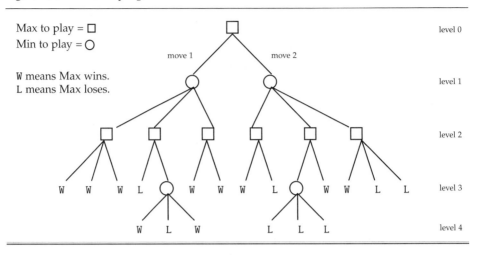

Max to play = □
Min to play = ○

W means Max wins.
L means Max loses.

level 0

move 1   move 2

level 1

level 2

W W W L   W W W L   W W L L   level 3

W L W   L L L   level 4

Starting from the very bottom of the tree, the labeling proceeds as follows:

- If it is Max's turn to play at a node,
  - the node is labeled W (Max wins) if there is at least one move from there to a state labeled W;
  - the node is labeled L (Min wins) if every move is to a state labeled L.
- If it is Min's turn to play at a node,
  - the node is labeled L (Min wins) if there is at least one move from there to a state labeled L;
  - the node is labeled W (Max wins) if every move is to a state labeled W.

The intuition here is that if it is Max's turn to play, and he has a move that takes him to a state where he wins, then this is a *winning state* even if there are many other moves that would take him to a loss.

For example, consider the rightmost node at level 2 in figure 10.3, where it is Max's turn to play. In this state, Max has three legal moves available to him: one leading to a win and two leading to a loss. Max can therefore win from this state by choosing the leftmost node, and so this state (at level 2) is labeled W.

The reasoning for Min is analogous. Consider the left node at level 3 in figure 10.3, where it is Min's turn to play. She has three legal moves available, two leading to Max's winning and the middle one leading to her winning. This node is labeled

Figure 10.4. A labeled game tree

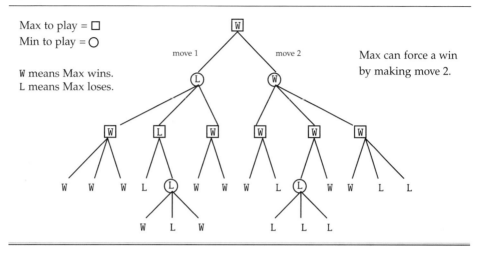

L, since by choosing the middle option, Min can guarantee a win. At one level up (level 2), Max has two choices, which are now both labeled L. So Max has no winning move, and this node is labeled L.

Continuing in this way from the bottom up leads to the labeling shown in figure 10.4. Then two things become clear:

- The initial state is a winning state for Max.

- The best move for Max to make is move 2, which can lead to a win no matter what Min does (and despite all the L labels on the leaves).

So as with planning, the game player can decide on a good first move if the search is carried ahead all the way to the goal. But unlike with planning, it is not sufficient to find a single path to the goal; all the possible responses and counterresponses must be considered all the way to the end.

10.2.2 A general game player

This process on one example game tree can be generalized to deal with any game, including games with ties. Here is how to label a node for state S in a game between two players P and Q, assuming it is P's turn to play, as being either a winning position for P, a winning position for Q, or `neither`:

Figure 10.5.   A general game player   gameplayer.pl

```
% This general game player needs these predicates to be defined:
%     - player(Player)
%     - game_over(State,Player,Winner)
%     - legal_move(BeforeState,Player,Move,AfterState)

% label(S,P,W): state S with player P to move is labeled winner W.
label(S,P,W) :- game_over(S,P,W).
label(S,P,P) :- win_move(S,P,_).
label(S,P,neither) :- \+ win_move(S,P,_), tie_move(S,P,_).
label(S,P,Q) :- opp(P,Q), \+ tie_move(S,P,_), \+ game_over(S,P,_).

% win_move(S,P,M):  P can win by making move M.
win_move(S,P,M) :- \+ game_over(S,P,_), opp(P,Q),
   legal_move(S,P,M,New), label(New,Q,P).

% tie_move(S,P,M):  P can avoid losing by making move M.
tie_move(S,P,M) :- \+ game_over(S,P,_), opp(P,Q),
   legal_move(S,P,M,New), \+ label(New,Q,Q).

opp(P,Q) :- player(P), player(Q), \+ P=Q.
```

1. If the game is over in state S, then label the node with the winner (P, Q, or neither) according to the rules of the game.

2. Otherwise, label the node with P as the winner if there is a legal move from S to a state S' where S' is labeled with P as the winner. This move is called a *winning move* for P in game state S.

3. Otherwise, label the node with neither as the winner if there is a legal move from S to a state S' where S' is not labeled with Q as the winner. This move is called a *nonlosing move* for P in game state S.

4. Otherwise, label the node with Q as the winner.

Except for condition 3 (having to do with ties), this summarizes what was done in the tree for Max and Min in figure 10.4. Regarding a tie, a node is labeled with neither when a player has no winning move but has a move to a state that is not labeled with the opponent's winning.

These principles can be encoded in a Prolog program, shown in figure 10.5. This defines a *general* game player. As with planning, for each specific game, a programmer will need to provide clauses that define the player, game_over, and legal_move predicates for that game. (The initial_state predicate is not used here.) Once these are provided, the predicate win_move can be used to see if there is a winning move from a state; and tie_move, to see if there is a move that avoids losing.

10.2.3 Playing Race to 21

To see how the general game-playing program works with a specific game like Race to 21, load both programs into Prolog. To understand how winning moves are found, it is best to start by looking at states very near to the end of a game. For example, in Race to 21, it is clear that if there are only one or two chips left, then the player whose turn it is to play has a winning move:

```
?- win_move(1,_,M).
M = 1

?- win_move(2,_,M).
M = 2
```

Here the move leads directly to a final state where the player is the winner (because there are no chips left). It is also evident that if there are three chips left, then there is no winning move:

```
?- win_move(3,_,M).
No
```

This is because after any legal move, the game is in a state that is a winner for the opponent. So 3 is a not winning position for the player who has to play. If there are four or five chips left, then there *is* a winning move:

```
?- win_move(5,_,M).
M = 2

?- win_move(4,_,M).
M = 1
```

The reason that 2 is a winning move for a player with five chips left is that $5 - 2 = 3$ is not a winning position for the opponent. The case with four chips is similar. What about six chips?

```
?- win_move(6,max,M).
No
```

The reason Max does not win with six chips is the following. If he takes one chip, then there are five left for Min, and this would be a winning position (for Min); if he takes two chips, then there would be four chips left, and this, too, wins for Min. So there is nothing Max can do with six chips to guarantee a win.

Similar reasoning would show that 9 is also not a winning position, nor is 12 or 15. In general, for Race to 21, a player cannot guarantee a win if the number of chips left is divisible by 3. In particular, at the start of the game, Max, who moves first, cannot guarantee a win:

```
?- win_move(21,max,M).
No
```

Once Max moves, by taking either one or two chips, Min will be able to make a winning move by leaving Max with eighteen chips, that number being divisible by 3:

```
?- win_move(20,min,M).
M = 2

?- win_move(19,min,M).
M = 1
```

So the behavior of win_move makes clear that if Min plays perfectly, Max will lose. Observe that this strategy of keeping the number of chips available to the opponent divisible by 3 is not programmed anywhere. It emerges out of looking at the entire game tree and labeling each of the nodes.

10.2.4 A second example: Tic-tac-toe

In some way tic-tac-toe is simpler than Race to 21, and playing it well is a challenge only for very young players. But there are some interesting complications, including the possibility of a tie.

The first decision in writing a tic-tac-toe program is how to represent the states and moves. A state of the 3×3 board in tic-tac-toe is determined by the markers in each of the nine possible positions. So a state can be represented by a list with nine elements, $[p_1, p_2, p_3, p_4, p_5, p_6, p_7, p_8, p_9]$, where each p_i is x or o or another character indicating blank, here a hyphen - (not to be confused the Prolog underscore, _). So the initial state of a tic-tac-toe game is represented by the list [-,-,-,-,-,-,-,-,-], where all the positions are vacant. The game is over in any state where one of the following conditions holds:

- There are three x marks making a straight line (x wins).

- There are three o marks making a straight line (o wins).

- Every p_i in the state is either x or o (the board is full).

A move in tic-tac-toe involves a player's putting a mark in one of the vacant positions. So a move is represented by a number m such that $1 \leq m \leq 9$, with the proviso that in the current state, $p_m = $ -.

Figure 10.6. A Prolog program for tic-tac-toe   `tictactoe.pl`

```
player(x). player(o).                    % This is the tic-tac-toe game.
initial_state([-,-,-,-,-,-,-,-,-],x).              % x moves first.
game_over(S,_,Q) :- three_in_row(S,Q).         % A winner
game_over(S,_,neither) :- \+ legal_move(S,_,_,_).  % A tie
three_in_row([P,P,P,_,_,_,_,_,_],P) :- player(P).
three_in_row([_,_,_,P,P,P,_,_,_],P) :- player(P).
three_in_row([_,_,_,_,_,_,P,P,P],P) :- player(P).
three_in_row([P,_,_,P,_,_,P,_,_],P) :- player(P).
three_in_row([_,P,_,_,P,_,_,P,_],P) :- player(P).
three_in_row([_,_,P,_,_,P,_,_,P],P) :- player(P).
three_in_row([P,_,_,_,P,_,_,_,P],P) :- player(P).
three_in_row([_,_,P,_,P,_,P,_,_],P) :- player(P).
legal_move([-,B,C,D,E,F,G,H,I],P,1,[P,B,C,D,E,F,G,H,I]).
legal_move([A,-,C,D,E,F,G,H,I],P,2,[A,P,C,D,E,F,G,H,I]).
legal_move([A,B,-,D,E,F,G,H,I],P,3,[A,B,P,D,E,F,G,H,I]).
legal_move([A,B,C,-,E,F,G,H,I],P,4,[A,B,C,P,E,F,G,H,I]).
legal_move([A,B,C,D,-,F,G,H,I],P,5,[A,B,C,D,P,F,G,H,I]).
legal_move([A,B,C,D,E,-,G,H,I],P,6,[A,B,C,D,E,P,G,H,I]).
legal_move([A,B,C,D,E,F,-,H,I],P,7,[A,B,C,D,E,F,P,H,I]).
legal_move([A,B,C,D,E,F,G,-,I],P,8,[A,B,C,D,E,F,G,P,I]).
legal_move([A,B,C,D,E,F,G,H,-],P,9,[A,B,C,D,E,F,G,H,P]).
```

A Prolog program for tic-tac-toe is shown in figure 10.6. As before, the predicates `player`, `initial_state`, `game_over`, and `legal_move` are defined. The predicate `three_in_row` is used to check if a player's mark (either `x` or `o`) completes one of the three horizontal lines, three vertical lines, or two diagonal lines (and hence the eight clauses). The `legal_move` predicate has nine clauses, one for each of the possible moves. In each case, it confirms that there is a `-` in the appropriate position for the move and replaces the `-` by the player's mark in the new state, using variables to leave all the other eight positions unchanged.

If this program is loaded with the general game player, it can show how to make a good move in various states of the game. For example, suppose X first put his mark in position 1, and then 0 put hers in position 2. The options X now has are the following:

```
?- win_move([x,o,-,-,-,-,-,-,-],x,M).
M = 4 ;                   % A surprising move for X, perhaps
M = 5 ;                   % The center
M = 7 ;                   % A corner but not 3 or 9
No
```

Among other things, this shows that player X can choose to move to position 4 and still be guaranteed a win.

Let us step back one move from this state to see what player 0 should have done differently when X had a single mark on the board:

```
?- win_move([x,-,-,-,-,-,-,-,-],o,M).
No

?- tie_move([x,-,-,-,-,-,-,-,-],o,M).
M = 5  ;
No
```

There is nothing 0 can do to guarantee a win after X chooses position 1. However, there is a move (and only one move) that will be sufficient to ensure that she does not lose, and that is the center square, position 5.

What X should do in the initial state:

```
?- win_move([-,-,-,-,-,-,-,-,-],x,M).
No

?- tie_move([-,-,-,-,-,-,-,-,-],x,M).
M = 1  ;      M = 2  ;      M = 3  ;      M = 4  ;      M = 5  ;
M = 6  ;      M = 7  ;      M = 8  ;      M = 9
```

As we might already know from actually playing tic-tac-toe, there is nothing that the first player can do to guarantee a win at the outset. Not so well known is the fact that *any* first move is as good as any other in terms of making sure that the player does not lose. So even with a game as simple as tic-tac-toe, there are perhaps some surprises that can be revealed by the game-playing program.

∗ 10.2.5 Playing an entire game

Although this adds nothing to the *thinking* behind game playing, it is fun to play an entire game from the initial state to a final state rather than just making a single next best move. A Prolog program that does this is shown in figure 10.7.

This program will work with the general game player and any game. The main predicate here is play_user, and its argument is used to indicate which of the two players in the game will be played by the *user* (that is, will not be played by the computer). So for tic-tac-toe, the query play_user(x) would play a game where the user is player X (plays first), and play_user(nobody) would play a game where the computer plays both sides.

Figure 10.7. Playing an entire game `playuser.pl`

```
% play_user(U): play entire game, getting moves for U from terminal.
play_user(U) :-
    initial_state(S,P), write('The first player is '), write(P),
    write(' and the initial state is '), write_state(S),
    play_from(S,P,U).

% play_from(S,P,U): player P plays from state S with user U.
play_from(S,P,_) :-                        % Is the game over?
    game_over(S,P,W), write('-------- The winner is '), write(W).
play_from(S,P,U) :-                        % Continue with next move.
    opp(P,Q), get_move(S,P,M,U), legal_move(S,P,M,New),
    write('Player '), write(P), write(' chooses move '), write(M),
    write(' and the new state is '), write_state(New),
    play_from(New,Q,U).

write_state(S) :- nl, write('    '), write(S), nl.

% Get the next move either from the user or from gameplayer.pl.
get_move(S,P,M,U) :- \+ P=U, win_move(S,P,M).     % Try to win.
get_move(S,P,M,U) :- \+ P=U, tie_move(S,P,M).     % Try to tie.
get_move(S,P,M,U) :- \+ P=U, legal_move(S,P,M,_). % Do anything.
get_move(_,P,M,P) :-
    write('Enter user move (then a period): '), read(M).
```

Apart from printing various pieces of information, the way this program works is that starting in the initial state, it uses `play_from` to obtain a next move, check that it is legal, move to the next state, and repeat until the game is over.

The `get_move` predicate is used to obtain the next move. In the case where the player is not the user (clauses 1, 2, and 3), this is done by first trying to find a winning move, then failing this, a nonlosing move, and then failing this, returning any legal move (and hoping for a mistake from the opponent).

The last clause for `get_move` handles the case when the next move needs to come from the user. A message is printed requesting a move, and a special Prolog predicate called `read` is used to obtain the move. (The details of `read` are not important here. Basically, it is the opposite of `write`: instead of producing output at the terminal, it consumes input provided at the terminal.)

An example of using `play_user` with tic-tac-toe appears in figure 10.8. In this case, the computer plays both X and 0. Not too surprisingly, although both players play perfectly, the game ends in a tie. Since `play_user` always returns the *first* move it finds, it will always play the same way. (To get some variation, one would need to *randomly* choose among the equally good moves.)

Figure 10.8.   An entire game of tic-tac-toe

```
?- play_user(nobody).
The first player is x and the initial state is
    [-, -, -, -, -, -, -, -, -]
Player x chooses move 1 and the new state is
    [x, -, -, -, -, -, -, -, -]
Player o chooses move 5 and the new state is
    [x, -, -, -, o, -, -, -, -]
Player x chooses move 2 and the new state is
    [x, x, -, -, o, -, -, -, -]
Player o chooses move 3 and the new state is
    [x, x, o, -, o, -, -, -, -]
Player x chooses move 7 and the new state is
    [x, x, o, -, o, -, x, -, -]
Player o chooses move 4 and the new state is
    [x, x, o, o, o, -, x, -, -]
Player x chooses move 6 and the new state is
    [x, x, o, o, o, x, x, -, -]
Player o chooses move 8 and the new state is
    [x, x, o, o, o, x, x, o, -]
Player x chooses move 9 and the new state is
    [x, x, o, o, o, x, x, o, x]
-------- The winner is neither
Yes
```

A more interesting run appears in figure 10.9 where the user is player 0. The first move player 0 makes here (by typing a 2 and then a period) is not a good one. The computer (playing **X**) immediately capitalizes on it and ends up winning.

∗ 10.2.6   A third example: Boxes

Let us now turn attention to a more challenging game. The game is called Boxes and its rules appear in figure 10.10. Figure 10.11 shows the first few moves of a typical Boxes game, starting at the top left. Max (moving first) chooses the rightmost vertical line, then Min chooses a vertical line beside it, then Max chooses an adjacent horizontal line, then Min chooses a connecting horizontal line, and then in the move depicted at the bottom left, Max chooses a horizontal line that completes the top right square. At this point, Max owns that square (and writes his name in it) and in the same move exercises his option to draw a second line, the bottom horizontal. The game would then continue with Min from there.

Figure 10.9. A game of tic-tac-toe with user input

```
?- play_user(o).
The first player is x and the initial state is
    [-, -, -, -, -, -, -, -, -]
Player x chooses move 1 and the new state is
    [x, -, -, -, -, -, -, -, -]
Enter user move (then a period): 2.      % A bad move entered.
Player o chooses move 2 and the new state is
    [x, o, -, -, -, -, -, -, -]
Player x chooses move 4 and the new state is
    [x, o, -, x, -, -, -, -, -]
Enter user move (then a period): 7.      % This is just fine.
Player o chooses move 7 and the new state is
    [x, o, -, x, -, -, o, -, -]
Player x chooses move 5 and the new state is
    [x, o, -, x, x, -, o, -, -]
Enter user move (then a period): 6.      % This is fine, too.
Player o chooses move 6 and the new state is
    [x, o, -, x, x, o, o, -, -]
Player x chooses move 9 and the new state is
    [x, o, -, x, x, o, o, -, x]
-------- The winner is x                 % But X still wins.
Yes
```

Figure 10.10. The game of Boxes

There are eight dots aligned as in the diagram, making the outline of three squares. At each turn, a player draws one of the undrawn horizontal or vertical edges of a square by connecting two adjacent dots. If this happens to be the last undrawn edge of a square, the player owns the square, and may optionally move again.

The first player to own two squares wins.
(There are no ties.)

Encoding the rules of this game in Prolog starts by deciding how to represent the states and moves. The lines and squares can be named as shown in figure 10.12. Each move will be a *list* of one or more lines drawn. (A list is needed here, since a player may draw multiple lines in a single move.)

Figure 10.11. The start of a game of Boxes

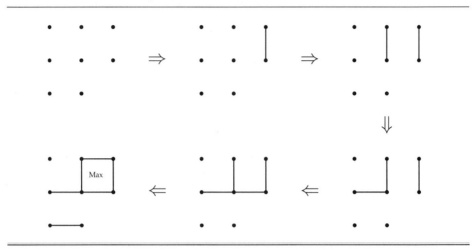

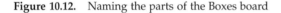

Figure 10.12. Naming the parts of the Boxes board

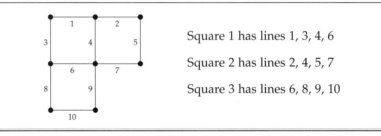

Square 1 has lines 1, 3, 4, 6

Square 2 has lines 2, 4, 5, 7

Square 3 has lines 6, 8, 9, 10

As for the states of Boxes, perhaps the simplest thing to do is to think in terms of situations and fluents (see section 9.4.1). A state will be a list of terms of the form draw(*player*, *line*), with the most recent drawings first. This allows calculating all the fluents that are needed to decide if a move is legal and when the game is over.

The full specification of the Boxes game in Prolog appears in figure 10.13. To summarize briefly how it works, the game is over if a player owns two squares. The successor state clauses for owns say that a player owns a square in a situation if either the player just drew a line that is the last available line for that square or the player already owned that square in the previous situation. The predicate last_available_line says that a line is the last one for a square in a situation if it is available, and nothing is available for that square once the line is drawn. The

Figure 10.13. A Prolog program for Boxes   `boxes.pl`

```
player(max).    player(min).            % This is the Boxes game.
square_lines(sq1,[1,3,4,6]).            % Lines for square 1
square_lines(sq2,[2,4,5,7]).            % Lines for square 2
square_lines(sq3,[6,8,9,10]).           % Lines for square 3
initial_state([],max).                  % Initially no lines are drawn.
game_over(St,_,W) :-                     % Winner W owns two squares.
   owns(W,Sq1,St), owns(W,Sq2,St), \+ Sq1 = Sq2.
% Player P owns Sq if just drew last line or owned Sq before.
owns(P,Sq,[draw(P,L)|St]) :- last_avail_line(L,Sq,St).
owns(P,Sq,[_|St]) :- owns(P,Sq,St).
% Line L is available and is the last of square not yet drawn.
last_avail_line(L,Sq,St) :-
   avail_line(L,Sq,St), \+ avail_line(_,Sq,[draw(_,L)|St]).
% Line L is from Sq and not yet drawn in state St.
avail_line(L,Sq,St) :-
   square_lines(Sq,Ls), member(L,Ls), \+ member(draw(_,L),St).
% The legal moves
legal_move(St,P,[L],[draw(P,L)|St]) :-  % Draw a line and stop.
   avail_line(L,_,St).
legal_move(St,P,[L|Rest],New) :-        % Draw a line and go on.
   last_avail_line(L,_,St), legal_move([draw(P,L)|St],P,Rest,New).
```

predicate `available_line` says that a line is available for a square in a situation if it is one of the lines for that square, and there is no previous draw action involving that line in the situation. Finally, the last two clauses of the program describe when a move is legal: either a list with a single line, or a list with more than one line, when a last available line for a square was just drawn.

Figure 10.14 shows the Boxes game in action:

- The first query asks if Max has a winning move from the configuration drawn on the right-hand side. The answer is that Max can win by drawing line 3 (completing a square) and then drawing line 8 in the same move.

- The second query asks a similar question for the configuration drawn there. In this case, Max can win by drawing line 7, but at this point, although he has the option of continuing with another line, he must not do so. Furthermore, this is the only winning move.

Figure 10.14.   Playing Boxes

```
?- win_move([ draw(min,6),draw(max,10),draw(min,2),draw(max,4),
              draw(min,9),draw(max,1) ],  max, Move).
Move = [3, 8]
Yes

?- win_move([ draw(min,5),draw(max,10),draw(min,2),draw(max,4),
              draw(min,9),draw(max,1) ],  max, Move).
Move = [7]   ;                   % Note: Draw one line only.
No

?- tie_move([             draw(max,10),draw(min,2),draw(max,4),
              draw(min,9),draw(max,1) ], min, Move).
No                             % So Min loses from here.

?- win_move([                          draw(min,2),draw(max,4),
              draw(min,9),draw(max,1) ],  max, Move).
Move = [8]    ;
Move = [10]   ;                % As above
No

?- win_move([],max,M).         % Can the first player guarantee a win?
No                             % ... After 2 minutes of computing
```

- The third query backs up one step and asks if Min can avoid losing from the configuration shown. The answer is that she cannot: the previous query showed that she would not win if she drew line 5; the other lines are similar.

- The next query backs up one more line and asks what Max can do to win in the displayed T configuration. One thing he can do is to draw line 10, which leads to the configuration of the previous query, where Min loses. The other thing Max can do is to draw line 8, which also works.

- The final query asks if Max can guarantee a win from the initial state. It takes a while to explore the entire game tree to answer this question, but the final answer is no.

10.3   Playing bigger games

It is not hard to see that every game considered in this chapter has to be one of the following three types:

- a game where both players can force a tie or better (as in tic-tac-toe);

- a game where the player who plays second can force a win (as in Boxes or Race to 21);

- a game where the player who plays first can force a win (none considered).

What does this mean? For a game of type 1, if your opponent does not make a mistake, you will not win no matter what you do. For a game of type 2, if you play first and your opponent does not make a mistake, you will not win no matter what you do. For a game of type 3, if you play second and your opponent does not make a mistake, you will not win no matter what you do.

So why should you even bother to play games like these? You could simply do the following:

```
?- initial_state(S,P), win_move(S,P,Move).
```

This would tell you, once and for all, what a proper first move should be. Then you could find a proper second move, and so on. *Where is the fun in playing?*

The answer is that for sufficiently complex games, it cannot be determined what the best first move is once and for all because the game trees are too large to explore fully:

- For checkers, the game tree is estimated to have 10^{70} nodes.

- For chess, the game tree is estimated to have 10^{120} nodes.

- For Go, the game tree is estimated to have 10^{750} nodes.

So the win_move predicate as written here is practical only for very small games. For big games, finding a best move must be possible without examining the entire game tree. This is why playing a game like chess remains challenging, and why it is still not known whether white (who plays first) can guarantee a win. (In 2007 checkers was solved by Jonathan Schaeffer and his team. It is a type 1 game like tic-tac-toe: both players can avoid losing.)

10.3.1 Numerical game trees and minimax

This section considers a second general game player, one that can decide on a best move without looking at the entire game tree. For this purpose, it is useful to imagine a *numerical game tree* similar to the one in figure 10.3 except that *numbers* are put on the leaves of the tree.

From now on, the two game players will always be called Max and Min, and a big positive number (say, 999) indicates that Max wins the game, and a big negative

Figure 10.15.   An example numeric game tree

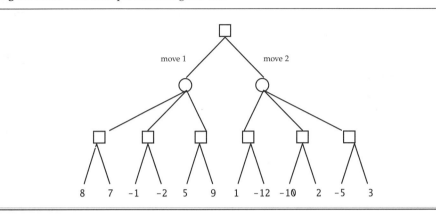

number (say, -999) indicates that Min wins the game. The number 0 is used when the game ends in a tie. (So big numbers are good for Max, and small numbers are good for Min.)

It is then a simple process to assign a numeric value to *every node* on the tree. Starting from the bottom of the tree, proceed as follows:

- If it is Max's turn to play, label the node with the *maximum* of the labels of the children of the node.

- If it is Min's turn to play, label the node with the *minimum* of the labels of the children of the node.

This labeling duplicates what was done previously with W and L (and also handles ties properly): a node labeled 999 is a winning position for Max; a node labeled -999 is a winning position for Min; and a 0 is neither. Overall because of the minimums and maximums, this numeric process is called *minimax*. (This finally also explains why Max and Min have the names they do.)

What makes this process interesting is that a numeric game tree need not go all the way to the end of the game but can stop at a certain depth, after which an *estimate* is made about the value of the state. A bigger number means that the state is estimated to be better for Max; a smaller number means that the state is estimated to be better for Min. (How to arrive at these estimates is discussed later.)

A tree of this type is shown in figure 10.15. The tree stops at depth 3, and estimated values are provided for all the leaf nodes. For example, according to this estimate, the leftmost state at level 3 (with a value of 8) is estimated to be slightly better for Max

Figure 10.16. A labeled numeric game tree

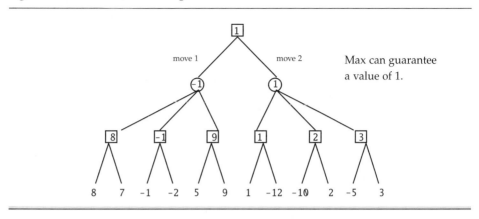

(worse for Min) than the state beside it (with a value of 7). In other words, if Max had to choose, he should choose to move to the leftmost state.

Applying the minimax procedure to this truncated tree results in a label for every node, as shown in figure 10.16. Max's best move here according to all the estimates is move 2, where he will be guaranteed a value of 1 or better no matter what Min does.

But why not simply truncate the tree at depth 1 and use the estimates from there instead of going to depth 3? The answer is that the estimates are expected to be more *accurate*, the closer the depth is to the end of the game. An estimate at level 1 may be much less useful than the values obtained by minimax with estimates at deeper levels. So there is a trade-off: the deeper the search using estimates, the more accurate the results will be, but the more nodes have to be considered to decide on a best move. In fact, as with planning (see section 9.3), the number of nodes to be considered grows *exponentially* with the depth of the tree.

* *A version of minimax in Prolog*

There are many ways to encode the minimax procedure in Prolog, but the easiest is to assume a number v and find a move (if one exists) that guarantees a value of v or better (that is, bigger for Max and smaller for Min). The property to be used in a program is that Max can guarantee a value of v or higher if he can move to a state where Min *cannot* guarantee a value of $v - 1$ or lower. Similarly, Min can guarantee a value of v or lower if she can move to a state where Max *cannot* guarantee a value of $v + 1$ or higher.

Figure 10.17. A minimax procedure in Prolog   minimax.pl

```
% Computing the values of moves for two players, Max and Min.
% The game-dependent predicate estval estimates values of states.
% The search of the game tree is limited to a depth given by D.

% can_get(S,P,D,V): P can get a value of V or better in state S.
can_get(S,max,_,V) :- game_over(S,max,W), winval(W,V1), V1 >= V.
can_get(S,min,_,V) :- game_over(S,min,W), winval(W,V1), V1 =< V.
can_get(S,max,0,V) :- \+ game_over(S,_,_), estval(S,max,E), E >= V.
can_get(S,min,0,V) :- \+ game_over(S,_,_), estval(S,min,E), E =< V.
can_get(S,P,D,V) :- \+ game_over(S,_,_), val_move(S,P,D,_,V).

% val_move(S,P,D,M,V): P can get a value of V or better with move M.
val_move(S,max,D,M,V) :- D>0, D1 is D-1, V1 is V-1,
    legal_move(S,max,M,S1), \+ can_get(S1,min,D1,V1).
val_move(S,min,D,M,V) :- D>0, D1 is D-1, V1 is V+1,
    legal_move(S,min,M,S1), \+ can_get(S1,max,D1,V1).

winval(max,999).       % The value of a state where Max has won
winval(min,-999).      % The value of a state where Max has lost
winval(neither,0).     % The value of a state with a tie
```

These ideas lead to the Prolog program shown in figure 10.17. The labeling predicate is called `can_get`. What `can_get` says for Max (and analogously for Min) is that Max can get a value of v or better if one of the following conditions holds:

- The game is over, and the final value v' according to the winner (as specified by the predicate `winval`) satisfies $v' \geq v$.

- The depth $d = 0$, and the estimated value of the state v' according to the game-specific predicate `estval` satisfies $v' \geq v$.

- The game is not over, and Max can get a value of v or better by making a move (as specified by the predicate `val_move`).

The predicate `val_move` is used for choosing a move. What it says for Max (and analogously for Min) is that assuming a depth $d > 0$, Max can guarantee a value of v or better if there is a legal move to a state where Min cannot get a value of $v - 1$ or better (for her) at depth $d - 1$.

The predicate `val_move` replaces `win_move` and `tie_move` as a general game-playing program. If the depth is very large, one will never hit the estimates, and so the values will be completely determined by the winner at the end of the game. So the query `val_move(S,max,10000,M,999)` asks for a move M for player Max in state S that will guarantee a win for Max, as `win_move(S,max,M)` did before. The query

Figure 10.18. Cutoffs in a game tree

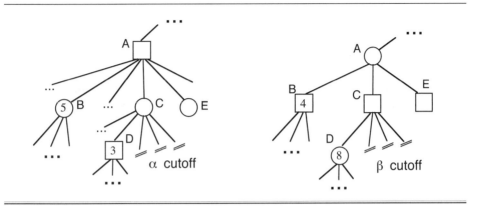

val_move(S,max,10000,M,0) asks for a move M for player Max in state S that will guarantee at least a tie. When the depth is smaller, and estimates of values have to be used (as provided by the estval predicate), then the guarantees are only relative to those estimated values.

10.3.2 Alpha and beta cutoffs

Minimax with estimates allows making decisions about how to move in a game without searching all the way to the end of the game. But because the search should be as deep as possible for the sake of accuracy, there may still be a very large number of nodes to consider in a game tree. However, sometimes it is not necessary to look at all those nodes to make the final decision.

Consider the portion of a game tree depicted on the left side in figure 10.18. The goal is to assign a value to the node labeled A, where it is Max's turn to play. To do this, values must be assigned to the nodes below A, where it is Min's turn to play. (Max will eventually chose the maximum of the values for B, C, E, and any other children of A.) Proceeding from left to right as usual, it has already been determined that the value of the node labeled B is 5. To get a value for the next node, C, the values of its children must be found. (Min will eventually chose the minimum of these values.) As part of this process, it has just been determined that the value of node D is 3.

Before continuing with the remaining children of C, observe the following. The value assigned to node C cannot be larger than 3, since Min chooses a minimum. However, whatever the value of C is, it will not change the value for A, since Max chooses a maximum, and the value of B is already larger than 3. The conclusion is that the search does not have to continue below C, since it cannot affect the result. Therefore perform an *alpha cutoff*, and jump immediately to node E, which may turn out to affect the value at A.

An analogous situation holds on the right of figure 10.18. In this case, the search is for a value for A, a node for Min. After it has been determined that B has value 4 and D has value 8, it is clear that C cannot get a value smaller than 8, since Max chooses a maximum. Since Min chooses a minimum at A, and the value of B is already smaller than 8, perform a *beta cutoff*, and jump immediately to node E, which may still affect the value at A.

The alpha and beta cutoffs allow deciding what moves to make (for Max or for Min) without examining an entire tree all the way to the leaves. These cutoffs can be very significant, especially if they happen high up in the game tree.

10.3.3   The application to chess

A minimax game player is able to decide on a best next move without looking at all the game states up to the end of the game. To use it, however, one needs to be able to estimate the values of states where the game is not over. (This is not unlike estimating the distance to the goal during planning in section 9.3.2.) So in addition to the four predicates `player`, `initial_state`, `legal_move`, and `game_over`, a fifth one is needed:

> estval(*state*, *player*, *v*)

This says that if it is the turn of *player* in *state*, then the number v is the estimated measure of how good the state is, from the point of view of Max.

Different games have different methods of estimating how well or how poorly Max is doing at nonfinal states of the game. For a game like chess, a typical estimate is something like (*material advantage* + *positional advantage*). The *material advantage* is of the form $9 \cdot Q + 5 \cdot R + 3 \cdot N + 3 \cdot B + P$, where Q, R, N, B, and P represent the advantage in queens, rooks, knights, bishops, and pawns, respectively. The *positional advantage* is much harder to quantify but usually includes things like mobility, control over squares, early development of pieces, and so on.

How well does this work for chess? Although chess-playing programs have existed for a long time, the first one to win against a world chess champion was *Deep Blue*, which won against Garry Kasparov in 1997. Here are some details on it:

- It used minimax with alpha-beta cutoffs, but on a special computer to speed up the generation of moves and the evaluation of states. (It was able to consider a staggering 200 million board positions per second.)

Figure 10.19. Chess rating and search depth

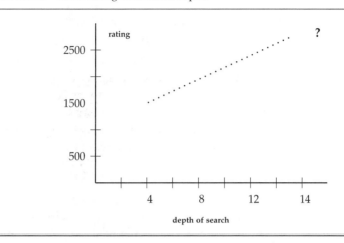

- It explored game trees to about depth 14, with occasional very deep searches. The estimates of the values of game states used 8,000 separate factors.

- It had a U.S. Chess Federation rating of 2650 in 1996; the rating of a chess grandmaster is 2500. (For comparison, the world chess champion as of January 2011, Magnus Carlsen, had a rating of 2814.)

What is perhaps most interesting about the effort in computer chess is that almost none of it is specific to chess. Instead, it is mostly directed toward speeding up the game tree search. This is not too surprising, since the U.S. Chess Federation rating of chess programs seems to be directly proportional to the search depth, as illustrated very roughly in figure 10.19. (It is worth noting, however, that this effort on search has not helped so far with *extremely* large games like the game of Go.)

Want to read more?

This chapter looked at the thinking behind playing strategic games. Getting computers to play these games, and especially chess, has been a mainstay of AI research from the very beginning. Alan Turing, the father of computer science, tried his hand at it, and one of the first minimax chess programs was due to Claude Shannon, the father of information theory. John McCarthy discovered alpha-beta cutoffs in 1956.

Much more of the history of computer chess can be found in the book by Levy and Newborn [50].

The reason for this fascination with chess is clear: it is intelligent behavior that can be exhibited in a very clear-cut way. Nobody disputes the achievement of a program that is able to defeat a world chess champion.

Since the time of the Deep Blue computer, there have been a number of progressively stronger chess programs, with names like Deep Fritz and Rybka. Although these programs appear to be outdistancing their human competitors, chess federations like FIDE do not actually rate them, chess competitions mostly exclude them, and chess champions often use them only to help improve their games against other humans. Chess commentators might mention what "the computer" would do in their analyses, but leave it at that.

Outside of chess, the games of Go and checkers are perhaps the most studied. As noted earlier, the game of checkers was solved by Jonathan Schaeffer [52], a researcher who had been working on a checkers program called *Chinook* for some time. (The late world champion, Marion Tinsley, lost a game to this program in 1992; he had not lost a game in forty years.) The game of Go, on the other hand, is interesting because it proved to be so difficult. Until the 1990s there were simply no computer programs that played Go competently [51]. Currently, there are much better programs, but they use statistical techniques beyond the minimax presented here. Statistical techniques are also used quite successfully in other games like bridge and backgammon that are outside the category of games considered here.

One interesting development in the area of strategic games is the recent attention to general game-playing, where the players do not know ahead of time the rules of the game they will be playing [49]. At the time of a competition, the game-playing programs are given the rules (specified in a certain language) as *input* and then have to figure out from there how to play and how to play well.

Exercises

1. Consider a game of tic-tac-toe where X begins by choosing position 2.

   a. Show that the general game player in `gameplayer.pl` finds no winning move for O from here.

   b. The usual move for player O here would be a center or a corner. Show that the general game player finds an equally good move for O.

Figure 10.20. A simple game tree

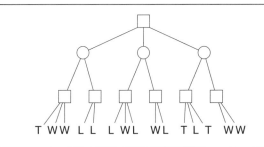

2. Consider the game tree depicted in figure 10.20. What is the move that Max should make from the root node? Answer by labeling every state of the game tree with W, L, or T (for a tie).

3. This question concerns the intuitive understanding of the labels on a game tree. Suppose players P and Q are playing a game, and each state of the game is labeled with P or Q (as the eventual winner) or neither for a tie.

   a. If a state is labeled with P as the winner, which of the following statements are true?

      (1) Throughout the game, no matter what either player does, P will eventually win.

      (2) Throughout the game, no matter what Q does, P will be able to choose a move that will eventually lead to a win.

      (3) Throughout the game, no matter what P does, Q will be unable to choose a move that will eventually lead to a win (for Q).

   b. If a state is labeled with neither as winner, which of the following statements are true?

      (1) Throughout the game, no matter what either player does, the game will eventually end in a tie.

      (2) Throughout the game, no matter what Q does, P will be able to choose a move that will eventually lead to a tie.

      (3) Throughout the game, no matter what Q does, P will be able to choose a move that will eventually lead to a tie or a win.

Figure 10.21. A numeric game tree

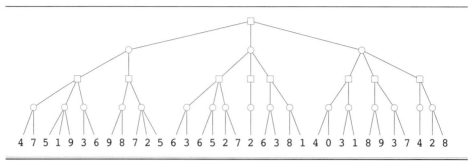

4. One of the reasons the Prolog general game player presented in the file `gameplayer.pl` may be hard to follow is because of the possibility of a tie. Write a simpler version of `label` and `win_move` (and any other predicate you need) for games where there is always a winner. Show that your program works properly on Race to 21.

5. Consider the numeric game tree to depth 4 in figure 10.21.

   a. Determine the numeric values for all the nodes in the tree.

   b. Indicate on the tree where alpha and beta cutoffs would occur, assuming that the tree is explored in the usual way, from left to right. Of the entire tree, how many leaf nodes do not need to be examined by using alpha-beta cutoffs?

6. Consider the following game, called Wythoff's Nim, a variant of Race to 21:

   When the game begins, there is a pile of green chips and a pile of red chips on the table. Each player takes turns removing at least one chip from the table, and the last player to take a chip wins. In a move, a player may take any number of green chips, or any number of red chips, or exactly the same number of green and red chips.

   To encode this game in Prolog, a game state can be represented using a list of two numbers $[p_1, p_2]$, where $p_1 \geq 0$ is the number of green chips, and $p_2 \geq 0$ is the number of red chips. The moves of the game can then be represented by one of the following terms:

   - $\text{green}(m)$, where $1 \leq m \leq p_1$, when m green chips are to be removed
   - $\text{red}(m)$, where $1 \leq m \leq p_2$, when m red chips are to be removed

- both(m), where $1 \leq m \leq p_1$ and $1 \leq m \leq p_2$, indicating that m green chips and m red chips are to be removed

For example, starting in state $[4, 2]$, here are all of the states that can be reached in one move: $[3, 2]$, $[2, 2]$, $[1, 2]$, $[0, 2]$, $[4, 1]$, $[4, 0]$, $[3, 1]$, and $[2, 0]$.

To generate legal moves for this game in Prolog, it is useful to be able to generate numbers between two bounds. You may use the built-in predicate between(x, y, z), which holds when $x \leq z \leq y$, and which can generate a z given an x and y.

a. Write Prolog clauses defining this game for two players, Max and Min. The initial state is unspecified, so you need to write clauses for `player`, `game_over`, and `legal_move` (using `between`).

b. Suppose the game is in state $[3, 1]$, where it is Max's turn to play. Draw the full game tree (with W and L at the leaves) starting at this state. Use the tree to determine the best next move for Max. Explain your reasoning. Show that your program selects this move.

c. Show by running your program that the best move, starting in state $[4, 6]$, is to take one chip from each pile.

d. Consider a sequence of game states defined by the following rule:

  - The 0th element of the sequence is the state $[0, 0]$;
  - For any $i > 0$, the ith element of the sequence is the state $[p_1, p_2]$, where p_1 is the smallest number that does not appear in an earlier state of the sequence, and where $p_2 = p_1 + i$.

  Use your program to explore what happens if the initial state of a game is one of the states in this sequence.

7. Use exercise 6d to describe a winning strategy for Wythoff's Nim. Given an arbitrary state of the game $[p_1, p_2]$, what is the best move to make?

8. Look on the Internet to discover the strange connection between winning strategies for Wythoff's Nim and the *golden mean*, that is, $(-1 + \sqrt{5})/2$, the remarkable number studied since the time of the ancient Greeks.

9. The game player presented in the file `minimax.pl` can find a move to guarantee a given numeric value, if one exists. However, it cannot find the *best* move to make, since it does not compare the values produced by all possible moves. Write a game player that does this. *Hint:* Use the built-in Prolog predicate `findall` to produce a list of *all* the legal moves from some state.

Case Study: Other Ways of Thinking

The discussion in previous chapters demonstrated how thinking supports intelligent behavior in a variety of domains, including puzzles, visual scenes, English sentences, actions, and games. Thinking uses what is known, and across the domains, the knowledge varied, but the thinking procedure was always the same: back-chaining. Even with complex extensions, like situations and fluents or minimax, the thinking procedure remained the same. This chapter, however, considers *other ways* of thinking, that is to say, other ways of using what is known.

These new modes of thinking can be illustrated with a simple example. Consider the following four sentences:

1. *If X is a polar bear, then X is white.*

2. *Thornton is a polar bear.*

3. *Thornton is white.*

4. *If X is a swan, then X is white.*

From (1) and (2), the sort of thinking considered so far would allow (3) to be concluded, which is a logical entailment of (1) and (2). This sort of reasoning is often called _deduction_: from (1) and (2), one can deduce (3).

But suppose only (1) and (4) are known. Nothing at all is known about the individual, Thornton. If he were actually observed to be white, one might *conjecture* that he is a polar bear, since it is known that polar bears are white. This sort of thinking is not deductive; it does not come with the guarantee of logical entailment. Thornton might be a swan or something completely different. Nonetheless, the conjecture that Thornton is a polar bear accounts for the color, as does the conjecture that he is a swan. This type of nondeductive thinking was called _abduction_ by the philosopher C. S. Peirce: from (1) and (3), one can abduce (2). This is the sort of reasoning that underlies _explanation_: according is what is known, Thornton being a polar bear would explain his being white.

Now assume that at first only (2) and (3) are known. Nothing at all is known about the color of polar bears or of swans. But then imagine (5) and (6) are observed:

5. *Shako is a polar bear, and Shako is white.*

6. *Peppy is a polar bear, and Peppy is white.*

One might want to generalize from these and *surmise* that all polar bears are white. Again, this sort of thinking is not deductive. The facts about the individuals do not logically entail that all polar bears are white; the very next polar bear could turn out to be a different color. C. S. Peirce called this type of nondeductive thinking *induction*: from (2) and (3) (and others like it), one can induce (1). This is the sort of reasoning that underlies a form of *learning*: from observing the color of polar bears Thornton, Shako, Peppy, and perhaps others, one learns that as a rule, polar bears are white.

So, to summarize:

- from (1) and (2), one can deduce (3);
- from (1) and (3), one can abduce (2);
- from (2) and (3), one can induce (1).

Finally, suppose (7) is added:

7. *Freddy is a either a polar bear or a swan.*

Based on what is known, one can conclude (that is, deduce) that Freddy is white. This is logically entailed by (1), (4), and (7). If (7) is true, then there are only two possibilities, and in either case, given (1) and (4), the color must be white. However, this conclusion could not be drawn using the current thinking procedure, back-chaining. There is no way to even represent a sentence like (7), since it is neither an atomic sentence nor a conditional. This chapter also explores what is involved with this sort of thinking, called *propositional reasoning*. (It is sometimes also known as Boolean reasoning.) Back-chaining is a special case.

The chapter is divided into four sections. The first section reexamines back-chaining as the starting point for discussing the other ways of thinking. Sections 2, 3, and 4 discuss explanation, learning, and propositional reasoning, respectively.

There is something of a paradox in using Prolog and back-chaining to look at new ways of thinking that go beyond back-chaining. And as the paradox is resolved, thinking itself will end up becoming the *subject matter* of the thinking. This reinterpretation will require a major conceptual shift, and this chapter is the most technically challenging one in the book.

Figure 11.1. A recap of back-chaining

There is a *knowledge base* of *clauses*, where each clause has a *head*, which is an atom, and a *body*, which is a sequence of atoms. There is also a *query*, which is a sequence of atoms. The task is to *establish* the query given the knowledge base.

The query $A_1, \ldots, A_n$ returns *success* or *failure* by back-chaining as follows:

1. If $n = 0$, the query returns *success*.

2. Otherwise, the query returns *success* only if there is a clause in the knowledge base whose head is A_1 (the first atom of the query) and whose body is $B_1, \ldots, B_m$, such that the query $B_1, \ldots, B_m, A_2, \ldots, A_n$ returns *success* (recursively) .

11.1 Back-chaining as subject matter

The back-chaining procedure that Prolog uses is summarized in figure 11.1. (This simplified version omits negation, equality, and any mention of variables or unification in the atoms.) In talking about back-chaining, it is assumed that any knowledge to be applied in thinking is represented symbolically in the knowledge base (KB). The KB can be about a world of family relationships, or a visual scene, or a game; the clauses in the KB will talk about these items and the relationships among them. An example is the clause in the family program in figure 3.1 that relates the `father` predicate to the `child` and `male` predicates.

But suppose one wants to think about *back-chaining* itself rather than about fathers and families. The clauses in the KB would have to talk not about people but about knowledge bases, clauses and queries. Instead of a predicate like $\mathtt{father}(x, y)$ that holds if person x is a father of person y, there might be a predicate like $\mathtt{est}(k, q)$ (short for establish) that holds when the query q can be established by back-chaining from the knowledge base k. The arguments to the predicate `est` would be Prolog terms standing for a knowledge base and a query. In sum, clauses, knowledge bases, and queries would be represented *as Prolog terms* so that they can then be used as arguments to predicates like `est`.

How is this done? To simplify matters, assume for now that predicates have no arguments. Then a clause can be represented as a Prolog term using a list of constants: the head of the list will represent the head of the clause, and the tail will represent the body of the clause.

Consider, for example, the Prolog clause

```
u :- p, b.
```

This can be represented by the Prolog term [u,p,b]. Similarly, a knowledge base can be represented as a list whose elements represent the clauses. Consider, for example, the following simple Prolog knowledge base:

```
a.
b.
u :- p, b.
p :- a.
```

This knowledge base can be represented using the following Prolog term:

```
[ [a], [b], [u,p,b], [p,a] ].
```

Of course, this list is not a knowledge base itself, but it can be used to represent one as a Prolog term. Each element of this list is a nonempty list representing a clause. (Atomic clauses are represented as lists with a single element.) Similarly, a query is represented as a list of atoms.

With these list representations, there are now sentences in Prolog that talk about the properties of knowledge bases and queries, just as previous sentences talked about properties of people. In particular, the predicate $est(k,q)$ should hold if the query represented by q can be established by back-chaining from the knowledge base represented by k. In other words, the following behavior is desired:

```
?- est([[a],[b],[u,p,b],[p,a]], [p,b]).
Yes

?- est([[a],[b],[u,p,b],[p,a]], [c]).
No
```

The first query should succeed because the knowledge base represented by the first argument (that is, the four clauses just listed) logically entails both p and b, the query represented by the second argument. The second query should fail because that same knowledge base does not logically entail c.

How should this est predicate be defined? Keeping in mind that one is working not with knowledge bases and queries but with symbolic representations of them as lists, one can encode what was said about back-chaining in figure 11.1:

The predicate $est(k,q)$ holds if one of the following holds:

1. q is the empty list (where k can be anything).

Figure 11.2. Querying the est predicate

```
?- est([[a],[b],[u,p,b],[p,a]], [b,a]).
Yes

?- est([[a],[b],[u,p,b],[p,a]], [u]).
Yes

?- est([[a],[b],[u,p,b],[p,a]], [p,d]).
No
```

Figure 11.3. Tracing the est predicate

```
Call: (5) est([[a],[b],[u,p,b],[p,a]], [u])
Call: (6) est([[a],[b],[u,p,b],[p,a]], [p,b])
Call: (7) est([[a],[b],[u,p,b],[p,a]], [a,b])
Call: (8) est([[a],[b],[u,p,b],[p,a]], [b])
Call: (9) est([[a],[b],[u,p,b],[p,a]], [])
Exit: (9) est([[a],[b],[u,p,b],[p,a]], [])
Exit: (8) est([[a],[b],[u,p,b],[p,a]], [b])
Exit: (7) est([[a],[b],[u,p,b],[p,a]], [a,b])
Exit: (6) est([[a],[b],[u,p,b],[p,a]], [p,b])
Exit: (5) est([[a],[b],[u,p,b],[p,a]], [u])
```

---

2. q has head a and tail t, and there is a list in k whose head is also a and whose tail is b, and $\text{est}(k, q')$ holds (recursively), where q' is the list formed by joining b and t.

This leads to the following two clauses for the est predicate:

```
% est(K,Q): query Q can be established from knowledge base K
est(_,[]).
est(K,[A|T]) :- member([A|B],K), append(B,T,Q), est(K,Q).
```

In the first clause, est holds trivially when the query is empty. In the second clause, the query is nonempty; it has head A and tail T; and one must find (using member) an element of the knowledge base K whose head is also A and whose tail (the body of the clause) is B. To establish the original query, one must be able to establish (recursively) a new query Q that is the result of joining B and T (using append). Note that these two clauses for est form a very concise description of back-chaining.

Some additional examples of using this predicate appear in figure 11.2. It is not hard to see that this program works just the way Prolog does, that is, $\text{est}(k, q)$ returns *success* when the query represented by *q* would return *success* in Prolog for the knowledge base represented by *k*. The partial trace in figure 11.3 shows that est does its work in the *same order* as Prolog's back-chaining would.

But so what? What is the point of all this? It shows that Prolog is well-suited for describing, among other things, how Prolog works. Once one can talk about thinking the way that Prolog does, one can also talk about *thinking in other ways*. So Prolog can be used to express other thinking procedures that work quite differently from Prolog itself. Understanding what those two simple clauses for the predicate est do and why is crucial to understanding the rest of this chapter.

11.1.1 A breadth-first thinking procedure

Let us examine a thinking procedure that differs from Prolog in a very minor way.

Perhaps the simplest part of back-chaining to modify is the *order* in which atoms are considered in a query. Consider a partial trace of a query that eventually fails:

```
Call: (10) est([[a],[b],[u,p,b],[p,a]], [u,c])
Call: (11) est([[a],[b],[u,p,b],[p,a]], [p,b,c])
Call: (12) est([[a],[b],[u,p,b],[p,a]], [a,b,c])
Call: (13) est([[a],[b],[u,p,b],[p,a]], [b,c])
Call: (14) est([[a],[b],[u,p,b],[p,a]], [c])
Fail: (14) est([[a],[b],[u,p,b],[p,a]], [c])
```

Note that before est can get to the atom c, it has to first deal with u. To deal with u, it has to go deeper and deal with p and b. To deal with p, it has to go deeper still and deal with a. Once it is done with a, it can go on to b. Once it is done with b, it finally gets to c, and then the query fails.

This sort of procedure is called a *depth-first procedure*, since the program handles new atomic queries that arise from the bodies of clauses *before* returning to the existing atoms in the query. In a *breadth-first procedure*, the program would consider existing atoms in a query before looking at new atoms that come from the bodies of clauses. It turns out that a breadth-first variant of est is very easy to express in Prolog:

```
% estbf(K,Q): query Q can be established from knowledge base K.
% The method is a breadth-first variant of back-chaining.
estbf(_,[]).
estbf(K,[A|T]) :- member([A|B],K), append(T,B,Q), estbf(K,Q).
```

The only difference between est and estbf is the order of arguments to append. A partial trace of the same query shows that the predicate estbf does not consider atomic queries in the same order as est does:

```
Call: (6) estbf([[a],[b],[u,p,b],[p,a]], [u,c])
Call: (7) estbf([[a],[b],[u,p,b],[p,a]], [c,p,b])
Fail: (7) estbf([[a],[b],[u,p,b],[p,a]], [c,p,b])
Fail: (6) estbf([[a],[b],[u,p,b],[p,a]], [u,c])
```

The procedure `estbf` detects the failure before even getting to the atom p.

So `estbf` is a thinking procedure that does *not* work like Prolog. There is no contradiction in saying this. Prolog uses a depth-first procedure, and its atomic queries (like `member` and `append` and even `estbf`) will always be handled in this way. The `estbf` procedure is breadth-first, however, and its atomic queries (like u and c) are handled in that way. *So Prolog is reasoning in a depth-first way about a thinking procedure that reasons in a breadth-first way.* This way of handling thinking procedures that are different from the back-chaining of Prolog is at the root of everything else discussed in this chapter.

Note that the breadth-first variant of back-chaining avoids some of the difficulties encountered with a depth-first procedure:

```
?- est([[a],[p,p]], [p,b]).        % Gets stuck in a loop.
ERROR: Out of global stack

?- estbf([[a],[p,p]], [p,b]).      % Does not get stuck.
No
```

Although the `estbf` predicate terminates here without getting stuck, it is not guaranteed to always terminate:

```
?- estbf([[a],[p,p],[p,a]], [p]).
ERROR: Out of global stack
```

It is possible to revise back-chaining to ensure termination. But it is easier to move to a very different sort of procedure that *is* guaranteed to terminate.

* 11.1.2 A forward-chaining thinking procedure

Let us now turn to a more substantial change in how to deal with a knowledge base. Instead of working backward from a query the way that Prolog does, one can work forward from the knowledge base. This is what was termed *forward-chaining* in section 2.5.

The idea with forward-chaining is to start by focusing on the clauses whose bodies are empty, that is, the atomic sentences of the knowledge base. Call an atom that is the head of such a clause *solved* (meaning "known to be true"). To establish a query by forward-chaining, proceed as follows:

Figure 11.4.   A forward-chaining procedure   `estfc.pl`

```
% estfc(K,Q) holds if query Q can be established from knowledge base K.
% The method is forward-chaining.
estfc(K,Q) :- allsolved(K,Q).
estfc(K,Q) :- nkb(K,K1), estfc(K1,Q).

allsolved(_,[]).
allsolved(K,[A|Q]) :- solved(K,A), allsolved(K,Q).

solved(K,A) :- member([A],K).

nkb(K,[[A]|K]) :- member([A|B],K), \+ solved(K,A), allsolved(K,B).
```

1. If all the query atoms are solved, the procedure returns *success*.

2. Otherwise, look for a clause in the knowledge base whose head is not solved but whose body consists of atoms that are all solved.

   a. If none is found, the procedure returns *failure*.

   b. If one is found, *extend the knowledge base* to include the head as a new atomic clause in the KB, and go back to step 1.

A Prolog program that realizes this procedure is shown in figure 11.4.

Whenever the predicates `est` and `estbf` return an answer, the predicate `estfc` will return the same answer. Here is a trace of a query:

```
Call: (6) estfc([[a],[b],[u,p,b],[p,a]], [u])
Call: (7) estfc([[p],[a],[b],[u,p,b],[p,a]], [u])
Call: (8) estfc([[u],[p],[a],[b],[u,p,b],[p,a]], [u])
Exit: (8) estfc([[u],[p],[a],[b],[u,p,b],[p,a]], [u])
Exit: (7) estfc([[p],[a],[b],[u,p,b],[p,a]], [u])
Exit: (6) estfc([[a],[b],[u,p,b],[p,a]], [u])
```

Note that in the recursive calls to `estfc`, the KB first grows to include p (since the atom in its body, a, is already solved), and then u (since the atoms in its body, p and b, are then solved). At this point, the resulting new KB contains atomic clauses for all the atoms in the query, and so the query is established.

Unlike the predicates `est` and `estbf`, the forward-chaining `estfc` procedure will never get stuck in a loop. To see this, note that each time `estfc` is used recursively, it is on a new KB that includes an additional solved atom. Once all the atoms mentioned in the KB have been considered, `nkb` must then fail, and the procedure terminates.

Figure 11.5. Making copies of terms

```
?- X=p(a), copy_term(X,T).
X = p(a),  T = p(a)
?- X=p(a,Z,b), copy_term(X,T).
X = p(a,_G249,b),  T = p(a,_G123,b)
?- X=[Y,W], W=a, copy_term(X,T), Y=a.
X = [a,a],  Y = a,  W = a,  T = [_G359,a]
```

11.1.3 Back-chaining with variables, negation, and equality

Now consider a final version of est that will correctly handle variables, negation, and equality. As before, a knowledge base is represented by a list of the representations of clauses, where a clause is represented by a nonempty list of the representations of the literals. Recall from section 9.2.3 that an atom can be used as a Prolog term; this means that an atom can be used to represent itself. Equalities are represented using a predicate eq; and negations, using a predicate not. For example, the clause

```
    q(a,X) :- p(Y,Z), \+ r(Y), Z=Y, s(X,Y).
```

is represented as a Prolog term by the following list:

```
    [q(a,X), p(Y,Z), not(r(Y)), eq(Z,Y), s(X,Y)]
```

So knowledge bases with variables can be represented, as in the following:

```
    ?- est([[p(a)],[p(b)],[q(X),p(X)]], [q(a)]).
    X = a
    Yes
```

The predicate est appears to work with variables. But consider this query:

```
    ?- est([[p(a)],[p(b)],[q(X),p(X)]], [q(a),q(b)]).
    No
```

The trouble here is that once q(X) unifies with q(a), the variable X is instantiated, and so q(X) will not unify with q(b).

A Prolog predicate that copies terms

The solution is a special built-in Prolog predicate copy_term(x, y), which holds if x and y are terms that are identical except that the variables appearing in y are all new, unrelated to those in x. Some examples of its use are shown in figure 11.5. As can be

Figure 11.6. The final version of back-chaining   est.pl

```
% est(K,Q) holds if query Q can be established from knowledge base K.
% This version performs Prolog back-chaining.
% It handles equality, negation, and variables.
est(_,[]).                                          % No query atoms
est(K,[eq(X,X)|T]) :- est(K,T).                     % Equality.
est(K,[not(A)|T]) :- \+ est(K,[A]), est(K,T).       % Negation.
est(K,[A|T]) :- member_copy([A|B],K), append(B,T,Q), est(K,Q).

% member_copy(X,L): X is an atomic element of L or a copy otherwise.
member_copy(X,L) :- member(X,L), X=[_].
member_copy(X,L) :- member(E,L), \+ E=[_], copy_term(E,X).
```

seen, `copy_term` behaves just like Prolog = except in the presence of (uninstantiated) variables.

A final version of the `est` predicate that handles all the new elements (equality, negation, variables) appears in figure 11.6. Here is how it works:

- The first clause is as before;

- The second clause handles a query whose first literal is an *equality* by unifying the two arguments and then continuing with the rest of the query.

- The third clause handles a query whose first literal is a *negation* by ensuring that the unnegated literal fails and then continuing with the rest of the query.

- The fourth clause handles a query whose first literal is an *atom*. It is as before except that `member_copy` is used instead of `member`.

The `member_copy` predicate here behaves just like `member` when the first argument happens to be a list with just one element (representing a clause that has no body). Otherwise, `member_copy` uses `copy_term`. This has the effect of finding a matching clause in the knowledge base but leaving its variables uninstantiated for later use. (Assume here that variables only appear in clauses with bodies.)

The following queries illustrate the behavior of the new `est` predicate:

```
?- est([[p(a)],[p(b)],[q(X),p(X)]], [q(a),q(b)]).
Yes

?- est([[p(a)],[p(b)],[q(X),p(X)]], [q(Y),not(eq(Y,a))]).
Y = b
Yes
```

This version of `est` now handles almost all of Prolog. (It does not yet work with numbers or built-in operations like `write` and `assert`. Also, it does not do the right thing when the same variable appears in both the query and knowledge base.) With a bit more work, *any* Prolog program and *any* query can be represented as terms and used as arguments to a predicate like `est`. So this program is a *language processor* for Prolog: a program that can take a symbolic representation of a Prolog program and execute it. What takes some getting used to, perhaps, is the fact that this processor for Prolog is written in the Prolog language itself.

11.2   Explanation

Explanation involves finding an atomic sentence such that if it were true, it would account for a given sentence's being true. For example, assuming it is known that all polar bears are white, one would like to be able to explain Thornton's being white by abducing that he is a polar bear. As it turns out, the final version of the `est` predicate from figure 11.6 makes this possible by using a variable `A` to stand for the new atomic sentence to be abduced:

```
?- est([[A],[white(X),polar_bear(X)]],[white(thornton)]).
A = white(thornton)      ;
A = polar_bear(thornton) ;
No
```

The query asks for an atomic sentence `A` such that if `A` is added to the knowledge base, the desired conclusion then follows. There are two such atoms. The first one, `white(thornton)` is technically correct but only in a trivial way, so one might not want to consider it as a possible explanation.

11.2.1   Diagnosis

Imagine that a knowledge base has the following facts:

A person will have sore elbows if she has a tennis elbow or sore joints in general. Arthritis will also lead to sore joints. A person will have sore hips if she has sore joints in general or a hip fracture. Only a tennis player will get tennis elbow.

A representation of this knowledge base is shown in figure 11.7. (The predicate `background` indicates that this list represents background knowledge.) One can then look for an explanation for a person Sue's having a sore elbow:

Figure 11.7.   A knowledge base about sore joints   joints.pl

---

```
% What is known about sore joints
background([ [sore_elbow(X), tennis_elbow(X)],
            [sore_elbow(X), sore_joints(X)],
            [sore_joints(X), arthritis(X)],
            [sore_hips(X), sore_joints(X)],
            [sore_hips(X), hip_fracture(X)],
            [tennis_player(X), tennis_elbow(X)] ]).
% The possible explanations to consider
assumable(tennis_elbow(_)).
assumable(arthritis(_)).
```

```
?- background(K), est([[A]|K],[sore_elbow(sue)]).
A = sore_elbow(sue)    ;
A = tennis_elbow(sue)  ;
A = sore_joints(sue)   ;
A = arthritis(sue)     ;
No
```

Thus there are four possible atoms A that could be added as clauses to the background knowledge K to get the desired conclusion. The first atom, sore_elbow, is the trivial explanation as before. The third atom, sore_joints, may or may not be useful as an explanation. The other two, tennis_elbow and arthritis, are likely the desired explanations for sore_elbow.

Often only explanations drawn from some prespecified assumption set or hypothesis set are of interest. A typical case of explanation is (medical) *diagnosis*. In diagnosis, some of the atoms are considered to be possible *symptoms*, and some of the atoms are considered to be possible *diseases*. Observations that are among the symptoms are given to a diagnostician, and an explanation is sought among the diseases. In general, what one is willing to assume depends on the problem, and that is what the assumable predicate in figure 11.7 is for:

```
?- background(K), assumable(A),
       est([[A]|K], [sore_elbow(sue)]).
A = tennis_elbow(sue)  ;
A = arthritis(sue)     ;
No
```

Note that the explanations that are generated depend on what needs to be explained. For example, suppose Sue also has sore hips:

Figure 11.8. A general explanation program `explain.pl`

```
% This program uses three predicates defined elsewhere:
%    est - the procedure that establishes a query
%    background - the background knowledge to be used
%    assumable - an atom that can be used in an explanation

% explain(Q,E): Q can be established if E is added to background KB.
explain(Q,E) :- background(K), merge(E,K,K1), est(K1,Q).

% merge(E,K,K1): adding the atoms E as atomic clauses to K produces K1.
merge([],K,K).
merge([A|E],K,[[A]|K1]) :-
   merge(E,K,K1), assumable(A), \+ member(A,E).
```

```
?- background(K), assumable(A),
       est([[A]|K], [sore_elbow(sue),sore_hips(sue)]).
A = arthritis(sue)      ;
No
```

In this case, only one explanation does the job; tennis elbow is no longer sufficient. In other cases, there may be no single atom that gives the desired explanation, and one may need to look for *multiple atoms* to assume.

11.2.2 A general explanation program

The general explanation program shown in figure 11.8 attempts to find one or more atoms to assume. The predicate `explain` takes two arguments: a query Q that is to be explained and an explanation E that it will generate as a list of atoms to assume. The `merge` predicate takes the list of atoms and adds them as atomic clauses to the knowledge base K, checking along the way that they are assumable and that there are no repeats in the list.

The `explain` predicate can be seen in action by looking at another diagnostic example, this time involving car trouble (see the knowledge base in figure 11.9). Some queries for this example appear in figure 11.10.

- The first query, without additional assumptions, cannot get an explanation of the car's not starting.

- The second query shows that a dead battery and being out of gas are both single-atom explanations for the car's not starting.

- The third query shows that being out of gas is the only single-atom explanation for the car's not starting when the radio is working.

Figure 11.9.   A knowledge base about car trouble   cars.pl

```
% The background knowledge
background([
    [wipers, not(dead_battery)],
    [radio, not(dead_battery), not(broken_speaker)],
    [ignition, key_turned, not(dead_battery)],
    [car_starts, not(out_of_gas), ignition],
    [gauge_shows_gas, not(out_of_gas), not(dead_battery)],
    [key_turned]]).

% Things that can go wrong
assumable(dead_battery).
assumable(out_of_gas).
assumable(broken_speaker).
```

Figure 11.10.   Explanations for car trouble

```
?- explain([not(car_starts)],[]).
No

?- explain([not(car_starts)],[A]).
A = dead_battery ;
A = out_of_gas   ;
No

?- explain([not(car_starts),radio],[A]).
A = out_of_gas   ;
No

?- explain([not(car_starts),not(radio),wipers],[A]).
No

?- explain([not(car_starts),not(radio),wipers],[A1,A2]).
A1 = broken_speaker,  A2 = out_of_gas  ;
A1 = out_of_gas,  A2 = broken_speaker  ;
No

?- explain([not(car_starts),not(radio),wipers],E).
E = [broken_speaker,out_of_gas]   ;
E = [out_of_gas,broken_speaker]   ;
ERROR: Out of global stack
```

- The fourth query shows that no single-atom suffices to explain all three facts: the car not starting, the radio not working, the wipers working.

- The fifth query shows that there is a double-atom explanation for these three facts. The explanation is that the car is out of gas *and* the radio speaker is broken (in either order).

- The sixth query looks for an arbitrary explanation under the same conditions. It finds the double explanation, but then continues to search indefinitely until all memory is exhausted.

The last query shows that it is possible to use `explain` without specifying how many atomic sentences are desired, but some care is needed.

11.3 Learning

As noted at the start of this chapter, (inductive) learning is a form of thinking that is similar to explanation except that instead of seeking an atomic sentence to account for a query's being true, it looks for a general *rule*, that is, a conditional sentence with variables to explain some observations. If it is known that Thornton and his friends are polar bears, and they are all observed to be white, it is reasonable to induce that all polar bears are white. Then on hearing of a new polar bear, one may wish to conclude that she also is white.

The general format for this type of thinking is similar to the `explain` predicate. Instead of

```
explain(Q,E) :- background(K), merge(E,K,K1), est(K1,Q).
```

which generates an explanation E (a list of atoms) that accounts for a given query Q, a predicate `induce` is defined as follows:

```
induce(Q,R) :- background(K), rule(R), est([R|K],Q).
```

The predicate `rule` generates a conditional sentence R with the property that if it is added to the background knowledge K, then Q can be established. For example, if the background knowledge contains `polar_bear(thornton)` and `polar_bear(shako)`, the desired behavior is the following:

```
?- induce([white(thornton),white(shako)],R).
R = [white(_G17), polar_bear(_G17)]
```

This induced rule (with the variable _G17 in it) says that polar bears are white. The next section discusses how to generate rules like this.

11.3.1 Inducing general rules

In the simplest case, a rule that explains some observations should have the following characteristics:

- The *head* of the rule should be a predicate in the relevant domain (like `polar_bear` or `white`) with variables as arguments.

- The *body* of the rule should be a sequence of literals. Each literal should be a possibly negated predicate in the domain. Moreover, the predicate should be different from the one in the head (to avoid recursion), and the arguments of the predicate should be among the variables in the head.

So for a rule whose head is `r(X,Y,Z)`, the body can contain the literals `not(p(Y))` and `q(X,Z,X)` but it should not contain `r(X,Z,X)`, which would make the rule recursive, nor `q(X,a,W)`, which uses arguments a and W that do not appear in the head.

The simplest way to satisfy these requirements is to assume that each problem domain specifies which predicates and which variables can be used. To do this, a special predicate called `predicate` can be used. It plays a role similar to that of the `assumable` predicate:

```
predicate(polar_bear(X),polar_bear,[X]).
predicate(white(X),white,[X]).
predicate(bigger_than(X,Y),bigger_than,[X,Y]).
```

The first argument to `predicate` is an atom that can be used in the head of a rule; the second argument is the predicate part of the atom as a constant; and the third argument is a list of the variables used in the head.

A definition for an `induce` predicate is presented in figure 11.11. The `rule` predicate uses the predicate hb (for "head-body") to generate an atom for the head and a list of literals for the body. To deal with the body, in the second clause of hb, each literal L (an atom or its negation) is checked to ensure that its predicate Q is different from the predicate in the head P, and its arguments U are among the arguments in the head V (using the auxiliary predicate subl). In addition, a negative literal is generated only if the rest of the body B is empty or begins with a negative literal.

11.3.2 An example of induction

To show the `induce` predicate in action, a new knowledge base about animals is provided in figure 11.12. There are a number of individuals that are animals of different types, and a number of predicates to learn about.

Figure 11.11. The induce predicate in Prolog induce.pl

```
% This program uses three predicates defined elsewhere:
%     est - the procedure that establishes a query
%     background - the background knowledge to be used
%     predicate - an atom that can be used in a rule

induce(Q,R) :- background(K), rule(R), est([R|K],Q).
rule([H|B]) :- hb(H,B,_,_), \+ B=[].

% hb(H,B,P,V): H is an atom with pred P and vars V and
% B is a list of literals with pred not P and vars among the V.
hb(H,[],P,V) :- predicate(H,P,V).
hb(H,[L|B],P,V) :- hb(H,B,P,V), lit(L,Q,U,B), \+ Q=P, subl(U,V).

% lit(L,P,V,B): L is a literal with pred P and vars V, where the
% neg case can only be used if the literals in B are also neg.
lit(A,P,V,_) :- predicate(A,P,V).              % the positive case
lit(not(A),P,V,[]) :- predicate(A,P,V).        % the 1st neg case
lit(not(A),P,V,[not(_)|_]) :- predicate(A,P,V).    % a 2nd case

% subl(L1,L2): the elements of list L1 are all elements of L2.
subl([],_).
subl([X|L1],L2) :- member(X,L2), subl(L1,L2).
```

Figure 11.12. A knowledge base about animals animals.pl

```
% An example knowledge base about animals
background([
  [animal(X),dog(X)],   % Dogs are animals.
  [animal(X),cat(X)],   % Cats are animals.
  [animal(X),duck(X)],  % Ducks are animals.
  % Some example animals
  [dog(fido)],    [dog(spot)],    [dog(rover)],
  [cat(kitty)],   [cat(kelly)],
  [duck(donald)], [duck(daffy)], [duck(huey)] ]).

% Some predicates to learn about
predicate(animal(X),animal,[X]).   predicate(dog(X),dog,[X]).
predicate(cat(X),cat,[X]).         predicate(duck(X),duck,[X]).
predicate(barks(X),barks,[X]).     predicate(quacks(X),quacks,[X]).
predicate(four_legged(X),four_legged,[X]).
```

What rule can be learned from observing that Fido barks:

```
?- induce([barks(fido)], R).
R = [barks(_G404), animal(_G404)]     % Every animal barks?
```

The answer is somewhat disappointing: the program induces that every animal barks. While this rule is certainly sufficient to explain Fido's barking, something more specific is desired. To find a more specific rule, the `induce` predicate must be given some *negative* examples:

```
?- induce([barks(fido),barks(rover),not(barks(kitty)),
        not(barks(donald))], R).
R = [barks(_G425), dog(_G425)]          % Every dog barks.
```

This is a much better rule. Similarly, what rule can be learned from observing that Fido and Kitty are four-legged but Daffy (the duck) is not:

```
?- induce([four_legged(fido),four_legged(kitty),
        not(four_legged(daffy))], R).
R = [four_legged(_G411), not(duck(_G411))]
        % Everything that is not a duck has four legs?
```

This induced rule may or may not be acceptable given what is known. At the very least, it should be restricted to *animals* only, so `induce` needs to be given information about a nonanimal individual, say, a tree:

```
?- induce([four_legged(fido),four_legged(kitty),
        not(four_legged(daffy)),
        not(four_legged(tree17))], R).
R = [four_legged(_G428), animal(_G428), not(duck(_G428))]
        % Every animal that is not a duck has four legs.
```

This induced rule has a body with two literals: the individual must be an animal and must not be a duck.

* 11.3.3 Classification: Training and testing

What is the point of inducing new rules? In general, one wants to observe the world, notice the properties of some individuals, induce some general rules about them, and finally, use the general rule to *predict* the properties of new individuals. So, for example, after observing that Fido and Rover both bark (but that Kitty and Daffy do not), the induced rule should be able to predict that Spot the dog will also bark.

This type of learning is often called *classification*: some *training examples* are given, some of which have a property (like barking) and some of which do not; then new *test examples* are classified into those that do and those that do not have the property.

The `induce` predicate can be used to find out if new individuals have a property. In fact, the new *atoms* learned from the training examples can be generated:

```
% Given a query Q as training data (as before), find a new
% atom A that can be established from an induced rule.
learned_atom(Q,A) :-
    background(K), induce(Q,R), est([R|K],[A]),
    \+ est(K,[A]), \+ member(A,Q).
```

The `learned_atom` predicate uses `induce` to generate a rule as before, then looks for an atom A that is not an element of the training data Q, and that can be established given that rule, but not without the rule. The result is the following:

```
?- learned_atom([four_legged(fido),four_legged(kitty),
            not(four_legged(daffy)),
            not(four_legged(tree17))], A).
A = four_legged(spot)    ;
A = four_legged(rover)   ;
A = four_legged(kelly)
```

In this case, enough is learned from the training examples to generate new examples: Spot, Rover, and Kelly are four-legged.

Unfortunately, this simple version of `induce` looks for ever longer rules to explain the observations it is given and never actually fails. So if `learned_atom` is asked to classify Donald or Huey as four-legged given the same training examples, instead of failing as it should, it would simply run forever.

There are ways of dealing with this issue. The easiest perhaps is to rewrite `induce` so that it eventually gives up and fails. For example, the length of the desired rule could be limited. But a better approach is to *commit* to the first induced rule found by the program. In other words, if a rule R has been found that accounts for the training data Q, the testing should be done with R, with no backtracking to look for other rules. Prolog provides a built-in predicate called `once` that does this: if `induce(Q,R)` in the body of `learned_atom` is replaced by `once(induce(Q,R))`, the program commits to the first rule found and `learned_atom` will then fail as it should, for instance, on classifying the test examples Donald and Huey as four-legged.

In performing such classification, the bulk of the work involves finding a rule that works well. When there are a number of predicates to choose from and a number of variables that are needed, it can be very time-consuming to find a rule that does the job properly. This makes it especially important to have training examples that include *near-misses*, individuals that do not have the desired property but are very similar to those that do. With near-misses, it is much easier to locate the negative literals that need to be included in the body of the induced rule.

11.4   Propositional reasoning

So far, it has been assumed that a knowledge base is made up only of atomic or conditional sentences. This allowed the use of a thinking procedure like back-chaining to draw all the necessary conclusions, and even to do explanation and learning.

But, of course, there are sentences of English that do not fit this pattern. Consider the following three sentences:

> *At least one of Alice, Bob, or Carol is guilty.*
> *If Alice is guilty, then so is Bob.*
> *If Alice is not guilty, then neither is Carol.*

From these sentences alone, there is no way to tell whether Alice and Carol are guilty. However, it is not hard to see that Bob must be guilty. The reasoning is as follows. If Alice is guilty, then Bob is also guilty. But if Alice is not guilty, then neither is Carol, and since one of the three must be guilty, it must be Bob. So either way, Bob must be guilty. In other words, the three sentences logically entail that Bob is guilty.

To be able to use knowledge in this sophisticated way, it is necessary to go beyond atomic and conditional sentences to represent what is known, and to go beyond back-chaining to calculate logical entailments. So it is useful to consider a new language for representing knowledge, a *propositional language*, which allows us the expression of negations and disjunctions in addition to the previous conjunctions and conditionals.

11.4.1   Conjunctive normal form

Perhaps the simplest representation of a propositional language in Prolog is to use the *conjunctive normal form*, or *CNF*. For present purposes, a CNF formula is a list of *disjunctive clauses*, or *dclauses* for short, where a dclause is a list of literals, and a literal is either an atom or its negation. A dclause is interpreted as the *disjunction* of its elements, and the entire CNF formula is interpreted as the *conjunction* of its elements. So the dclause [p,q] is interpreted as saying that p or q is true, and the CNF formula [[p,q],[not(r)]] is interpreted as saying that p or q is true and r is false.

Note that dclauses are interpreted differently from clauses. Previously, a list like [p,q,r,s] represented the conditional "If q and r and s then p." That same list as a dclause represents the disjunction "p or q or r or s."

And yet there is a definite connection between the two interpretations. Consider a conditional like this:

> If q and r and s then p.

That conditional says the same thing as the following disjunction:

$\text{not}(q)$ or $\text{not}(r)$ or $\text{not}(s)$ or p.

To see why, ask what it takes for the conditional to be *false*. This happens when q, r, and s are true, but p is false. Now what does it take for the disjunction to be false? This happens when all the disjuncts are false, that is, when q, r, and s are true, but p is false. So the conditional and the disjunction are *equivalent*: they are either both false or both true. This means that the conditional "If q and r and s then p" can also be represented by a dclause: `[p,not(q),not(r),not(s)]`. (The order of the literals in a dclause does not matter.)

In the example with Alice, Bob, and Carol, let the atoms a, b, and c stand for the guilt of Alice, Bob, and Carol, respectively. Then the three given facts can be represented as a CNF formula:

`[ [a,b,c], [not(a),b], [a,not(c)] ]`

This gives the following:

- The first dclause says that Alice is guilty or Bob is guilty or Carol is guilty (which is just another way of saying that at least one of them is guilty).

- The second dclause says that Alice is not guilty or Bob is guilty (which is an equivalent way of saying that if Alice is guilty, then so is Bob).

- The third dclause says that Alice is guilty or Carol is not guilty (which is an equivalent way of saying that if Alice is not guilty, then neither is Carol).

So every conditional can be represented as a dclause (containing precisely one unnegated literal), and once it is determined how to calculate logical entailments for CNF formulas in general, that procedure will work for conditionals too.

Although every clause can be rewritten as a dclause, the converse is not true. For example, there is no way to represent `[not(p)]` as a clause. Although there was a form of negation in queries and in the bodies of clauses, there is no way to have a simple negative fact (like *Alice is not guilty*) in a Prolog knowledge base.

11.4.2 Satisfiability

How does logical entailment work for CNF formulas? So far, a collection of sentences $S_1, S_2, \ldots, S_n$ logically entails a sentence S if S has to be true when the S_i are all true. Another way of saying this is that the sentences $\{S_1, S_2, \ldots, S_n, \text{not}(S)\}$ cannot all be true. A set of sentences is said to be *satisfiable* if they can all be true, and unsatisfiable otherwise. So to compute if a collection of sentences S_i entails another S, it is sufficient to compute whether a certain set of sentences (formed by adding the negation of *S* to the other S_i) is satisfiable or not.

But how does one test for satisfiability? For a set of dclauses without variables, there is a very simple account of satisfiability:

A set of dclauses (without variables) is satisfiable if and only if there is a way to pick a literal from each dclause without picking both an atom and its negation.

This derives from the fact that a disjunction will be true if one of the disjuncts is true (that is, the literal chosen for that dclause), and a conjunction will be true if all of the conjuncts are true (that is, all the dclauses are true). So, for example, the CNF formula

```
[ [p], [not(p),not(q)], [not(q)] ]
```

is satisfiable: pick p from the first dclause, not(q) from the second, and not(q) (already picked) from the third. This means that the dclauses can all be true: it happens when p is true and q is false.

However, the CNF formula

```
[ [p], [not(p),not(q)], [q] ]
```

is unsatisfiable: pick p from the first dclause, which forces the choice of not(q) from the second (to avoid having an atom and its negation), and then there is nothing to pick from the third. (In other words, the first two dclauses logically entail not(q).) Similarly, the CNF formula

```
[ [p,q], [not(p),q], [not(q),p], [not(p),not(q)] ]
```

is unsatisfiable: no matter what is chosen for the first three dclauses, both p and q are picked, with nothing left to choose from the last one. (In other words, the first three dclauses logically entail both p and q.)

11.4.3 Computing satisfiability

A predicate for testing whether a list of dclauses (without variables) is satisfiable is presented in figure 11.13. It uses the predicate `satpick` to go though the dclauses, picking a literal from each one using the predicate `pickone`. For each dclause, there are three possibilities (and so three clauses for the `pickone` predicate):

- No new picking is needed if the head of the dclause has already been picked.
- The head of the dclause can be picked if its negation has not been picked.
- A literal from the tail of the dclause can also be picked.

Figure 11.13. A satisfiability program sat.pl

```
% The dclauses in DL are satisfied by picking Lits.
sat(DL,Lits) :- satpick(DL,[],Lits).

% satpick(DL,P,Lits): the dclauses in DL can be satisfied by
% picking the literals in Lits, given that those in P are taken.
satpick([],P,P).
satpick([D|DL],P1,Lits) :- pickone(D,P1,P2), satpick(DL,P2,Lits).

pickone([L|_],P,P) :- member(L,P).          % L is picked.
pickone([L|_],P,[L|P]) :- \+ member_neg(L,P).  % ~L is not picked.
pickone([_|D],P,P2) :- pickone(D,P,P2).     % Use D instead.

member_neg(A,P) :- member(not(A),P).
member_neg(not(A),P) :- member(A,P).
```

The predicate member_neg is used to check if the negation of a literal has already been picked. It does this by either adding or removing a not on the given literal.

It is not hard to confirm that this predicate does the right thing:

```
?- sat([[p],[not(p),not(q)],[not(q)]],L).
L = [not(q), p]
Yes

?- sat([[p],[not(p),not(q)],[q]],L).
No

?- sat([[p,q],[not(p),q],[not(q),p],[not(p),not(q)]],_).
No
```

11.4.4 Logical entailment reconsidered

The notion of logical entailment can now be enlarged to deal with knowledge bases that are lists of dclauses. Continue to assume that there are no variables in the dclauses, and for simplicity, that the queries are as before, a list of atoms or their negations, all of which are to be established. It is then easy to do logical entailment: negate the literals in the query and let the sat predicate do the heavy lifting, as shown in figure 11.14.

With this procedure, one can go beyond what was possible with back-chaining. For example, the puzzle with Alice, Bob, and Carol can now be solved:

```
?- estsat([[a,b,c],[not(a),b],[a,not(c)]], [a]).
No
```

Figure 11.14.   Entailment using satisfiability   estsat.pl

```
% Dclauses DL entails Q using sat (defined elsewhere).
estsat(DL,Q) :- negs(Q,NQ), \+ sat([NQ|DL],_).

% negs(Q,NQ): NQ is the negation of the literals in Q.
negs([],[]).
negs([not(A)|T],[A|NT]) :- negs(T,NT).
negs([A|T],[not(A)|NT]) :- \+ A=not(_), negs(T,NT).
```

```
?- estsat([[a,b,c],[not(a),b],[a,not(c)]], [b]).
Yes

?- estsat([[a,b,c],[not(a),b],[a,not(c)]], [c]).
No
```

The given facts entail that Bob is guilty, but they do not entail the guilt (or innocence) of Alice or Carol.

The back-chaining examples shown in figure 11.2 can be repeated with the conditionals translated into dclauses:

```
?- estsat([[a],[b],[u,not(p),not(b)],[p,not(a)]], [b,a]).
Yes

?- estsat([[a],[b],[u,not(p),not(b)],[p,not(a)]], [u]).
Yes

?- estsat([[a],[b],[u,not(p),not(b)],[p,not(a)]], [p,d]).
No
```

Of course, the way these queries are answered (using the sat predicate) is very different from the back-chaining method used until now.

* 11.4.5   First-order reasoning

When a propositional language is enlarged to include variables, it is usually called a *first-order language*. Reasoning correctly with a first-order language is much more complicated than what has been done so far. For satisfiability, it is no longer sufficient to pick a literal from every dclause; a literal must be picked from every dclause for every value of the variables in that dclause.

For example, the formula [[not(p(a))],[not(q(b))],[p(X),q(X)]] is considered to be satisfiable, since q(X) can be chosen when X is a, and p(X) otherwise. But the formula [[not(p(a))],[not(q(a))],[p(X),q(X)]] is unsatisfiable, since

Figure 11.15. An unsatisfiability program unsat.pl

```
% Dclauses in DL are unsat, after making N copies of them.
unsat(N,DL) :- copies(N,DL,DL2), nopick(DL2,[]).

% copies(N,X,Y): Y is the result of making N copies of list X.
copies(0,_,[]).
copies(N,X,Y) :-
    N>0, N1 is N-1, copies(N1,X,L), copy_term(X,X2), append(X2,L,Y).

% nopick(DL,P): there is no way to pick literals from the
% dclauses in DL, given that the ones in P have been picked.
nopick([[]|_],_).
nopick([[L|D]|T],P) :- unpickable(L,T,P), nopick([D|T],P).

% The literal L cannot be picked.
unpickable(L,_,P) :- member_neg(L,P).    % Negation of L is picked.
unpickable(L,T,P) :- nopick(T,[L|P]).    % Cannot add L to picked.

% As before
member_neg(A,P) :- member(not(A),P).
member_neg(not(A),P) :- member(A,P).

%----------------------------------------------------------------
% Dclauses DL entails Q using unsat.
estunsat(N,DL,Q) :- negs(Q,NQ), unsat(N,[NQ|DL]).

% As before
negs([],[]).
negs([not(A)|T],[A|NT]) :- negs(T,NT).
negs([A|T],[not(A)|NT]) :- \+ A=not(_), negs(T,NT).
```

there is no literal to choose when X is a. (Specifically, the CNF formula without variables, `[[not(p(a))],[not(q(a))],[p(a),q(a)]]`, is unsatisfiable according to what was done before.) One complication here is that *more than one value* per variable may have to be considered to handle cases like the following: the formula `[[not(p(a)),not(p(b))],[p(X)],[p(Y)]]` is unsatisfiable (when X is a and Y is b), and so `[[not(p(a)),not(p(b))],[p(X)]]` is unsatisfiable too.

This suggests that for first-order reasoning it is easier to work with unsatisfiability than with satisfiability:

> *A set of dclauses (with variables) is unsatisfiable if and only if there are (possibly multiple) values for the variables such that the resulting set of dclauses without variables is not satisfiable.*

A program that realizes this definition appears in figure 11.15. To deal with the multiple values for variables, it begins by making *copies* of all the dclauses using the built-in `copy_term` predicate. (It uses a parameter N to decide how many copies to make.) It then uses the predicate `nopick` to confirm that there is no way to pick a literal from each dclause in the resulting list. Below the dashed line in the figure, the `estunsat` predicate is like the `estsat` predicate in figure 11.14 except that it uses the success of `unsat` rather than the failure of `sat` to do all the hard work:

```
?- estunsat(1, [[p(a)],[not(p(X)),q(X)]], [q(a)])
Yes

?- estunsat(1, [[p(a)],[not(p(X)),q(X)]], [q(b)])
No
```

Note that for some queries it is necessary to use a parameter N > 1:

```
?- unsat(1, [[not(p(a)),not(p(b))],[p(X)]]).     % Wrong.
No

?- unsat(2, [[not(p(a)),not(p(b))],[p(X)]]).     % Right.
Yes
```

Unfortunately, there is no way to know in advance how large a value of N will be needed to obtain the correct answer.

With a first-order language, more advanced reasoning problems can be handled. Consider the following puzzle (a generalized version was discussed in section 4.4):

There are three blocks, A, B, C, in a stack, with the top one (A) green
and the bottom one (C) not green.

Is there a green block directly on top of a non-green one?

It is clear that the answer must be yes. If B is green, then it is a green one directly on a non-green one (C); if, on the other hand, B is not green, then the top block (A) is a green one directly on a non-green one (B). Either way, the conclusion follows.

What makes this puzzle challenging is that we know there has to be a green block directly on top of a non-green one, and yet we cannot say which one it is. With back-chaining, whenever it was known that *something* had a property, enough information was always given to figure out what that something was. First-order reasoning using `estunsat` is more general and does not have this limitation:

```
?- estunsat(2,
    [ [on(a,b)], [on(b,c)],          % The facts
      [green(a)], [not(green(c))] ],  % More facts
    [ on(X,Y), green(X), not(green(Y))] ).  % The query
Yes
```

Observe that the only thing that prevents representing all the given facts as a set of *clauses* in Prolog (and using normal back-chaining) is the fact about the bottom block not being green. But to handle this negative fact properly and to fully use what is known requires thinking in this new advanced way.

Want to read more?

This chapter explored ways of thinking that went beyond simple back-chaining. Remarkably enough, these new ways of thinking were all formulated in terms of back-chaining.

The idea of using a programming language to write a language processor for that very language (a *meta-interpreter*) is a practice developed to a fine art in the LISP community [53], which uses this idea in a number of ways, including adding new primitive constructs to the language. In this chapter it was used to explore variants of the Prolog processor and to handle abduction and induction by making temporary additions to the underlying knowledge base.

The section on explanation took a first glance at an area of research called *abductive logic programming* (for example, see [54]). The section on learning introduced the area of *inductive logic programming* (for example, see [56]). These two continue to be active areas of research, although techniques more closely allied with probability theory have gradually come to dominate the study of both diagnosis and learning.

The section on propositional reasoning is perhaps the most open-ended part of the book. Its generalization of clauses to dclauses allowed representing a much wider range of knowledge, in particular, *incomplete knowledge*, when certain facts must be considered even though their truth is unknown (like the guilt of Alice). When variables and a few other features are included, the resulting first-order logic is the typical starting point for logical reasoning within AI, for example in [4].

Computing satisfiability (for CNF formulas without variables) has become an active area of AI research. It turns out that many of the problems considered in this book (including constraint satisfaction and planning) can be reformulated directly in terms of satisfiability. This is significant because there have been great advances in recent programs that compute satisfiability [55].

Computing unsatisfiability (for CNF formulas with variables) is also an active area of research called *automated theorem-proving* [57]. The emphasis is on taking (small) parts of mathematics, formalizing them as a set of axioms in a first-order logic, and then asking if they entail some mathematical conjecture of interest. In 1996 an automated theorem-proving program written by William McCune and colleagues was able to prove Robbins' Conjecture, a statement in algebra whose status had remained open for sixty years.

All the reasoning in this book comes out as a special case of first-order reasoning. This means (in theory) leaving Prolog behind and continuing the work using a first-order logic instead. Prolog is a conceptual ladder of great value, but now one can kick the ladder away and explore along different paths.

12   Can Computers Really Think?

This is a book about thinking. Looking at a wide range of behaviors that appear to depend on thinking, it showed how they could be realized in computer programs: solving recreational puzzles, interpreting visual scenes, understanding English expressions, planning courses of action, playing games, and some forms of explanation and learning. Only simple versions of these activities were considered, of course, but in each case, thinking—bringing knowledge to bear on the activity—could be understood as a form of computation.

What can be learned from this? Perhaps the following:

- It is possible to get computers to do fairly impressive things even with small programs. (All the programs in this book are well under one hundred lines long.) What is needed is a programming language that allows stating what needs to be known to perform the task.

- It is indeed possible to interpret at least some forms of thinking as computation. What needs to be known can be represented as a collection of (atomic and conditional) sentences, from which conclusions can be drawn using back-chaining.

- The real issue is not so much whether intelligent behavior can be produced at all but *how well*. Almost all the tasks considered (puzzles, language, planning, games, and so on) worked in simple versions, but as the problems got bigger and more complex, the basic methods did not scale well.

Not surprisingly, the bulk of the research in artificial intelligence (AI) is concerned with how to achieve intelligent behavior in complex situations where simple techniques do not work (like playing chess and Go, rather than tic-tac-toe, for instance). The book showed some of the ways of dealing with this complexity:

- how to do better than basic generate-and-test;
- how to represent action and change for large worlds;
- how to play games without searching the entire game tree; ...

Of course, there is a lot of thinking that the book did *not* talk about at all. What about the thinking that goes into designing a bridge or composing a piece of music? What about following the dialogue in a play? What about the sort of thinking that occurs when recalling a childhood event or daydreaming? What about meditation? What about the role of emotion? An account of thinking that is true to the very wide range of mental experiences people have would go well beyond what was considered here.

But nonetheless, even within a limited context, and despite all the restrictions, this book still raises a *philosophical* question. If it is true that thinking (or some forms of it) can be understood as computation, does it then not follow that given the right program, *a computer is able to think?*

For many people, this is a very troubling idea. Thinking and the intelligent behavior it gives rise to feel very special to us. At its most elevated, we might say, thinking *defines* what it means to be human. The idea that a gadget like an electronic computer might also be able to think is unsettling.

Looking back at what was accomplished in previous chapters, was it really possible to program a computer to think about the grandfather relation, the objects in a scene, the words in a sentence, the ways to achieve a goal? Or was the computer just programmed to behave *as if* it were thinking? Is there a difference?

This final chapter briefly explores these philosophical questions.

12.1 What computers can do

Can a computer really think? Before answering, consider a question that is even more basic: Can a computer really add two numbers? Many of us, would say yes: a suitably programmed computer can take two numbers as input and return their sum as output. Nobody disputes this. If this is not adding two numbers, then what is?

But nothing is taken for granted in philosophy. In fact, some might be tempted by an account like the following:

> Computers *cannot* do addition, really. All they can do is mechanically shuffle around uninterpreted symbols. It is we, the human beings, who interpret this shuffling. In some cases, we might interpret it as addition, say. But this is up to us, and someone else might interpret the shuffling completely differently, like solving a puzzle or playing some sort of mysterious game. At any rate, for the computer itself, no arithmetic is involved.

If this is the way one chooses to talk about computers, the discussion stops here. There is really no point in talking about whether they can think if one is not even willing to concede that they can add.

This is not a particularly *helpful* way of talking, however. Imagine we are studying the bewildering game of Go and wondering whether a computer has ever won against a Go champion. Suppose we get an answer like this:

> No computer has ever beat a Go champion because a computer cannot even *play* the game of Go. All it can do is move around meaningless symbols.

This way of talking is not helpful because it does not make the simple distinctions we are looking for. We want to be able to say that yes, a computer did win against a chess champion (once), but no, a computer has not yet beat a Go champion. But in talking this way, we are allowing that computers can indeed do things like add numbers, solve Sudoku puzzles, and play world-class chess. (You can't *win* at chess if you can't even *play* chess!)

In essence, we are saying that the computer's *external behavior* (as given by the inputs and outputs) is enough for us to judge. We do not need to know about the hidden internal state of the computer or whether there are other interpretations of the inputs and outputs. Fortunately, this is the way most people choose to talk about computers.

(As a side note, there is something right about shifting the question about what computers can do to the question about what people can do. When we ask, "Can a computer play decent Go?" what we are really asking is, "Is there a suitable computer program?" that is, a program that when run on a general-purpose computer produces the external behavior we want in a reasonable amount of time. And to go further, it is not just a program's *existence* that matters; we might know that there must be such a program without anyone's knowing how to write it. Our question is really, "Has anyone been able to write a suitable program?" So the question is really about *people*! When we say that the Deep Blue computer beat a chess champion, and we applaud that achievement, it is really the team from IBM that produced Deep Blue that we are applauding. Of course, some day, we may be more willing to give credit to the machine itself; but that's for another day.)

Now let us return to the original question: Can a computer really think? Can it understand English? Can it be intelligent? Here we do not seem to be talking about the computer's external behavior but about its *internal workings*, not just what a computer can do, but what it can be.

12.2   The Turing Test

In the 1950s, Alan Turing wrote a now famous philosophical paper [66] arguing that terms like *thinking, understanding, being intelligent* are just too vague to be worth spending time arguing about. One can imagine, for instance, two critics going back and forth never being able to agree on whether *real* thinking or *real* understanding was taking place. Instead, Turing proposed, we should return to behavior in the following thought experiment.

Imagine that you have a long-distance typed conversation over a terminal with two other parties. One of them is a person, and the other is a computer program. The conversation is natural, free-flowing, and about *any* topic you desire. Neither party is stonewalling or trying to steer the conversation in any way. Now imagine that no matter how long the conversation goes on, you cannot figure out which of the two parties you are talking to is the person and which is the computer. We would say that the computer has passed the Turing Test.

Roughly speaking, Turing's position amounts to this. If we insist on using terms like *thinking* or *understanding*, we should be willing to accept that anything that passes this test is thinking or understanding as much as a person is. We are of course perfectly free to say that something is not thinking if it does not look like we do, or does not have a brain, or is not connected to a physical world the way we are, and so on. We are free to say this, but in the end, this is just a form of chauvinism, not so different from sexism or racism. We should concede that anything that can behave as intelligently as we do is as intelligent as we are.

(We might be wrong, of course. But we could be wrong about the *person* we have been talking to as well. This "person" might actually be some sort of zombie from outer space, somehow able to fake a conversation without any understanding, or without any internal mental life. These are possibilities, but they are just too far-fetched to be worth spending any time on.)

So for Turing, external behavior is what counts. To paraphrase the Forrest Gump movie character, *Intelligent is as intelligent does!*

Turing's argument is compelling, and most computer scientists today probably accept it. This explains why scientists in artificial intelligence see their job as dealing with *intelligent behavior* of various sorts and spend almost no time discussing whether *real* understanding (say) is taking place. This is what was done in this book: it studied what was needed to get the desired *external behavior* in a variety of domains.

12.3 The Chinese Room

But philosophers are an obstinate lot. They are not going to back down on the issue of whether *real* understanding is taking place just because someone like Turing says they should. Perhaps the most successful attack on Turing's position came from the philosopher John Searle in the 1980s. He devised a different thought experiment to argue that there was much more to understanding (or thinking, or being intelligent) than merely getting the external behavior right. Here is (a slight variant of) his argument.

Imagine that there is already a computer program that is somehow able to pass the Turing Test, but in Chinese, not in English. Let us call the computer program that does this `chinese.pl`, assuming it is written in Prolog. So Chinese characters can be presented to this program (encoded in some way), and it will produce responses (also encoded in some way) that cannot be distinguished even over a long period of time from those of a person who really understands Chinese.

Now imagine that Searle does not know Chinese, but knows Prolog very well. He is put in a room with a book that contains the text of the `chinese.pl` program. When someone outside the room slips him pieces of paper with Chinese written on them, he does not understand them, but he can follow what `chinese.pl` would do given these as input. He traces the behavior of the program, writes on a piece of paper the output that the program would produce, and hands that back, again without understanding what any of it means.

So there is a person, Searle, who is receiving Chinese messages and producing Chinese responses no different from those of a native Chinese speaker (since `chinese.pl` is assumed to pass the Turing Test). His external behavior, in other words, is *perfect*. And yet Searle does not know Chinese. Searle's conclusion: getting the external behavior right is not enough, and so Turing is wrong.

A counterargument is that Searle is not producing this behavior, but Searle together with the book. Although Searle does not understand Chinese, the *system* consisting of Searle and the book does. So Turing is not wrong. Searle's reply to this objection is beautiful in its simplicity: Imagine that he *memorizes* the book and then destroys it. Then there is no longer a system to talk about; there is just Searle. So Turing is wrong.

Is this the last word on the topic? Remember, nothing is obvious in philosophy. Consider this: How can we be so sure that Searle does not come to *learn Chinese* after memorizing the book? If he did, then the argument would collapse. The answer is that we do not know what happens after he learns the book simply because we do not have a clear picture of what this imagined chinese.pl program would have to be like (assuming it can exist at all). But we can get some clarification by turning to a simpler case, addition again.

12.4   The Summation Room

Imagine a room with a person in it who does not know how to add numbers. Messages are passed to the person on a sheet of paper containing a list of twenty numbers, each of which has ten digits. The book inside the room that he is able to use is a very large one: it has ten billion chapters, and each chapter has ten billion sections, and each section has ten billion subsections, and so on, up to depth twenty. The preface of the book has the following instructions:

> Take the first number in the list of twenty and go to that chapter; then take the second number in the list and go to that section; then take the third number and go to that subsection; and so on until all twenty numbers have been used up. At the end of this process, there will be a number written in the book with at most twelve digits. Write that number on a slip of paper and hand it back outside the room.

Unbeknownst to the person in the room, the book is constructed in such a way that the twelve-digit entries in the book are in fact the *sums* of the twenty numbers that led to the entry.

Now the person in the room, following the procedure in the book, is clearly not adding. He is producing the correct sums, of course, but only by looking them up. This is no different from phoning a friend and getting the answers from her. And what if the person were to somehow memorize the contents of the book and follow the instructions mentally? To an observer, the person would be examining the numbers, reflecting for a while, and then writing down their sum. From the outside, it would look just like the numbers were being added, but they are not.

This, in a nutshell, is Searle's argument but now applied to addition. The person in the room is producing the right external behavior but does not know how to add.

So does this mean that Searle is right after all? Not quite. There is a serious flaw in the argument with the Summation Room: *the book needed for the thought experiment cannot possibly exist.* It would have to contain 10^{200} entries, but the entire physical universe only has about 10^{100} atoms. So a thought experiment that relies on this book is vacuous. It might work if we only had to add *two* ten-digit numbers, say, but for *twenty* or more, this is too much for our universe.

However, there is a smaller book that would do the job for the twenty numbers. Consider a book that contained the procedures PROC0, PROC1, PROC2, and PROC3 from chapter 1. This book can certainly exist. In fact, it would be more like a small pamphlet, and the instructions there would allow the person in the room to produce the correct sums.

However, notice what happens this time when the person in the room memorizes the instructions in the pamphlet: *he learns how to add*. In fact, most of us learned how to add by being given instructions like those in the pamphlet. So the man in the room does get the right answers, but now he also knows how to add.

This is enough to cast some doubt on Searle's Chinese Room argument. Perhaps adding *two* ten-digit numbers is simple enough that a big table of answers would allow someone to fake it. But adding *twenty* ten-digit numbers appears to be complex enough that a book that does the job would also end up teaching the person in the room how to add. Beyond some level, if you need to get the sums out, you will not be able to fake it; you will need to do the addition. So why should we think that *Chinese* (however that book turns out) is going to be any easier to fake? It might be more sensible to conclude that once a behavior is *complex* enough (on the order of adding twenty ten-digit numbers, say), insisting that the behavior be right will be enough to rule out various forms of tricks or fakery.

12.5   A final word

So does this settle the question as to whether a computer can think? No, not at all. At best, it casts doubt on Searle's refutation of Turing's position, which was that we should not even ask this question in the first place. And new and improved arguments on this topic may yet appear.

But no matter what one's position on the philosophical issues, we are still left with what might be called *the AI question*: If it is indeed true that tricks and fakery are not sufficient to generate intelligent behavior such as passing some form of the Turing Test, then *what is*? In the end, it is *this* question that is perhaps the most profound one to emerge out of the entire discussion, and one that will not be resolved by merely arguing one way or another.

And where to look for a possible answer is what this book has been about.

Want to read more?

The issues presented in this chapter are part of what is usually called the *philosophy of mind*, an area of research well represented in most departments of philosophy and in various articles in [59].

This area began more or less with the writings of René Descartes (1596–1650), who wondered how an intangible mind could interact with a physical body (the so-called mind-body problem). Although there was always a fascination with a variety of automata, attention shifted decisively to computers as soon as they became widely known. Turing's paper introducing the Turing Test [66] was perhaps a watershed point in this evolution, although he did what he could to stand outside the area and quell further discussion. Searle's paper on the Chinese Room [64] was another milestone that resulted in a flurry of replies and commentary, including my own Summation Room argument [61]. Although the ideas in Searle's paper may seem frustratingly naive to many computer scientists, they have withstood the test of time.

There are many other aspects of the philosophy of mind that have not even been touched on here. Among them are the following: Jerry Fodor argues for a "mentalese" that has many of the properties of natural languages [60]; Daniel Dennett and many others study properties of consciousness [58]; and there are many who argue that the human mind cannot be computational, based on considerations such as Gödel's Incompleteness Theorem [62] and even quantum mechanics [63].

But perhaps the most thought-provoking philosophy related to thinking and computation is the work of Brian Cantwell Smith, for example [65]. His writing can be hard to read and is not about the philosophy of mind at all, but more on the other side of the street, the *philosophy of computation*. Smith argues (convincingly) that computation must be understood as more than shuffling around uninterpreted symbols. His view is that in some cases the interpretation of the symbols matters to the computation, although in many cases that interpretation is outside the "causal reach" of the person or computer using the symbols. His attempt to formulate the approach to knowledge taken in this book, but taking into account this richer notion of computation, is what he calls the *knowledge representation hypothesis* (see [1], p. 6).

Appendix A
Some Computer Basics

To make good use of this book, you need to be able to perform some simple operations on a computer. (You do *not* need to know how to program a computer.) Mainly these involve creating, deleting, editing, saving, and printing ordinary text files, as well as viewing and printing PDF files.

If you are using this book as part of a course, find the website site for this book, which contains a number of useful files.

A.1 Working with computer files

Here is a checklist of operations you should be able to do comfortably as you start to use the book:

1. View these instructions on a computer screen. Go to the book website which has a file called basics.pdf that contains this appendix in PDF format.

2. Print these instructions on a computer printer.

3. Save these instructions in a file on your computer called basics.pdf. You should also be able to come back to your computer later, find your copy of the file on your computer, and view it on your screen.

4. Delete the file basics.pdf from your computer, and go back to reading the online version of the file at the book website for the next step.

5. Go to the book website and find the file basics.pl. Click on the file, and download it to your computer. This is a text file that contains a simple program in the language Prolog. Your computer won't be able to do much with the file yet.

6. Make a copy of the file basics.pl and call it origbasics.pl. This one is for safekeeping.

7. View the contents of the file basics.pl in a text editor on your computer. You can use a basic editor like Notepad (Windows) or TextEdit (Mac) or nedit (Linux), or a fancier one like Microsoft Word or vi or emacs. *Windows and Mac users*: You will *not* be able to simply double-click the file; you will need to start the editor first and then open the file from there.

8. Change the line in the file that says

   ```
   myname('Sydney J. Hurtubise').
   ```

   so that your name appears between the single quotes.

9. Save the changed file as `mybasics.pl` on your computer. This needs to be saved as an *ordinary text file,* meaning no bold or italics, or anything with fonts or special formatting. These files are sometimes called text-only or plain-text or ASCII or no-formatting.

10. Exit the editor leaving the file `basics.pl` unsaved and in its original state. It should be identical to `origbasics.pl`.

11. Print the file `mybasics.pl` on your printer and confirm that your name appears between the single quotes.

That's it. If you can successfully perform all these tasks, you are as computer-literate as you need to be.

A.2   Files available online

Here are all the files that should be available online at the book website for downloading. First, there are the following special files:

`basics.pdf`: This appendix as a PDF file
`basics.pl`: A sample text file
`applescript.txt`: A file for Mac OS X users (figure B.1, page 281)
`wordUtils.pl`: A Prolog utility file used in chapter 8 (page 170)

Finally, there are all the example Prolog programs that are presented in the text:

`family.pl`: The family example in Prolog (figure 3.1, page 42)
`likes.pl`: The likes example (figure 3.11, page 56)
`blocks.pl`: A blocks-world program (figure 4.2, page 67)
`left.pl`: A better procedure for the `left` predicate (figure 4.6, page 80)
`map.pl`: Coloring the map of figure 5.1 (figure 5.2, page 88)
`sudoku.pl`: A Sudoku solver (figure 5.5, page 93)
`factorial.pl`: A program for n! (figure 5.7, page 99)
`sendmore1.pl`: SEND+MORE=MONEY v1 (figure 5.8, page 100)
`sendmore2.pl`: SEND+MORE=MONEY v2 (figure 5.9, page 102)

cap.pl: Testing if one queen can capture another (figure 5.12, page 105)

queens.pl: A solution to the eight-queens problem (figure 5.13, page 105)

logic1.pl: A solution to the first logic problem (figure 5.15, page 108)

logic2.pl: A solution to the second logic problem (figure 5.16, page 109)

zebra.pl: A solution to the zebra problem (figure 5.17, page 111)

schedule-top.pl: A classroom scheduler (figure 5.19, page 114)

schedule-aux.pl: Previously scheduled periods (figure 5.20, page 114)

regions.pl: The types of regions and their properties (figure 6.4, page 123)

sketch.pl: The sketch map interpretation (figure 6.6, page 124)

polyrules.pl: Permissible vertices in Prolog (figure 6.10, page 127)

polyinterp.pl: Interpreting the edges in figure 6.7 (figure 6.11, page 128)

cuboid.pl: Finding a cuboid in an image (figure 6.15, page 131)

occlusion.pl: Finding vertices with occlusion (figure 6.17, page 134)

blocks2.pl: The blocks-world program redone (figure 7.3, page 148)

nldb.pl: A world of people, parks, trees, hats (figure 8.4, page 160)

lexicon.pl: A lexicon in Prolog (figure 8.5, page 161)

np.pl: A parser of noun phrases in Prolog (figure 8.6, page 163)

yesno.pl: A parser for yes/no questions (figure 8.14, page 171)

declarative.pl: A parser for declaratives (figure 8.15, page 174)

plan.pl: A general planner in Prolog (figure 9.3, page 184)

coins.pl: The three-coins problem in Prolog (figure 9.4, page 184)

monkey.pl: The monkey and bananas problem in Prolog (figure 9.6, page 187)

bplan.pl: A general but bounded planner (figure 9.8, page 189)

puzzle2x3.pl: A 2x3 version of the 15-puzzle (figure 9.11, page 191)

splan.pl: A staged planner in Prolog (figure 9.13, page 195)

raceto21.pl: A Prolog program for Race to 21 (figure 10.2, page 212)

gameplayer.pl: A general game player (figure 10.5, page 216)

tictactoe.pl: A Prolog program for tic-tac-toe (figure 10.6, page 219)

playuser.pl: Playing an entire game (figure 10.7, page 221)

boxes.pl: A Prolog program for Boxes (figure 10.13, page 225)

minimax.pl: A minimax procedure in Prolog (figure 10.17, page 230)

estfc.pl: A forward-chaining procedure (figure 11.4, page 246)

est.pl: The final version of back-chaining (figure 11.6, page 248)

joints.pl: A knowledge base about sore joints (figure 11.7, page 250)

explain.pl: A general explanation program (figure 11.8, page 251)

cars.pl: A knowledge base about car trouble (figure 11.9, page 252)

Appendix B
Getting Started with SWI-Prolog

To be able to follow the many Prolog examples in the book and to run your own programs, you will need to have access to a Prolog system installed on the computer you are using. To simplify matters, the book only discusses the SWI-Prolog system. If for some reason, you are forced to deal with another dialect of Prolog, see appendix D for some of the differences you may run into.

Ideally, a computer expert will install SWI-Prolog for you on your computer and tell you what to do with your Prolog files. From that point on, everything else you need to know is covered in this book starting in chapter 3.

In case there is no computer expert around, you will need to do the installation yourself. Take it slowly, make sure everything works as you go, and get as much help as you can. Section B.1 deals with the installation of SWI-Prolog, and section B.2 covers how to load and run your own Prolog programs.

> **Warning**. *The instructions in this appendix may go out of date. Computers change, operating systems (Windows, Mac, Linux) change, and Prolog systems change. If too much has changed, these instructions may no longer work and you will need help from an expert.*

B.1   Installing SWI-Prolog

This section concerns installing the free SWI-Prolog software on a computer that you control. If you are using a *shared computer*, as in a lab at a university, you will not be able to install any software yourself. If SWI-Prolog is already installed, you are in luck; find out how to start it, and then go on to the next section. If SWI-Prolog is not installed, you will need to ask around to see what your options are; another dialect of Prolog may be installed, or you may be out of luck.

With Windows

To install SWI-Prolog under Windows, begin by downloading an installation package from `http://www.swi-prolog.org/download/stable/`. The latest version of SWI-Prolog should run under the latest version of Windows. (Note: You can always safely use a 32-bit version.) Then follow the installation instructions.

With Mac OS X

To install SWI-Prolog under Mac OS X, begin by downloading an installation package from `http://www.swi-prolog.org/download/stable/`. You will need to know which version of Mac OS X you are using (which you can see by selecting "About This Mac" under the Apple menu): 10.4 (Tiger), 10.5 (Leopard), 10.6 (Snow Leopard), or later. Then follow the installation instructions. (Note to experts: If MacPorts is installed, SWI-Prolog can be installed from there. Either way, the SWI-Prolog binary will be installed as `/opt/local/bin/swipl`.)

With Linux

The SWI-Prolog binary comes preinstalled on some Linux systems. If so, you are in luck as there is no easy way to do the installation. There is an RPM file at `http://www.swi-prolog.org/download/stable/`, but it may not be right for your system. There are sources online, but if you have never installed a Linux program from sources before, you will definitely need help.

B.2   How to load SWI-Prolog programs

Once you have installed SWI-Prolog, you are ready to use it with some Prolog programs that you have written yourself or downloaded and saved on your hard drive. For example, assume you have saved the file `family.pl` (figure 3.1). This program is available on the book website (see appendix A) and will be used here as an example.

With Windows

Once SWI-Prolog has been installed on a Windows system, any file whose name ends with `.pl` (such as `family.pl`) will be known to the system as a Prolog program. You can double-click the file, and this will start SWI-Prolog *and* automatically load that Prolog program. It is therefore unnecessary to use the square bracket notation to manually load the program, as done in figure 3.2. (However, additional Prolog programs in the same folder as the file can be loaded with the square bracket notation as required.) When you are finished with Prolog, close the Prolog window to exit.

Figure B.1. An AppleScript for SWI-Prolog

```
on run
  set prolog to "/opt/local/bin/swipl"
  set myprompt to "Where do you keep your Prolog programs?"
  set dir to POSIX path of (choose folder with prompt myprompt)
  tell application "Terminal"
    activate
    do script "cd \"" & dir & "\"; " & prolog in window 1
  end tell
end run
```

With Mac OS X

Unfortunately, running SWI-Prolog with a Mac is not as easy as it could be. It is best to begin by preparing an AppleScript. Start the AppleScript Editor (often located in the Utilities folder within the Applications folder). In the untitled window that it presents, insert the text from the figure B.1 exactly as is. (The text can be cut and pasted from the file applescript.txt that is on the book website. See appendix A.) Then do a "Save As" to save the script: choose the file format "application," use a name like "Start-SWI," and save it to your desktop.

Once "Start-SWI" has been saved, Prolog can be used as follows:

1. To start Prolog, double-click the "Start-SWI" icon on your desktop.

2. It will ask you where you keep your Prolog programs. Navigate to a folder, such as the folder that contains family.pl, and hit the "Choose" button.

3. From within Prolog, you can now load any Prolog program in that folder by using the square bracket notation (as done in figure 3.2).

4. When you are done with Prolog, quit the Terminal application.

With Linux

After installing SWI-Prolog, there should be a binary called swipl. To use it, first connect using cd to the directory that contains your Prolog programs like family.pl, and then start Prolog. From there, interact with Prolog, as shown in figure 3.2.

Appendix C
Getting Your Prolog Programs to Work

I assume that SWI-Prolog has been installed, and that the family.pl program works for you just like in figure 3.2. (Otherwise, see appendix B.) This appendix considers how to use some of the features of SWI-Prolog to get new Prolog programs that you write to work as intended. (There are, of course, many ways of doing this, but what follows are my recommendations.)

When you are using SWI-Prolog on your computer, keep *two windows* open and work as follows:

1. Start your text editor (see appendix A), and either type in or open the current version of your own Prolog program. Save the file (with a name like something.pl), but keep this window open.

2. Start Prolog and load the current version of your program (as described for family.pl in appendix B). This will be your second window.

3. Try some Prolog queries in the Prolog window.

4. If the queries all work as expected, then you are done. You may want to save some queries and their results for the record. Then quit Prolog and the text editor.

5. If some queries do not work as expected, find out what went wrong, make some changes in the text editor window, save the file, and then reload the program into Prolog. Then go back to step 3.

Let us go through these steps to see what can go wrong.

C.1 Getting program files to load

One problem you may have is that you try to load a program file (using the square brackets), but the file is not found:

```
?- [block].
ERROR: source_sink 'block' does not exist
```

The special predicate ls can be used to see what files are in the current folder and are available to be loaded:

```
?- ls.
blocks.pl       grid.pdf        myfamily.pl
daisy.jpg       monkey.pl       planner.pl
Yes

?- [blocks].
% blocks compiled 0.00 sec, 2,088 bytesYes
```

Note that ls lists all the files in the current folder. Only the files whose names end with .pl, such as blocks.pl, can be loaded. It is sometimes necessary to load two or more files, which can be done as follows:

```
?- [planner,monkey].
% planner compiled 0.00 sec, 1,432 bytes
% monkey compiled 0.00 sec, 2,012 bytes
Yes
```

The next thing to worry about is that Prolog finds your file but cannot load it without an error:

```
?- [myfamily].
ERROR: myfamily.pl:4:0: Syntax error: Operator expected
% myfamily compiled 0.00 sec, 1,400 bytes
Yes
```

This error means that myfamily.pl is not yet a legal Prolog program. Typically, punctuation of some sort is wrong. Here is a listing of the myfamily.pl file:

```
child(henry,hanna).

male(henry)
female(hanna).

mother(X,Y) :- child(Y,X), female(Y).
```

As can be seen, there is a missing period at the end of the second clause. Prolog reports where it runs into trouble. The myfamily.pl:4:0 on the error line means that it was at line 4 column 0. (The actual error is typically somewhere nearby. It is a good idea to use a text editor like Notepad or TextEdit that allows you to easily get to a line in a file by its line number.)

Here is what you need to do: Go to the text editor window, find the grammatical error, change the file, and save the new version of the file. Then go back to the Prolog window, and use the special predicate make to reload the file into Prolog:

```
?- make.
% myfamily.pl compiled 0.00 sec, 64 bytes
% Scanning references for 1 possibly undefined predicates
Yes

?- child(X,hanna).
X = henry
Yes
```

SWI-Prolog keeps tracks of all the files that were loaded (using the square brackets). The predicate `make` reloads any of those files that have changed on the hard drive since they were last loaded. (Ignore any `Scanning references` messages). Because of `make`, you will not need to type the names of the files again.

C.2 Getting the right answers from queries

Once your program loads without errors, it is time to see if it responds to queries in the right way. In this case, unfortunately, it does not:

```
?- mother(hanna,henry).
No
```

Now you have to go through the logic of the program and see what went wrong.

It is easy to make mistakes in queries, too. Suppose you find yourself repeatedly typing and mistyping a long query that involves variables X, Y, Z, say. Then one simple thing to do is to add a new predicate to the program file like this:

q(X,Y,Z) :- ... *long query with* X, Y, *and* Z.

After reloading the file with `make`, you can then test the long query using just q. Once the query is working, simply remove the clause for q from the program.

To isolate an error, it is good practice to consider each predicate in the file in turn, and check using queries that it is behaving the way you expect it to. Start with the simplest ones (that appear only in atomic sentences), then move on to those that are not recursive, and then finally deal with the recursive ones.

In this case, the `child` and `female` predicates appear to be working:

```
?- child(henry,hanna).
Yes

?- female(hanna).
Yes
```

Sometimes, the best way to find out what is wrong with a predicate is to trace the execution of queries that use it.

C.2.1   Tracing the execution

In the simplest case, simply add `trace, leash(-all)` to the front of a query:

```
?- trace, leash(-all), mother(hanna,henry).
   Call: (8) mother(hanna, henry)
   Call: (9) child(henry, hanna)
   Exit: (9) child(henry, hanna)
   Call: (9) female(henry)
   Fail: (9) female(henry)
   Fail: (8) mother(hanna, henry)
No
```

With this trace, you can see the problem: you are checking that henry is female instead of hanna. It is now easy to fix the program (change the argument of female from Y to X in the mother clause), and then reload the saved file using make.

As programs get larger, you often want more control on how the tracing should appear. If you put `trace, leash(+all)` at the front of the query (that is, use +all instead of -all), you get the trace presented line by line, after which you enter a single-character command. There are a number of options (typing a ? will show them), but here are the main ones:

- space or c (for creep) tells Prolog to go to the next line as usual;
- a (for abort) tells Prolog to give up on the entire query;
- s (for skip) tells Prolog to jump ahead without stopping or printing anything until the current atomic query either succeeds or fails.

With s you can skip over parts of the query that you know are working properly.

Finally, it is possible to restrict a trace to a given list of predicates. For example, by inserting `trace([mother,female])` at the front of a query, only the parts of the trace involving those two predicates will be printed. (The `leash` predicate is not used in this case.)

C.2.2   Interrupting the execution

Another common problem is that instead of getting the wrong answer to a query, you get no answer at all! This can happen when the program goes into a loop (because of a recursive predicate) or just takes too long (because of a very large search space).

In these cases, the execution can be interrupted by typing a Control-C (holding down the `Ctrl` key and typing a C). Prolog then displays the following and waits for a character to be typed:

```
Action (h for help) ?
```

There are a number of options here (typing a ? will show them), but the main two are as follows:

- c (for continue) tells Prolog to continue as if it had not been interrupted;

- a (for abort) tells Prolog to give up on the entire query.

Of course, aborting a query like this is a desperation measure, but sometimes it is the only way to regain control and go on to try something else. Almost certainly some tracing will be needed to find out what went wrong.

C.3 Saving a record of program execution

Once a program is finally behaving the way it should, the only thing left to do is to make a record of the way it responds to queries. The simplest way to do this is to use the special predicates `protocol` and `noprotocol`. Here is the idea:

```
?- protocol('myfile.txt').
Yes
```

Some queries are now entered and their responses are produced.

```
?- noprotocol.
Yes
```

The result of this is that a text file called `myfile.txt` is created in the same folder as the Prolog program. All the queries and their responses between the `protocol` and `noprotocol` will be saved to this file. (The text file will also contain a spurious first and last line, but these are easy to remove.)

As a final note, it is sometimes useful to use the `protocol` feature of SWI-Prolog to deal with a very long trace. By sending the trace to a file, it can be examined later, parts can be edited out, and the trace can be printed.

Appendix D
Other Prolog Systems

There are many implementations of Prolog other than the SWI-Prolog that is used in this book. Fortunately, many of the more recent systems (including SWI-Prolog, SICStus Prolog, ECLiPSe, and GNU Prolog) use the same *ISO Standard* Prolog dialect. Variations are found mainly in older systems (such as C-Prolog, Open Prolog, LPA Prolog, Quintus Prolog, and Amzi! Prolog). There are many other Prolog systems out there, however, which can be found by searching online. Each of these systems has its own advantages and disadvantages regarding special features (including language additions), speed of execution, and in some cases, commercial support.

Before talking about language differences, it is worth noting that even in systems that use the *same dialect* of Prolog, the behavior of the systems is not always precisely the same. It should be possible to run the same queries on the same programs to get the same answers, but there are variations. For example, in this book, it is assumed that the system responds to queries by printing Yes (for success) or No (for failure), as it does in release 5.6.43 of SWI-Prolog. But more recent versions of SWI-Prolog, including release 5.6.63, print true or false instead.

This book uses a very small subset of SWI-Prolog. For anyone trying to run the examples here or write their own programs on a different Prolog system, here are some things to watch for:

Negation. The symbol \+ is used to indicate negation (see chapter 3, page 49). Many earlier Prolog systems used the more mnemonic not instead.

Comments. Comments in a Prolog program are indicated with a % and continue to the end of the line (see chapter 3, page 44). In other Prologs, comments are placed between /* and */ characters.

Loading files. Program files are loaded using square parentheses (see appendix B). So the query [myfile] is how the program file myfile.pl is loaded. In other Prolog systems, the query consult(myfile) is used instead.

Reloading files. In SWI-Prolog, if a file is reloaded (using the square brackets or with the special SWI-Prolog query make introduced in appendix C), the new definition replaces the previous one. In other Prologs, new clauses are *added* to the old ones, unless the special query reconsult is used.

Dynamic predicates. In SWI-Prolog, predicates are not dynamic unless the special `:-dynamic` declaration is included in the file (see chapter 8). In some Prolog systems, *all* predicates are considered to be dynamic. (So if a predicate that does not appear in a program is used in a query, the query will *fail* rather than cause an *error*, as it does in SWI-Prolog.)

Assert and retract. The predicates `assert` and `retract` are used here to add and remove clauses for dynamic predicates (see chapter 8). Other Prolog systems may use predicates with slightly different names for this purpose.

Member and append. The predicates `member` and `append` are built-in predicates in SWI-Prolog. In some older systems, these need to be defined by the user. (The definitions appear in chapter 7 under the names `elem` and `join`).

Copying terms. A special predicate `copy_term` is used in chapter 11. This is a built-in SWI-Prolog predicate, but it is difficult to duplicate otherwise. One definition that often works is based on `assert` and `retract`:

```
copy_term(X,Y) :-
    assert(mycopy(X)), mycopy(Y), retract(mycopy(X)).
```

Sending output to a file. The predicates `protocol` and `noprotocol` are used to send the output produced by Prolog to an external file (see appendix C). Other conventions are used in other systems, including `tell` and `told` for output, and `see` and `seen` for input.

Tracing. Prolog systems vary considerably on how they handle tracing. The SWI-Prolog conventions are described in appendix C.

There are many tutorials and FAQs about Prolog that can be found online. For more information about SWI-Prolog, see `http://www.swi-prolog.org/`. A survey that has a lot of information about many of the older versions of Prolog can be found at `http://www.faqs.org/faqs/prolog/`.

References

Chapter 1   Thinking and Computation

[1] Ronald J. Brachman and Hector J. Levesque. *Knowledge Representation and Reasoning*. San Francisco: Morgan Kaufmann, 2004.

[2] Gilles Fauconnier and Mark Turner. *The Way We Think: Conceptual Blending and The Mind's Hidden Complexities*. New York: Basic Books, 2003.

[3] Jerry A. Fodor. *The Mind Doesn't Work That Way*. Cambridge, MA: MIT Press, 2000.

[4] Frank van Harmelen, Vladimir Lifschitz and Bruce Porter, eds. *Handbook of Knowledge Representation*. Amsterdam: Elsevier, 2008.

[5] Philip Johnson-Laird. *Mental Models*. Cambridge, MA: Harvard University Press, 1986.

[6] Steven M. Kosslyn, William L. Thompson, and Giorgio Ganis. *The Case for Mental Imagery*. Oxford: Oxford University Press, 2009.

[7] Douglas B. Lenat and R. V. Guha. *Building Large Knowledge-Based Systems: Representation and Inference in the Cyc Project*. Boston: Addison-Wesley, 1990.

[8] Harry Lewis and Christos Papadimitriou. *Elements of the Theory of Computation*. 2d ed. Upper Saddle River, NJ: Prentice Hall, 1997.

[9] Steven Pinker. *How the Mind Works*. New York: W. W. Norton, 1999.

[10] Zenon W. Pylyshyn. *Computation and Cognition: Toward a Foundation for Cognitive Science*. Cambridge, MA: MIT Press, 1986.

[11] Stuart J. Russell and Peter Norvig. *Artificial Intelligence: A Modern Approach*. 3d ed. Upper Saddle River, NJ: Prentice Hall, 2009.

[12] Alan Turing. On computable numbers, with an application to the *Entscheidungsproblem*. Reprinted in *The Undecidable*, ed. Martin Davis, 115–153. Mineola, NY: Dover Publications, 2004.

Chapter 2   A Procedure for Thinking

[13] Apostolos Doxiadis and Christos Papadimitriou. *Logicomix*. New York: Bloomsbury Publishing, 2009.

[14] Herbert B. Enderton. *A Mathematical Introduction to Logic*. San Diego, CA: Academic Press, 2001.

[15] Elliott Mendelsohn. *Introduction to Mathematical Logic*. 5th ed. London: Chapman and Hall/CRC, 2009.

Chapter 3   The Prolog Language

[16] Alain Colmerauer and Philippe Roussel. The birth of Prolog. In *History of Programming Languages*, ed. Thomas Bergin Jr. and Richard Gibson Jr., 331–351, New York: ACM Press, 1996.

[17] Carl Hewitt. Planner: A language for proving theorems in robots. In *Proceedings of the International Joint Conference on Artificial Intelligence*, Washington, DC, 1969, 295–301.

Chapter 4   Writing Prolog Programs

[18] Kenneth A. Bowen. *Prolog and Expert Systems Programming*. New York: McGraw-Hill, 1991.

[19] Ivan Bratko. *Prolog Programming for Artificial Intelligence*. 3d ed. Boston: Addison-Wesley, 2000.

[20] William F. Clocksin and Christopher S. Mellish. *Programming in Prolog*. 4th ed. Berlin: Springer-Verlag, 1994.

[21] Daniel Crookes. *Introduction to Programming in Prolog*. Englewood Cliffs, NJ: Prentice Hall, 1988.

[22] Tony Dodd. *Prolog: A Logical Approach*. Oxford: Oxford University Press, 1990.

Chapter 5   Case Study: Satisfying Constraints

[23] Steven A. Cook. The complexity of theorem-proving procedures. In *Proceedings of the Third Annual ACM Symposium on Theory of Computing*, Shaker Heights, Ohio, 1971, 151–158.

[24] Rina Dechter. *Constraint Processing*. San Francisco: Morgan Kaufmann, 2003.

[25] Michael R. Garey and David S. Johnson. *Computers and Intractability: A Guide to the Theory of NP-Completeness*. New York: W. H. Freeman, 1979.

[26] Alan Mackworth. Consistency in networks of relations. *Artificial Intelligence* 8 (1977): 99–118.

[27] Ugo Montanari. Networks of constraints: fundamental properties and applications to picture processing. *Information Science* 7 (1974): 95–132.

[28] Moshe Vardi. Constraint satisfaction and database theory: A tutorial. In *Proceedings of the Nineteenth ACM Symposium on Database Systems*, Dallas, Texas, 2000, 76–85.

Chapter 6   Case Study: Interpreting Visual Scenes

[29] Norm Badler. *Temporal Scene Analysis: Conceptual Descriptions of Object Movements*. Ph.D. dissertation, Department of Computer Science, University of Toronto, 1975.

[30] Anthony G. Cohn and Jochen Renz. Qualitative spatial representation and reasoning. In [4], 551–583.

[31] Sven Dickinson. The evolution of object categorization and the challenge of image abstraction. In *Object Categorization: Computer and Human Vision Perspectives*, ed. S. Dickinson, A. Leonardis, B. Schiele, and M. Tarr, 1–37. Cambridge: Cambridge University Press, 2009.

[32] William Eric Leifur Grimson. *Object Recognition by Computer: The Role of Geometric Constraints*. Cambridge, MA: MIT Press, 1991.

[33] Zenon W. Pylyshyn. *Seeing and Visualizing: It's Not What You Think*. Cambridge, MA: MIT Press, 2003.

[34] Ray Reiter and Alan Mackworth. A logical framework for depiction and image interpretation. *Artificial Intelligence* 41 (1989): 125–155.

[35] Antonio Torralba. Contextual priming for object detection. *International Journal of Computer Vision* 53 (2003): 169–191.

[36] John Tsotsos. *A Framework for Visual Motion Understanding*. Ph. D. dissertation, Department of Computer Science, University of Toronto, 1980.

[37] David Waltz. Understanding line drawings of scenes with shadows. In *The Psychology of Computer Vision*, ed. Patrick Winston, 19–92. New York: McGraw-Hill, 1975.

Chapter 7   *Lists in Prolog*

[38] John McCarthy. *LISP 1.5 Programmer's Manual.* Cambridge, MA: MIT Press, 1962.

[39] Leon Sterling and Ehud Shapiro. *The Art of Prolog.* 2d ed. Cambridge, MA: MIT Press, 1994.

Chapter 8   *Case Study: Understanding Natural Language*

[40] John L. Austin. *How to Do Things with Words.* 2d ed. Cambridge, MA: Harvard University Press, 1975.

[41] Noam Chomsky. *Syntactic Structures.* 2d ed. Berlin: Mouton de Gruyter, 2002.

[42] Daniel Jurafsky and James H. Martin. *Speech and Language Processing.* 2d ed. Upper Saddle River, NJ: Prentice Hall, 2008.

[43] Terry Winograd. *Understanding Natural Language.* New York: Academic Press, 1972.

Chapter 9   *Case Study: Planning Courses of Action*

[44] Fahiem Bacchus and Froduald Kabanza. Using temporal logic to express search control knowledge for planning. *Artificial Intelligence* 116 (2000): 123–191.

[45] Malik Ghallab, Dana Nau, and Paolo Traverso. *Automated Planning: Theory and Practice.* San Francisco: Morgan Kaufmann, 2004.

[46] Hector J. Levesque and Gerhard Lakemeyer. Cognitive robotics. In [4], 869–886.

[47] John McCarthy. Programs with common sense. Reprinted in *Readings in Knowledge Representation*, ed. Ronald J. Brachman and Hector J. Levesque. San Francisco: Morgan Kaufmann, 1986.

[48] Ray Reiter. *Knowledge in Action: Logical Foundations for Specifying and Implementing Dynamical Systems.* Cambridge, MA: MIT Press, 2001.

Chapter 10 Case Study: Playing Strategic Games

[49] Michael Genesereth, Nathaniel Love, and Barney Pell. General game playing: Overview of the AAAI competition. *AI Magazine* 26 (2005): 62–72.

[50] David N. L. Levy and Monroe Newborn. *How Computers Play Chess*. New York: W. H. Freeman, 1990.

[51] Martin Müller. Computer Go. *Artificial Intelligence* 134 (2002): 145–179.

[52] Jonathan Schaeffer, Neil Burch, Yngvi Björnsson, Akihiro Kishimoto, Martin Müller, Rob Lake, Paul Lu and Steve Sutphen. Checkers is solved. *Science* 317 (2007): 1518–1522.

Chapter 11 Case Study: Other Ways of Thinking

[53] Harold Abelson and Gerald Jay Sussman. *Structure and Interpretation of Computer Programs*. Cambridge, MA: MIT Press, 1996.

[54] Marc Denecker and Antonis Kakas. Abduction in logic programming. In *Computational Logic: Logic Programming and Beyond*, 402–437. LNAI 2407. Berlin: Springer Verlag, 2002.

[55] Carla P. Gomes, Henry Kautz, Ashish Sabharwal, and Bart Selman. Satisfiability solvers. In [4], 89–134.

[56] Nada Lavrak and Saso Dzeroski. *Inductive Logic Programming: Techniques and Applications*. Chichester, UK: Ellis Horwood, 1994.

[57] Larry Wos, Ross Overbeek, and Ewing Lusk. *Automated Reasoning: Introduction and Applications*. Englewood Cliffs, NJ: Prentice Hall, 1984.

Chapter 12 Can Computers Really Think?

[58] Daniel C. Dennett. *Consciousness Explained*. Boston: Little, Brown, 1991.

[59] Paul Edwards, ed. *The Encyclopedia of Philosophy*. New York: Macmillan, 1967.

[60] Jerry A. Fodor. *The Language of Thought*. Cambridge, MA: Harvard University Press, 1975.

[61] Hector J. Levesque. Is it enough to get the behavior right? In *Proceedings of the Twenty-First International Joint Conference on Artificial Intelligence*, Pasadena, California, 2009, 1439–1444.

[62] John R. Lucas. Minds, machines, and Gödel. Reprinted in *Minds and Machines*, ed. Alan Ross Anderson, 43–59. Englewood Cliffs, NJ: Prentice-Hall, 1964.

[63] Roger Penrose. *The Emperor's New Mind: Concerning Computers, Minds, and the Laws of Physics*. Oxford: Oxford University Press, 1989.

[64] John Searle. Minds, brains and programs. *Behavioral and Brain Sciences* 3 (1980): 417–424.

[65] Brian C. Smith. The owl and the electric encyclopaedia. *Artificial Intelligence* 47 (1991): 251–288.

[66] Alan Turing. Computing machinery and intelligence. *Mind* 59 (1950): 433–460.

Index of Technical Terms

These are the main technical terms presented in the book. They are introduced at the page number indicated, where the words appear underlined.